Turned Inside Out

6/13/23

For Michael —

A wonderful guy with a big
heart, + a wonderful student!

Warmly,
SS

Turned Inside Out

Reading the Russian Novel in Prison

◆

Steven Shankman

NORTHWESTERN UNIVERSITY PRESS

EVANSTON, ILLINOIS

Northwestern University Press
www.nupress.northwestern.edu

Copyright © 2017 by Northwestern University Press.
Published 2017. All rights reserved.

Printed in the United States of America

10   9   8   7   6   5   4   3   2   1

Library of Congress Cataloging-in-Publication Data

Names: Shankman, Steven, 1947– author.
Title: Turned inside out : reading the Russian novel in prison / Steven Shankman.
Description: Evanston, Illinois : Northwestern University Press, 2017. | Includes
    bibliographical references and index.
Identifiers: LCCN 2016049618| ISBN 9780810134928 (cloth : alk. paper) | ISBN
    9780810134911 (pbk. : alk. paper) | ISBN 9780810134935 (e-book)
Subjects: LCSH: Russian fiction—History and criticism. | Russian fiction—Study
    and teaching. | Prisoners—Books and reading—United States. | Dostoyevsky,
    Fyodor, 1821–1881—Criticism and interpretation. | Lévinas, Emmanuel—
    Criticism and interpretation. | Grossman, Vasiliĭ—Criticism and interpretation. |
    Imprisonment in literature.
Classification: LCC PG3095 .S44 2017 | DDC 891.73009—dc23
LC record available at https://lccn.loc.gov/2016049618

For my students, inside and out

I am inside-out
Nerves bared to the air.

—Gareth Reeves, *Nuncle Music*

In Levinas, I sense . . . the experience of a man who has been
in prison. It's there in every line, and perhaps this is another
reason why it speaks to me so vividly.

—Václav Havel, *Letters to Olga*

The openness of the I exposed to the other is the bursting open
or the turning inside-out [*à l'envers*] of interiority.

—Levinas, "God and Philosophy"

The "I" [*le moi*] is . . . a being divesting itself, emptying itself
of its being, turning itself inside-out [*à l'envers*].

—Levinas, *Otherwise Than Being*

The fundamental question . . . that has tormented me all my
life long . . . is the existence of God.

—Dostoevsky, letter to Maikov

Yes, for real Russians the questions of God's existence and of
immortality, or, as you say, the same question turned inside
out, come first and foremost.

—Alyosha to Ivan Karamazov,
The Brothers Karamazov

To be religious—it is not to believe in the existence of God—
which is an abstraction—but to have a question about God—
the question about God is prayer—The Question put to the
person concerned—call.

—Levinas, *Prison Notebooks*

La métaphore des métaphores—Dieu.

—Levinas, *Prison Notebooks*

Faith is not a question of the existence or non-existence of
God. It is believing that love without reward is valuable.

—Levinas, "The Paradox of Morality"

This wasn't a religion class, [but] it was a spiritual sanctuary for me. This class transformed my personal spirituality. I felt God, the spirit, the humbling force, or some higher power within human interaction.

—Leslie, outside student, spring 2009,
Oregon State Penitentiary

The secret of man is the secret of his responsibility.

—Havel, *Letters to Olga*

CONTENTS

ACKNOWLEDGMENTS

The writing of this book began with a paper I delivered in Denver in October 2009 for a panel on teaching Dostoevsky in the twenty-first century at the annual meeting of the Association of Literary Scholars, Critics, and Writers (ALSCW). I was buoyed by the encouragement I received on that occasion from a number of Dostoevsky scholars who have continued to be wonderfully receptive to this project. These include Susan McReynolds, Gary Saul Morson, and Robin Feuer Miller. Special thanks to Susan McReynolds for her generous willingness to engage with me at length about my ideas, and for suggesting that I submit my manuscript to Northwestern University Press. Sincere thanks as well to Homi Bhabha and Luke Menand for inviting me to share an early version of the argument of this book at the Harvard Humanities Center in November 2010. On that occasion, I had the good fortune to meet Svetlana Boym, for whose interest in my project I was most grateful, and whose recent and much too early passing I recall with sadness. I am grateful as well for the invitation to give a plenary address on the subject of this book at the annual meeting of the North American Levinas Society in May 2011 at Texas A&M University in College Station, Texas.

This book emerged directly from my experience teaching Russian novels in prison through the Inside-Out Prison Exchange Program. I am especially grateful to the visionary founder of Inside-Out, Lori Pompa, for creating the model for the kind of class that made this book possible, as well as to Inside-Out's former assistant director, Melissa Crabbe. It was Melissa's persistence and savvy that paved the way for the Inside-Out program to get the green light from the Oregon Department of Corrections so that I, and other college instructors in the state of Oregon, could begin to offer Inside-Out classes in Oregon prisons. Simone Davis and Barbara Roswell, both Inside-Out instructors who have been members of the national steering committee of Inside-Out, solicited an essay from me for their coedited volume *Turning Teaching Inside-Out*. That essay was an early articulation of the central argument of this book.

I owe a special debt of gratitude to Nancy Green, former education coordinator for both the Oregon State Penitentiary and the Oregon State Correctional Institution, who helped us to win the confidence of the Oregon Department of Corrections so that we could begin teaching

Inside-Out courses in Oregon. Without Nancy's continuous, unflagging, and devoted support of Inside-Out and of my own teaching in the program, this book would never have been written.

Others have supported my teaching behind bars in crucial ways, including Shaul Cohen, Jerry Long, Ken Singer, Don Strand, and Mike Yoder. Most of my Inside-Out courses were taught through the Robert D. Clark Honors College at the University of Oregon. I would like to thank Professor Dick Kraus for his timely and courageous early support of my efforts to get Inside-Out started at the University of Oregon, as well as to David Frank, who believed in the program and helped it to grow at Oregon in amazing ways. Other key supporters at Oregon were Dave Hubin and the late Dave Frohnmayer, the distinguished and longtime president of the University of Oregon, who was also a kind and caring friend.

I am grateful to colleagues at Oregon for supporting my work in various ways. Jenifer Presto and Katya Hokanson shared with me their impressive knowledge of Russian literature. I am very grateful to my Russian teachers Yelaina Kripkov, Valeriia Tretiak, and Alena Nekrasova. Heghine Hakobyan, Slavic Librarian at the University of Oregon, was not only a dynamic teacher of conversational Russian, but she generously helped me work through key passages in Dostoevsky and Vasily Grossman in Russian and was an invaluable proofreader.

My sincerest thanks to Tony Topoleski, to Bert Meisenbach, and to my inside student Kevin G. for reading—at various stages in its evolution—the entire manuscript and for their valuable comments and critiques. I am grateful to Anna Pucilowski for composing the bibliography. My gratitude, as well, to Sister Helen Prejean, with whom I have discussed this project on a number of occasions, and whose work and friendship have inspired me.

Thanks also to Randi Getsushin Brox, Bill Cadbury, Steven Cassedy, Steve Durrant, Dorothy Figueira, Carmela Hill-Burke, Warren Ginsberg, Evlyn Gould, Georges Hansel, Rabbi Yitzhak Husband-Hankins, Luba Jillings, Sasha Kashirin, Peter Laufer, Shlomo and Debbie Rose Libeskind, Lee Minoff, Gareth Reeves, Sharon Schuman, Taylor Smith, Yves Sobel, Dmitry Spivak, Mark Unno, Val Vinokur, Susan Wadsworth-Booth, and Gene Webb. My wife, Marsha Maverick Wells, with her keen editorial skills, made excellent suggestions for improving the book's organization. I have been blessed, for many years, with her companionship as a fellow traveler in countless ways, including in matters of the spirit.

I am grateful to Mike Levine for his interest in the project and for guiding the manuscript through to its acceptance for publication. My thanks to the readers for their generous responses to the manuscript, as well as to Anne Gendler for her efficient editorial work and to Steve Moore for compiling the index and for his excellent editorial suggestions.

The Oregon Humanities Center awarded me a Provost's Senior Humanist Fellowship at a particularly timely moment, and provided the occasion to give a work-in-progress talk that helped me to clarify the book's argument and organization.

Portions of this book, in earlier drafts, have been published previously. I am grateful for the permissions I have received to incorporate these materials into this book. Parts of the prologue and the epilogue appeared in "Turned Inside-Out: Reading the Russian Novel in Prison after Levinas," in *Turning Teaching Inside-Out: A Pedagogy of Transformation,* ed. Simone Davis and Barbara Roswell, 143–53 (Palgrave Macmillan, 2013); material in chapter 1 in "Narrative, Rupture, Transformation: Dostoevsky in Prison and on the Road," *Comparative Critical Studies* 10, volume supplement (2013): 27–37; parts of chapters 3 and 5 in "God, Ethics, and the Novel: Dostoevsky and Vasily Grossman," *Neohelicon* 42, no. 2 (December 2015): 371–87; and material from chapter 5 in "The Death of a Certain God Inhabiting the World behind the Scenes: Loss and Hope in Levinas and Vasily Grossman," in *Loss and Hope: Global, Interreligious and Interdisciplinary Perspectives*, ed. Peter Admirand, (London: Bloomsbury Academic, 2014), 149–62.

In 2010 my students Katie D., Madeline, and James (students are known only by their first names, occasionally with initials following their first names, in Inside-Out classes) coedited a marvelous anthology of essays and testimony from the first three Inside-Out classes I taught at the Oregon State Penitentiary. This anthology is titled *Turned Inside-Out: Literature, Art, and Testimony from the Inside-Out Prison Exchange Program.* I am grateful to these students—one from the Oregon State Penitentiary and two from the Robert D. Clark Honors College at the University of Oregon—for graciously allowing me to borrow the title of their anthology for this book. This book would never have been written were it not for my students, both inside and out, who have been—and who continue to be—a constant source of inspiration.

Turned Inside Out

PROLOGUE

My scholarly writing is almost always inspired by my teaching, by what
happens in the classroom. This is especially true of this particular book,
which emerged directly from what has been, for me, the remarkably
engaging and even transformative experience of teaching in a rather
unusual classroom. Since the spring quarter of 2007, I have been teaching college classes in literature and ethics in the prison environment to
a mix of university students and incarcerated men at two correctional
institutions in Salem, Oregon. I designed these classes in accordance with
the pedagogical approach of the Inside-Out Prison Exchange Program,
which emphasizes the centrality of conversation and dialogue rather than
straight lecture. Students sit not in rows but in a circle. The circles can
be large or small, but inside and outside students always sit side-by-side.

When I took the Inside-Out training in the summer of 2006, most of
the classes taught in the program were in criminal justice. I wanted to
teach literature and ethics inside, particularly the novels of Dostoevsky.
From the moment I first started teaching, I had the idea—uninformed
and romantic though it may have been, for I hadn't stepped into a
prison until I took the Inside-Out training in 2006—that what and how
I taught needed to be compelling enough to have traction in a class
taught inside a prison. But why teach Dostoevsky in the prison context?
During that training in 2006, I was struck by a quote contained in the
Inside-Out training manual and attributed to Dostoevsky remarking
that you could gauge the level of a civilization by looking at its prisons.
And of course everyone knows the title of Dostoevsky's famous novel
Crime and Punishment, and that the novel is about a murder. Dosto-
evsky, moreover, spent time in prison and he wrote about that experience.
So reading Dostoevsky in a literature class taught in a prison seemed a
good fit.

I taught my first class in spring 2007 on Dostoevsky's *House of the
Dead* and *Crime and Punishment*, the first major novel Dostoevsky wrote
after he was released from his four-year prison sentence followed by six
years in exile in Siberia. I taught that first class at an advanced lower-
division level because, as a novice Inside-Out instructor teaching in the
Oregon State Penitentiary, a maximum-security facility in Salem, I wasn't
sure that the inside students would possess the necessary academic skills

for more advanced, upper-division work. Since this was a lower-division class, officially the third quarter of a year-long survey class taught in the Clark Honors College at the University of Oregon, I felt it wasn't appropriate to focus the class in the way I would have preferred, that is, on ethics as understood by Emmanuel Levinas.

The first class I taught inside, on Dostoevsky's *House of the Dead* and *Crime and Punishment*, went surprisingly well, but I hadn't yet been able to justify, to myself, exactly what I was doing in teaching my Inside-Out classes and why. Why teach literary texts in this particular setting to a mix of undergraduates and incarcerated men? At the beginning of each course, Inside-Out instructors meet separately with their inside and outside students before the two groups come together for their first combined class in prison. I recall meeting my first set of inside students for the very first time as a group during the first week of the academic quarter in March 2007. We're asked, as instructors, to let our students know at that first meeting precisely why we're doing what we're doing. I wasn't sure.

I recall entering the Oregon State Penitentiary (OSP) for that first meeting. I felt I was in over my head. OSP is a dingy, old, traditional penitentiary that first opened in 1851. The classrooms are located in the rather cramped area of the prison devoted to education on the fourth floor of the institution. There's no elevator. The class was set to begin at 6 P.M. I entered the prison at 5:30, got processed through the various labyrinths of security, and passed through several steel gates that opened and then decisively and ominously clanged shut behind me. I then began the long climb up to the fourth floor. During the Inside-Out training, I was always with colleagues, most of whom hadn't been in prison before. Now I was alone and anxious about what I had gotten myself into. What did I, a pampered member of the privileged middle class who had enjoyed a comfortable upbringing and the luxury of studying for a Ph.D. in the field of comparative literature, have to say to a group of men who had faced personal challenges and demons I could hardly imagine?

As I climbed the stairs past big windows with bars looking out onto the grounds and buildings of the prison complex surrounded with barbed wire, I felt the air becoming thinner and thinner and then noticed that my nose was bleeding. I was fortunately able to staunch the blood in the bathroom before I entered the classroom to meet my inside students for the first time. Not an auspicious beginning for a class consisting of students sentenced for serious crimes, including murder, taught in a maximum-security prison on Dostoevsky's novel *Crime and Punishment*, which is centered on a bloody double murder! Fortunately, our meeting went well, as did the class. But I hadn't yet found the raison d'être of my teaching of literature in prison through the unique opportunities provided by the approach of the Inside-Out Prison Exchange Program.

I wanted to teach the writings of Emmanuel Levinas, who was so profoundly influenced by Dostoevsky, but I was concerned, when I conceived my first Inside-Out class, that Levinas's prose would be forbidding for those not schooled in the history of philosophy, and especially in phenomenology, with its sometimes specialized vocabulary. My outside students were wonderful but, because the class was a lower-division one, they were mainly freshmen and sophomores, and therefore very young. The inside students, it turned out, were much better readers and writers than I had imagined. I felt it was important, for future classes, to recruit older and therefore more emotionally mature outside students. After debriefing with my outside students at the end of my first Inside-Out course, I decided to teach my next Inside-Out course as a senior-level colloquium in the Clark Honors College, and to bring Levinas and his notion of ethics front and center.

In my next Inside-Out class in spring 2008, I taught a senior-level colloquium on "Literature and Ethics." We read *The Brothers Karamazov* and Levinas's short book *Ethics and Infinity*, which consists of a series of interviews with Levinas that gives a reasonably accessible overview of his thought. This class was, for me, a breakthrough experience for several reasons. First, there was the consistent interplay between Dostoevsky's great novel and Levinas's text, which made several explicit references to Dostoevsky and to *The Brothers Karamazov* in particular. Second, Levinas's thought—and Dostoevsky's novel—began to reveal, for me, much of what makes the Inside-Out experience so powerfully transformative. We not only read about the ethical encounter in both Levinas and Dostoevsky, but the class itself, it seemed to me, powerfully enacted this encounter in its interpersonal dynamics, thus affirming the profundity of the texts we were reading together.

I continued to teach "Literature and Ethics" at both the Oregon State Penitentiary, the state's one maximum-security prison, and at the Oregon State Correctional Institution, a medium-security facility. In spring of 2009, we read Cervantes's *Don Quixote* and Dostoevsky's *The Idiot*, whose protagonist, Prince Myshkin, was modeled on Cervantes's hero. We also read a selection of transcriptions of the last set of lectures Levinas delivered at the Sorbonne in 1975–76 on "God and Onto-theo-logy." In 2010 we read Vasily Grossman's *Life and Fate* alongside a collection of interviews with Levinas gathered in the book *Is It Righteous to Be?* In 2011 I began teaching at the Oregon State Correctional Institution. I again taught Levinas and *The Brothers Karamazov*, which revealed extraordinary new depths to me in Dostoevsky's novel and its relation to Levinas's thought. In 2012 I again taught Grossman and Levinas. In 2013 I taught Dostoevsky's *Demons* at the Oregon State Penitentiary.

By ethics Levinas means the face-to-face, concrete encounter with a unique human being for whom I am uniquely and inescapably responsible. Face-to-face! Those of us who teach Inside-Out classes will immediately think of the Wagon Wheel, the signature Inside-Out icebreaking exercise we use with our students. The Wagon Wheel consists of two concentric circles of facing chairs. The inside students sit in the outside circle, the outside students in the inside circle. The facilitator asks a "fill-in-the-blank" question. Inside and outside students share their responses for several minutes. Then, with a signal from the facilitator, those in the outside concentric circle, consisting of inside students, rise up from their seats and move to their right, sitting in a chair facing a different outside student. This procedure is repeated until each and every inside student sits, face-to-face, opposite each and every outside student. It is crucial that it be the outside students who sit in the stationary, inside circle. Were the inside students to sit in this stationary position, it could create the impression that the inside students are being made objects of the curious gaze of a group of tourists from the outside.

The face-to-face encounter is central to the way in which Levinas explains the ethical relation. "The best way of encountering the Other," Levinas says, "is not even to notice the color of his eyes! When one observes the color of his eyes one is not in social relationship with the Other. The relation with the face can surely be dominated by perception, but what is specifically the face is what cannot be reduced to that." Levinas continues:

> There is first the very uprightness of the face, its upright exposure, without defense. The skin of the face is that which stays most naked, most destitute. It is the most naked, though with a decent nudity. It is the most destitute also: there is an essential poverty in the face; the proof of this is that one tries to mask this poverty by putting on poses, by taking on a countenance. The face is exposed, menaced, as if inviting us to an act of violence. At the same time, the face is what forbids us to kill.[1]

In the Wagon Wheel, one feels both responsible and vulnerable at the same time.

Dostoevsky draws on his prison experience in a remarkable passage in *The Brothers Karamazov*. The novel's moral beacon, Father Zosima, remarks that it isn't truly possible to be "a judge of anyone." Zosima continues:

> For no one can judge a criminal, until he recognizes that he is just such a criminal as the man standing before him, and that he perhaps is more than all men to blame for that crime. When he understands that, he will be able to be a judge. Though that sounds absurd, it is true. If I had been righteous myself, perhaps there would have been no criminal standing before me.[2]

But how can "I" possibly be responsible—as Dostoevsky's revered Father Zosima insists—for someone else's crime?

I asked my students to think about this extraordinary passage from *The Brothers Karamazov*. An inside student named Terry remarked that he'd been thinking deeply about this passage ever since he first encountered it the week before. He resolutely refused to allow anyone else to take responsibility for his crime. "If I did not commit my crime," Terry insisted,

> people would not have had their precious lives cut short by my selfish act. Putting it any other way feels like an avoidance of the truth and a violation of the memory of the lives of my victims.[3]

Danny, an outside student, broke the hushed silence that followed Terry's disarmingly honest words. Danny said that his best friend from high school, at the age of nineteen, was killed in a fight in a parking lot after a major league baseball game. Since his friend's death, Danny said, he "swiftly passed judgment on his murderer, and there was not a doubt in my mind," he observed in his final paper, "that he [i.e., the murderer himself] was solely responsible for his actions." After reading Father Zosima's words, especially within the context of the feelings of deep friendship that developed between the inside and outside students in our class, Danny said that he had now reflected upon the ways in which he may have contributed to the murder. "My actions in high school condoned violence. Fighting others was a rite of passage. It exemplified masculinity and dominance, and was even glorified. I have accepted the possibility that my involvement in these actions helped create an atmosphere that shaped the outcome" of his friend's death.[4]

This, for me, was one of the most extraordinary moments of my teaching literature and ethics in the Inside-Out program. Let me try to explain why.

First, there is the absolute honesty of this exchange, an honesty that is rare in a conventional academic setting, and that encourages students to be vulnerable and to take risks. A large part of what makes Inside-Out classes so special is the fact that inside and outside students come to class, like Prince Myshkin in Dostoevsky's *The Idiot*, without an agenda. In the class I taught in spring 2009 on *Don Quixote* and *The Idiot*, the students and I had the opportunity to reflect on the relation of Prince Lev Nikolaevich Myshkin's surprisingly consistent—indeed, his disruptive—openness toward the Other to the particular atmosphere that made the class such a special experience for the students. We noted how often the notion of emptiness came up in the course of the novel. This occasioned some remarks, on my part, on the doctrine of kenosis, of Christ's emptying and humbling himself, that was so central to Dostoevsky's understanding of the Eastern as opposed to the Western church. Roman Catholicism, for Dostoevsky, equated spiritual with temporal power, and hence with a triumphalist notion of Christianity epitomized by the Crusades. Even Don Quixote, despite or rather because of his idealism, continually exerts his will upon others, not restraining himself from physical violence in pursuit of his ideals, although his weapons are generally hapless and ineffective. Don Quixote has an agenda. What is remarkable about Prince Myshkin, the students maintained, was that, in his relations with others, he has no agenda. In the complex, materialistic, competitive, and upwardly mobile social world depicted by Dostoevsky in his novel *The Idiot*, virtually everyone has an agenda. This fact is exemplified in Ganya Ivolgin's quest for marriage with the beautiful but tragically unstable Nastasya Filippovna, whom Ganya tries to purchase as if she were a thing rather than a human being.

Inside and outside students, in the respective worlds from which they come and which they leave behind when they cross the threshold of an Inside-Out classroom, typically encounter those who have an agenda. Honors college students often make remarks in honors college classes at the University of Oregon, as do Dostoevsky's characters in fashionable St. Petersburg society, in order to impress those who are capable of advancing their careers. They have an agenda. Inside students come to distrust many of the people around them in the prison environment. Even gestures of apparent kindness and openness can be viewed with suspicion as insincere forms of manipulation. Inside and outside students come to study together without an agenda. Students know each other only by their first names. Once the class is over, no further contact is permitted between inside and outside students. This helps to ensure that inside students are not tempted to use their acquaintance with outside students as a way to cultivate contacts that might lessen their sentences. Outside

students, in turn, are discouraged from possibly misusing their friend-
ships with inside students.

Second, this moment confirms for me the reason why I was drawn to
teaching literature—great literature—inside. When I was trained to teach
Inside-Out, the paradigmatic class was in criminal justice. And that made
good sense. If the subject you are studying is criminal justice, it seems
perfectly fitting for a professor to bring his or her college students inside
to give them a firsthand experience of the prison environment. But the
teaching of literary texts? This question haunted me the first time I taught
an Inside-Out class. Why do it here, in this particular environment? Why
drive an hour and a quarter from Eugene to Salem, and then back again,
with a group of University of Oregon undergraduates to study literary
texts when you can do the very same thing back in the classroom in
Eugene? Inside-Out classes bring together students from the outside and
students from the inside. The two groups come from very different worlds
to study together. Reading a shared, great literary text creates community.
A great text has the potential of eliciting powerful individual responses.
Indeed, it *requires* such responses. While outside students often have
better training as academic analysts of literary texts, the inside students
teach the outside students how to read great texts from a profoundly
experiential perspective.

Third, the exchange between Terry and Danny illustrates key aspects
of the ethical encounter upon which Levinas insists. For Levinas, the "I"
is inescapably responsible for the Other. No one can take my place. As
Father Zosima's brother Markel says earlier in the novel (book 6, chapter
2a), "Each of us—before [the faces of] everyone and for everything—is
responsible [*Vsiakii iz nas pred vsemi vo vsem vinovat*], but I more than
all the others [*a ia bolee vsekh*]."[5] I more than all the others! This is what
Terry was insisting, as was Nat, another inside student, in his written
response to this passage, in which Nat remarked that "I can ask mercy for
all others, and refuse it for myself." "It cannot be said," Levinas remarks,
"that we are 'I's in the world. The way in which my 'I' is an I is something
utterly singular in the world." Levinas continues:

> And therefore, *I* am responsible, and may not be concerned about
> whether the other is responsible for me. The human, in the highest,
> strictest sense of the word, is without reciprocity. I didn't discover
> that, Dostoevsky did. It is his great truth: "We are all guilty in every-
> thing in respect to all others, and I more than all the others." This
> "I more than all the others" is the important point here, even if that
> means in a certain sense to be an idiot.[6]

Precisely because of this untransferable responsibility of the I, it is only "I" who can save the world. For Levinas, what the Other does is his or her affair. If there is injustice in the world, *I* need to step up. No one can take my place. I am responsible for the Other, for the world. I can do more. If only I had been more righteous, perhaps there wouldn't be a criminal standing before me now. Perhaps, as Danny observed, if I had worked to create a more peaceful, more loving environment in my high school, I might have thereby prevented the death of my best friend. I am responsible!

What is my role in the phenomenon of crime? Of mass incarceration? What have I done to address the deep social ills that have created the current crisis? "If only I were [more] righteous," Father Zosima notes in *The Brothers Karamazov*, "there would perhaps be no criminal standing in front of me now." What is my role in the phenomenon of crime, and of punitive incarceration? Dostoevsky asked the same question after his experience of serving four years in prison in western Siberia. "How much youth," the narrator of *House of the Dead* asks, "lay uselessly buried within those prison walls, what mighty powers were wasted here in vain!" The narrator continues,

> After all, one must tell the whole truth; those men were exceptional men. Perhaps they were the most gifted, the strongest of our people. But their energies were vainly wasted, wasted abnormally, unjustly, hopelessly. And who was to blame, whose fault was it [*a kto vinovat*]? And that's just it, who was to blame [*kto vinovat*]?[7]

The answer is provided by Father Zosima's brother Markel who, on his deathbed in *The Brothers Karamazov*, says: *I am responsible*. "Each of us—before [the faces of] everyone and for everything—is responsible, but I more than all the others." This sentence, which was to become the mantra of Levinas, to which we have already alluded, is repeated by a number of characters in Dostoevsky's last and greatest novel.

In this book, I read the Russian novel, specifically the novels of Dostoevsky (1821–1881) and Vasily Grossman (1905–1964), in the wake of the moving and influential writings of Emmanuel Levinas (1906–1995). Levinas was born and raised, in the shadow of a prison, in the town of Kaunas, in Lithuania, where his father owned a bookstore that sold mainly Russian books. The young Levinas encountered a preoccupation with ethics, as he would come to understand ethics, in Russian literature and especially in Dostoevsky's novels, which he read in the original. The Russian novel asks all the big questions, including the question about whether or not God exists and the relation of this question to ethical responsibility. "Yes, for real Russians," Alyosha Karamazov tells his brother Ivan, "the questions of God's existence and of immortality . . . come first and foremost."[8] The great philosopher of ethics, Emmanuel Levinas, first found these kinds of fundamental questions addressed in the Russian novel, particularly in the novels of Tolstoy and Dostoevsky. "The Russian novelists ceaselessly wonder," Levinas writes, about "the philosophical problem understood as the meaning of the human, as the search for the famous 'meaning of life [*sens de la vie*].'"[9]

Before he wrote his major novels, Dostoevsky spent four formative years in prison in Siberia for his involvement in allegedly fomenting political unrest. Levinas, before he wrote his major philosophical works, was taken by the Germans as a French prisoner of war and spent five years in captivity.[10] Václav Havel, when he was imprisoned as a political dissident in what was then Soviet-dominated Czechoslovakia, became a devoted reader of Levinas and immediately recognized, in Levinas, the sensibility of a writer who had himself been in prison. Dostoevsky reflects on his captivity mainly in his semiautobiographical prison memoir, *The House of the Dead* (1861). Levinas's notebooks and writings on his captivity have only recently been published (2009).[11] Reading the Russian novel after Levinas means, for me, reading the novels of Dostoevsky and Vasily Grossman for the inspiration that Levinas found in them.

Levinas declared that, in the aftermath of the Shoah, theodicy—explaining evil as somehow part of a divine plan—was no longer possible. Rejecting the traditional ontological understanding of God as a supreme "being" and acknowledging, with Nietzsche, "the death of a certain god inhabiting the world behind the scenes,"[12] Levinas sought to "think God" (*penser Dieu*) on the basis of ethics, outside of ontology.[13] This bold, innovative effort to think God outside of ontology preoccupied Levinas especially from the time he wrote *Otherwise Than Being* (1974) and "God and Philosophy" (1975). It preoccupies Levinas in *Of God Who Comes to Mind* (1982) and persists as a topic for reflection to the end of his life as a writer and thinker.[14]

The novelist who had the most profound impact on Levinas's understanding of ethical responsibility was Dostoevsky, who was tormented by the question of God's existence or nonexistence. Levinas, a practicing Jew, found his own efforts to think God outside of ontology and on the basis of ethics confirmed by Vasily Grossman, a self-proclaimed nonbeliever who wrote the novel *Life and Fate*, the massive Soviet-era version of Tolstoy's *War and Peace*. In this book, I will read the novels of Dostoevsky and Grossman in the context of Levinas's radical quest to think God on the basis of ethics, that is, through the experience of being turned inside out by the Other, a transformative experience which, for Dostoevsky, occurred during his incarceration in Siberia, and especially as he recalled that experience in his *Writer's Diary* in 1876, five years before his death; and in the context of my own teaching of these texts in prison, since 2007, as part of the national Inside-Out Prison Exchange Program.[15]

The compound adjective "Inside-Out" in the title of the Inside-Out Prison Exchange Program refers to the fact that each class taught under the auspices of the program consists both of incarcerated students— students on the *inside*—and of their classmates from outside the prison walls. For me, however, "inside-out" suggests something that happens emotionally to many of those participating in the class. Many of us find ourselves turned inside out, emptied of ego as we experience a tran- scendence of labels and categories—"student," "teacher," "murderer," "prisoner," "criminal"—and respond to the Other as fully human. The class becomes a community of learning based on the dignity, and the absolute uniqueness, of every individual participating in the class. It is often a transformative experience for those involved. We not only read about and discuss ethics in these classes, but the students enact the ethical encounter in which the ego (the "*moi*"), as Levinas describes this encoun- ter, is experienced as "a being divesting itself, emptying itself of its being, turning itself inside out [*à l'envers*]."[16]

This book is divided into five chapters and, in a manner often practiced by Dostoevsky in his novels, preceded by a prologue and followed by an epilogue.

Chapter 1, "Incarceration and Transcendence," explains what Levinas means by transcendence, by the experience of being turned inside out at first by what he calls the no-exit quality of Being, and then by my respon- sibility for the Other. It relates this experience of being turned inside out to Levinas's incarceration as a prisoner of war for five years. And it reads *Crime and Punishment*, the first of Dostoevsky's four great novels, in the light of Dostoevsky's semiautobiographical prison memoir *House of the Dead* (1861).

In chapter 2 I attempt to describe, as precisely as possible, what Levi- nas means by "thinking God on the basis of ethics" by commenting on a few key texts (from the mid-1970s through the mid-1980s) of Levinas's later oeuvre.

Chapter 3 reads Dostoevsky's major novels—*Crime and Punishment, The Idiot, Demons,* and *The Brothers Karamazov*—through the lens of the later Levinas as the novelist's attempt to think God on the basis of ethics, on the basis, that is, of the I's being turned inside out by its responsibility for the Other. And it ponders the powerful influence of Dostoevsky's experience of incarceration on the novelist's understanding of ethical responsibility.

Chapter 4 connects Dostoevsky's hostility toward Jews and Judaism, which became particularly virulent in the last few years of his life, to his personal struggles with religious belief. Here I focus on some key passages in Franz Rosenzweig's great book *The Star of Redemption* in which Rosenzweig reflects on the differences between Judaism and Christianity in regard to the question of belief which, for Rosenzweig, is of more concern to the Christian than to the Jew.

Chapter 5 considers Jewish attitudes toward God, and specifically toward the ontological understanding of God, a topic broached in the previous chapter in reference to Dostoevsky's disturbing, and disturbingly pervasive, hostility toward Jews. The work of both Grossman and Levinas bears witness, I shall argue, to the loss of a belief "in a certain god [*un certain dieu*] inhabiting the world behind the scenes."[17] But in the wake of this loss there is born, or revived, a hope in the continued manifestation of acts of human goodness amidst total moral devastation, manifestations that both authors—one (Levinas) an observant Jew and the other (Grossman) a secular Jew and a self-proclaimed nonbeliever—associate with the word "God."

This book builds on my previous scholarly work on the great philosopher of ethics Emmanuel Levinas, especially my book *Other Others: Levinas, Literature, Transcultural Studies* (SUNY Press, 2010). *Turned Inside Out* offers an original and, I hope, a persuasive reading of Dostoevsky's major novels, as well as an original reading of another great but less well-known Russian novelist, Vasily Grossman. A number of scholars have read Dostoevsky's novels from a religious perspective. Val Vinokur, Jill Robbins, Alain Toumayan, and others have discussed Levinas's reading of Dostoevsky, but no one, apart from Peter Atterton in a seminal essay,[18] has focused on Levinas's preoccupation with Dostoevsky's attempt to think God through ethics, outside of ontology. This book engages in the conversation, begun by Jacques Rolland and continued in Susan McReynolds's and Val Vinokur's recent work, that ponders the relation of Dostoevsky's antisemitism to his theological thought as this finds expression in his fiction.[19] Scholars such as Joseph Frank[20] and Paul Contino[21] have noted the influence of Dostoevsky's prison experience on his thought, but no book or article has brought these two emphases—the carceral and the ethical/theological—together within a single, overarching argument. And no book on Dostoevsky and Russian fiction of which I am aware makes this argument by framing it through the lens of its author's having taught these materials in the very kind of environment—that is, the prison environment—that had such a formative influence on the young Dostoevsky.

This book is addressed to those with an interest in Levinas and to readers of some of the classic novels of Russian literature. The book should have an appeal, as well, to those interested in prisons and in pedagogy. Perhaps readers who are not familiar with Levinas will find themselves intrigued by his compellingly articulated formulations about the relation of ethical responsibility to the significance, that is, the meaningfulness, of the word "God."

Turned Inside Out finds its focus in Levinas, whose philosophical ideas first took shape in response to his early immersion in the classics of Russian literature, especially Dostoevsky, and whose prose, as Václav Havel remarks, clearly bears the traces "of a man who has been in prison. It's there in every line, and perhaps this is another reason why it speaks to me so vividly."[22] In the following pages, and especially in the epilogue, I shall continue to reflect on why reading the Russian novel in prison after Levinas has—at least in my experience teaching inside—had such a powerfully transformative effect both on incarcerated men with no previous university education, or with very little, and on the college students who venture to study with them as classmates inside the prison walls.

Chapter 1

Incarceration and Transcendence

Dispossession, Transcendence, Incarceration: Dostoevsky's *Notes from the House of the Dead* and Levinas as Prisoner

Both Dostoevsky and Levinas spent formative early years in prison. The reasons for their incarceration were very different. Dostoevsky was sentenced as a result of his participation in the Petrashevsky circle of utopian socialists. He was tried and convicted of treason and sentenced to death. Dostoevsky's death sentence was famously reprieved at the last moment, just as he was facing a firing squad in Semenevsky Square in St. Petersburg. His sentence was then commuted to four years of hard labor. Dostoevsky was first incarcerated in the Peter and Paul Fortress in St. Petersburg in 1849, when he was twenty-eight years old. He spent part of his time in the prison in the Peter and Paul Fortress in solitary confinement. He arrived in Tobolsk prison in western Siberia in January 1850 and was released four years later, when he was thirty-two.

Levinas was taken as a French prisoner of war in Rennes with the Tenth French Army in June 1940. As a Jew, he was isolated and separated by his Nazi captors, along with other Jewish French prisoners of war, from his fellow non-Jewish French officers. His imprisonment in various labor camps, first in France and then in Nazi Germany, lasted five years, from 1940 to 1945. His incarceration began when he was thirty-four years old. He was released from a labor camp not far from the infamous Bergen-Belsen concentration camp when he was thirty-nine. As Levinas himself explains on a number of occasions in his writings, it was his French officer's uniform that saved him, under the Third Geneva Convention, from being deported to a concentration camp, for the Germans—remarkably!—adhered to the Geneva Convention in this regard.[1]

I am focusing this study around the subject's undergoing the trauma of being turned inside out (*à l'envers*) and on the relation of this trauma

15

both to ethical responsibility and to the related emergence of the word "God" in the Bible. For Levinas, the glorious road to the subject's being turned inside out by, and responding to, the Other is a two-step process, as he came to see in composing *Existence and Existents* (*De l'existence à l'existent*, more accurately translated "From Existence to the Existent [i.e., to the concrete human being who exists]") and *Time and the Other*, two philosophical works that were conceived and, in the case of the first, largely drafted during his years of captivity. One can try to exit the anonymous rumbling of Being—which Levinas names the *il y a*, the "there is"—through what Levinas calls "hypostasis," that is, through a positing of oneself as a knowing subject. Levinas, who is no irrationalist, associates knowing with an assertive grasping of the true, and hence even with violence. Knowing, for Levinas, is burdened with a likely forgetting—a forgetting not, as in Heidegger, of Being, but rather of one's prior and infinite obligation to the Other, an obligation that precedes knowing and its light. Knowing, for Levinas, is associated with solitude. We can truly exit both the *il y a* and the essential solitude of the knowing subject, for Levinas, through the ethical relation, through a responding to, and a taking responsibility for, the Other.

The I, before being turned inside out by an awakening to its responsibility for the Other, first undergoes a thoroughly disorienting and indeed maddening exposure to what Levinas calls the "there is," the *il y a*, the horrifyingly impersonal and "irremissibile" (i.e., "no-exit") nature of Being. Levinas's reflection on the "there is," he notes in a conversation with Philippe Nemo, "starts with childhood memories. One sleeps alone, the adults continue life; the child feels the silence of his bedroom as 'rumbling' [*bruissant*]."[2] Levinas goes on to say that his friend Maurice Blanchot comes close to articulating what Levinas himself means by the chilling anonymity of the "there is" when Blanchot, in his fiction, speaks of "a night in a hotel room where, behind the partition, 'it does not stop stirring' [*ça n'arrête pas de remuer*]; 'one does not know what they are doing next door.'"[3]

I shall now draw my own example of what I believe Levinas means by the *il y a* from a famous episode entitled "Time Enough at Last" of the venerable television series *The Twilight Zone* (1959–64), created by Rod Serling and broadcast in classic black and white. The episode's protagonist, Henry Bermis, is a bank teller, a voracious reader, and a misanthrope who had been having lunch in the bank's vault. Bermis hears a tremendous explosion and then exits the vault to find himself the last person alive on a planet Earth that has just been destroyed by a hydrogen bomb. The bank teller is socially awkward and an avid reader who wears very thick glasses. After at first experiencing total despair at his situation of complete isolation, he spots an intact library in the distance. He approaches the building and suddenly finds himself among piles of books. He is greatly heartened. He passionately looks forward to all the time he can now spend with his many books. As he begins to dive into his first tome, he stumbles over a rock. His only pair of glasses falls from his face; the lenses lie shattered on the ground. He is now utterly alone in an anonymous universe, and unable to read any of the many books that surround him. There is now no apparent exit from the anonymous rumbling and the rubble of the there is, nor will there ever be any such exit, certainly not through books—and certainly not through the ethical relation, as this is a totally solitary world without others.

Neither Heideggerian anxiety about death nor Sartrean "nausea," as Levinas remarks in *Existence and Existents*, the book he drafted in captivity, accounts for the "horror" generated by the *il y a*, a horror in which "the subject is stripped of his subjectivity, of his power to have private existence. The subject is depersonalized. . . . Horror turns the subjectivity of the subject, his particularity qua *entity*, inside out [*à l'envers*]. It is participation in the *there is*, in the *there is* which returns in the heart of every negation, in the *there is* that has 'no exits' [*sans issue*]."⁴ Horror, for the then incarcerated author of *Existence and Existents*, turns the subjectivity of the subject, his particularity qua *entity*, inside out. In the preface to *Existence and Existents*, Levinas says that this book was "begun before the war" and was "continued and written down for the most part in captivity." With his typical modesty, Levinas remarks that "the *stalag* [Nazi prisoner-of-war camp for noncommissioned, or enlisted, officers] is evoked here not as a guarantee of profundity nor as a claim to indulgence, but as an explanation for the absence of any consideration of those philosophical works published, with so much impact, between 1940 and 1945."⁵

Levinas's description of the *il y a*, of the subject's being turned inside out by its encounter with the no-exit quality of Being in *Existence and Existents*, was doubtless influenced by his experience of incarceration as a profound *dépouillement*—a "dispossession"—of the bourgeois self,⁶ which is content to seek its own needs and comforts, and which is content to enjoy itself. The prisoner, despite his physical "*installation*" in prison, Levinas remarks in his prison notebooks, always feels himself "about to leave" [*sur le point de partir*].⁷ Dostoevsky, likewise, notes that "every convict feels that he is," when in prison, "so to speak, *not at home* [*ne u sebia doma*], but on a visit [*v gostiakh*]."⁸ "Le bourgeois est un homme installé [the bourgeois is a man who sets himself up, who installs himself],"[9] Levinas writes. Incarceration offers the I the opportunity of transcending the bourgeois self in order to become a responsible self. In *Crime and Punishment*, which Dostoevsky published after his semiautobiographical prison memoir *Notes from the House of the Dead*, the police investigator Porfiry Petrovich, who is convinced that Raskolnikov is the murderer he is seeking, urges the young man to confess. Perceiving Raskolnikov's resistance, Porfiry Petrovich asks Raskolnikov if he is "afraid of the bourgeois shame [*styda burzhuaznogo*]"[10] of confessing his guilt. In Dostoevsky, as in Levinas, the term "bourgeois," which is foreign to the prison context, is associated with a conventionality that must be transcended if the I is to assume responsibility for the Other.

Joseph Frank, in his great biography of Dostoevsky, titles one of his chapters on *House of the Dead* "A World of Moral Horror" and observes that "life in the barracks" for the incarcerated Dostoevsky was "a never-ending, rasping assault on Dostoevsky's sensibility at one of its sorest points; there was no escape" from what Dostoevsky, in a letter to his brother Mikhail written just after his release from prison in 1854, describes as "the eternal hostility and quarreling around one, the wrangling, shouting, uproar, din."[11] Upon first entering the prison camp in Omsk, there was no escape for Dostoevsky from the horror of what Levinas would later call the "there is." At the beginning of his incarceration in Siberia, the protagonist of *House of the Dead* says he preferred the risk of exposing himself to deadly diseases in the hospital rather than remain in the prison, for "life was unbearable there, more unbearable than the hospital, [more] *morally* unbearable [*nravstvenno tiazhelee*]."[12] Nor could Dostoevsky imagine escaping the "there is" through books, as the bank teller in the episode from *The Twilight Zone* longed to do, for the prisoners were not allowed to have books, with the exception of the New Testament. As the protagonist Gorianchikov observes toward the end of *House of the Dead*, "living without books, I had no choice but to become absorbed [*uglublialsia*] in myself."[13]

Levinas, in contrast, had access to books beyond the Bible during his five years of incarceration. His prison notebooks record his responses to many writers, including Shakespeare, Dante, Goethe, Vigny, Proust, Goncharov (*Oblomov*), Ariosto (*Orlando Furioso*), Racine (*Phèdre*), Dostoevsky, and Tolstoy. In his prison notebooks, Levinas discusses his own plans to write novels. It was during his years as a prisoner of war that Levinas drafted, as we previously mentioned, his book *Existence and Existents*, with its profound reflections on Shakespeare's *Macbeth* and *Hamlet*. It is even a bit uncanny, given the fact of his later incarceration in a Nazi prison camp, that Levinas titled his first book, which he published in 1935, *On Escape (De l'évasion)*. Even in this early work, before his incarceration, Levinas was interested in escape, in transcendence, in what Jacques Rolland calls the philosopher's early attempt at "getting out of being by a new path."[14]

In *Ethics and Infinity*, Levinas remarks on what I have been calling the two stages of the subject's being turned inside out: first by the "there is" and then by the other in front of me. The I, confronting the impersonality of the "there is," is stripped of its agency. The ego then posits Being, which had just previously been experienced as anonymous, as something in which I inchoately participate, as a something. Levinas calls this something a "hypostasis" of Being (existence) by an existent who, through this very act of hypostasis, differentiates himself from the anonymity of Being. Being is thus posited and, in a sense, dominated. But then—as early as *Time and the Other*, which Levinas published within two years of his release from prison—Levinas speaks of a second and "an entirely different movement [*un tout autre movement*],"[15] an entirely different way of being turned inside out:

> To escape the "there is" one must not be posed [or "pose oneself," *se poser*] but deposed; to make an act of deposition, in the sense one speaks of deposed kings. This deposition of sovereignty by the *ego* is the social relationship with the Other. The dis-inter-ested relation. I write it in three words to underline the escape from being [i.e., from ested-ness] it signifies.[16]

Levinas concerns himself with the obligations incumbent on the subject, on the I. I am responsible for the Other. Citing Dostoevsky's sentence "Each of us is responsible for everything, before everyone, but I more than all the others," Levinas insists that "it is I who support all."[17] But isn't the Other, Philippe Nemo asks Levinas, also responsible for me? "Perhaps," Levinas answers, "but that is *his* affair."[18] The other's responsibility for me, Levinas insists, is his affair. Nevertheless, it is hard to imagine, in Levinas's personal experience of incarceration, of five years of waiting and suffering, that Levinas did not wonder why others were not being turned inside out by the suffering of Levinas and the other victims of Nazi cruelty and oppression. It is hard to imagine that Levinas did not experience the "there is" of his captivity as a time in which others failed to rise to the dignity of their responsible selves and do something to stop the anonymous rustling of Being surrounding Levinas and his fellow Jewish prisoners.

Here is how Levinas, thirty years after his release in his essay "The Name of the Dog" (1975), describes the trauma of having been "stripped" by his Nazi captors of his human skin, of his humanity:

> The French uniform still protected us from Hitlerian violence. But the other men, called free, who had dealings with us or gave us work or orders or even a smile—and the children and women who passed by and sometimes raised their eyes—stripped us [*nous dépouillaient*] of our human skin. We were subhuman, a gang of apes. A small inner murmur, the strength and wretchedness of persecuted people, reminded us of our essence as thinking creatures, but we were no longer part of the world. Our comings and goings, our sorrow and laughter, illnesses and distractions, the work of our hands and the anguish of our eyes, the letters we received from France and those accepted for our families—all that passed in parenthesis. We were beings entrapped in their species; despite all their vocabulary, beings without language. Racism is not a biological concept; anti-Semitism is the archetype of all internment.[19]

Antisemitism is the archetype of all internment. All internment, for Levinas in this passage, strips the subject of his human skin and exposes the I to the relentless anonymity of the "there is." "In horror," Levinas writes in *Existence and Existents*, a subject is stripped (*dépouillé*) of his subjectivity. The verb *dépouiller* from this passage in *Existence and Existents* recalls Levinas's description, in his prison notebooks, of his experience of captivity as *un dépouillement*,[20] a destitution and a dispossession, a having been stripped bare. The passage from *Existence and Existents* looks forward to Levinas's description, in the later essay "The Name of the Dog" cited above, of how his Nazi captors and other Germans in the vicinity of the camp had stripped (*dépouillaient*) Levinas and his fellow Jewish prisoners of their human skin. Levinas would have to wait patiently for five years for a responsible other, having been turned inside out, to dispel the horror of the "there is" for those held captive in their detention camp.

Dostoevsky, whose writings so consistently express a hostility to Jews, himself paradoxically experienced this same archetypal "anti-Semitism," this same subjection to horror of the "there is" without the possibility of escape while in prison, as described above by Levinas. We recall here Joseph Frank's description of Dostoevsky's speaking of the prison camp at Omsk as a world of moral horror. Dostoevsky experienced the dehumanization of persecution in his prison camp in Siberia. Though he eventually

made friends and experienced remarkable acts of kindness from some of
his fellow convicts, he was terribly isolated by the fact of his social class.
He was a gentleman, a member of the educated class, while at least half
of the other inmates were from the peasant class. In a letter from Omsk
on February 22, 1854, that he wrote to his brother Mikhail just after his
release, Dostoevsky expresses the full force of his resentment toward the
peasant convicts who had so relentlessly persecuted him:

> They are a coarse, irritated, and embittered lot. Their hatred for the
> gentry passes all limits, and for this reason they displayed hostility at
> the sight of us, along with a malicious joy at seeing us in such a sad
> plight. They would have devoured us if given the chance.[21]

The reader of *House of the Dead* is constantly reminded of the isolation
and the persecution by the peasant majority of Alexander Petrovich Gorianchikov and the other gentlemen in the prison camp in Omsk.

Compared with the animosity expressed in this letter, Dostoevsky's
attitude toward his fellow inmates is often tempered in *House of the
Dead*, which began to appear in serial form seven years later, in 1861. In
House of the Dead, in contrast to the bitterness he expresses in the letter
to his brother Mikhail, Dostoevsky bears witness to the subject's, or the
ego's, having being turned inside out in the prison camp through the ethical relation—through the I's assuming responsibility for the other.

The narrator of *House of the Dead* describes his experience of a kind
of transcendence in reading these prison memoirs as if he were reading a
travel narrative that was revealing to him an entirely new world: "This
absolutely new, till then unknown world; the strangeness of some facts;
some peculiar observations on these lost creatures," he says, "carried me
away" (*uvlekli menia*).[22] The staid, self-contained narrator of *House of
the Dead* is "carried away," transported, by his reading of the text he
has found, written by a certain Alexander Petrovich Gorianchikov, that
describes the ten years Gorianchikov spent in prison serving a sentence
for the murder of his wife.

Dostoevsky was himself deeply affected by his incarceration. He
entered prison as a young radical from a privileged class with advanced,
European ideas about social equality, and who thought he knew what
was best for Russia but who was, certainly at first, unable to connect
emotionally with the largely peasant population of convicts whom he
had initially found so repellent. Eventually, Dostoevsky's first impressions of his fellow convicts were dramatically reversed. In the process,
he gained, or aspired to cultivate, a sense of fraternal intimacy with

Russia's peasant class as well as with many of those less fortunate than himself.

Dostoevsky does not directly discuss his own personal experiences in prison in *Notes from the House of the Dead*. He chooses, instead, to relate these experiences indirectly, through a narrator who says he has chosen two or three chapters from the manuscript by Gorianchikov which he has discovered and which the author himself refers to as "Scenes from the Dead House" ("Stseny iz Mertvogo doma"). In the first section of *House of the Dead*, Dostoevsky records his protagonist Alexander Petrovich's first impressions of life in prison. We sense, in these pages, the thinness of the persona Dostoevsky has created for the alleged author of these prison chronicles. The veil has been all but lifted. Dostoevsky is speaking here of his own experiences, of the transcendence before the face of the other prisoners that he himself experienced in the prison camp.

The narrator speaks of how, just before entering the prison, he had formed what proved to be an accurate idea of what he could expect when he arrived. Very soon thereafter, however, he "began to find a mass of the strangest surprises." He began to appreciate "the surprising nature" of his existence in the prison and confesses that "this wonder did not leave me throughout the long years of my imprisonment; I could never get used to it."[23] The narrator encounters many surprises. He is struck by the high level of literacy in the prison population, who were mostly peasants; half could read[24] in comparison with only 10 to 15 percent in Russia's general population. The narrator becomes starkly aware, from the very beginning of his stay, of how his rank as a "gentleman" (*dvorianin*)[25] inspires instant and sometimes shockingly callous contempt in his fellow inmates, many of whom, as we have noted, were from the peasant class. He also feels affection for those from different religious backgrounds, including Muslims and the one Jewish inmate, Isai Fomich Bumshtein. The narrator encounters a selfless Muslim named Aley, to whom he teaches the Russian language by reading with him the New Testament in a Russian translation, one of the few books not prohibited in the prison. He is overwhelmed by Aley's kindness, by the Muslim Aley's openness to Christ's Sermon on the Mount while, at the same time, remaining a Muslim.[26]

In his first month as a prisoner, the narrator stunningly concedes to himself that his fellow prisoners are "no worse than other men."[27] He had "suddenly become a man of the same humble class, a convict like the rest."[28] He understands what Levinas will mean by the "saying" as opposed to the "said," with how it is gestures rather than mere words that convey the kindness of prisoners who, like Osip, were "incapable of keeping up a conversation," who "would smile or answer 'yes' or 'no,' and that was all."[29] Or consider Shushilov who, like a caring mother of a young child, would regularly substitute the word "we" for "you" when addressing our protagonist. Shushilov "would never say, for instance, 'You have so many shirts, your jacket is torn,' . . . but always '*We* have so many shirts now, our jacket is torn.'" In spite of a desperate need of money, Shushilov is deeply hurt when he infers that our narrator suspects that a recent act of kindness on the part of Shushilov was motivated by the hope that our narrator would repay Shushilov in much-needed cash in order to allow him to make good on a pressing debt. Shushilov, on the brink of tears, stuns our narrator by telling him, "Alexandr Petrovitch, you think . . . that I do for you . . . for money . . . but I . . . e-ech!" Shushilov begins to sob and our narrator observes that "this was the first time I had seen a man crying in prison."[30]

Ethical Transcendence in Dostoevsky's *Summer Notes on Winter Impressions*

In *House of the Dead*, then, Dostoevsky bears witness, as does Levinas, to kindness, to an infinite kindness that gives without an expectation of reciprocation or reward. The true I, for both Dostoevsky and Levinas, is the responsible I. In his European travels as recorded in *Winter Notes on Summer Impressions*, which he published the year after the appearance of *Notes from the House of the Dead*, Dostoevsky comments on what he perceives to be the absence of brotherhood in the cities of western Europe. Dostoevsky sees everywhere in France the flourishing of the principle of bourgeois individuality at the expense of true *fraternité*, of the brotherhood he himself experienced in the prison in Omsk. In "the French nature—to be sure, in the Western nature in general," Dostoevsky writes, brotherhood "has not shown up." Dostoevsky continues:

> What has shown up is a principle of individuality, a principle of isolation, of urgent self-preservation, self-interest, and self-determination for one's own *I*, a principle of opposition of this *I* to all of nature and all other people. . . . Well, brotherhood could not come from such a self-conception. Why? Because in brotherhood, in true brotherhood, it is not the separate personality, not the *I*, that must plead for the right of its own equality and equal value with *everyone else*, but rather this *everyone else* must *on its own* come to the one demanding his right to individuality, to this separate *I*, and on its own, without his asking, must recognize his equality.[31]

In the last sentence of this quotation, Dostoevsky is firmly stressing the *I*'s responsibility for the rights of the Other that must precede the demand of the *I* for its *own* rights. As Levinas puts it, "the Rights of Man are originally the rights of the *other* man" (the italics are mine).[32] Am I my brother's keeper? The Rights of Man, for Levinas, depend on my responding affirmatively to this question posed by the biblical Cain.[33]

True transcendence, the rupture of the I, for Dostoevsky, came not through travel, where the sovereignty of his ego remained largely intact, and especially not through travel in the bourgeois, post-Enlightenment France of the Second Empire in the early 1860s, but rather in the prison camp in Siberia. During his first month in prison, our narrator remarks that, just before his arrival in prison, he was gifted with a copy of the New Testament in the binding of which several rubles had been inserted by a group of exiles in Siberia. These men, he says, "had long been accustomed to look at every 'unfortunate' as a brother [*brat*], to show pure and disinterested sympathy and compassion for them, as though they were their own children."[34] Our narrator reports on another such benefactor, a widow who, though very poor, did all she could to help the convicts in the prison at Omsk. After the narrator is released, he reports, he went to visit this benefactor and observes, "All that one could see in her was an infinite kindliness [*beskonechnaia dobrota*]."[35] He goes on to observe that "some people maintain . . . that the purest love for one's neighbor is at the same time the greatest egoism. What egoism there could be in this case," he insists, "I can't understand."[36]

I have been arguing that it is in his semiautobiographical prison memoir rather than in his travelogue that Dostoevsky records his experience of being turned inside out by the Other. There is at least one moment in *Winter Notes on Summer Impressions*, however, when Dostoevsky experiences a transcending of his ego before the face of the Other—several faces, in fact. Dostoevsky is in the Haymarket area of London. It is evening. There is a huge crowd of people of starkly contrasting appearances: well-dressed gentlemen gambling in a casino, beautifully dressed women, and people in rags. He is first struck by the beautiful face of a woman whose delicacy of features belies a deep sadness as she apparently feels herself coerced into a demeaning sexual relationship with a wealthy young man who has just bought her a glass of gin. Dostoevsky then observes "little girls around twelve years of age" who "take you by the hand and ask you to go with them." The author continues:

> I remember in the crowd of people on the street I once saw a little girl not more than six years old, all in rags, filthy, barefooted,

hollow-cheeked, and beaten: her body was covered with bruises that could be seen through her rags. She walked as though unconscious of herself, without hurrying, going nowhere, wandering, God knows why, in the crowd; perhaps she was hungry. No one paid attention to her. But what struck me most of all was that she walked with a look of such sorrow, of such hopeless despair, on her face [*na litse*] that to see this little creature, already crushed by such malediction and despair, was somehow unnatural and terribly painful.[37]

One is reminded here of Levinas's description of the face as "without defense" and as "the most destitute also: there is an essential poverty in the face. . . . The face is exposed, menaced, as if inviting us to an act of violence. At the same time, the face is what forbids us to kill."[38] The face, for Levinas, is that which commands me to give to the other. After seeing this young girl's face, Dostoevsky tells his reader, "I turned around and gave her a half-shilling."[39]

The Face of the Peasant Marey

What clearly transformed Dostoevsky during his time in Omsk Prison in Siberia, what suddenly and definitively turned him inside out, as he later came to understand perhaps only fully in retrospect, was a now well-known experience he later describes in *A Writer's Diary* (February 1876). Dostoevsky was twenty-nine years old at the time, still in his first year of captivity. Like Raskolnikov at the end of *Crime and Punishment* when he first entered prison in Siberia, so did Dostoevsky at first feel profoundly ill at ease with most of his fellow prisoners, who were peasants. Dostoevsky, in contrast to the peasants, as we have noted, was, like his protagonist Raskolnikov in *Crime and Punishment*, a political prisoner from an educated class. In *A Writer's Diary*, Dostoevsky describes the contempt he at first felt for the illiterate peasants who shared his captivity. On the second day of Easter week during his first year of captivity, a fellow political prisoner, a Pole rather than a native Russian, tells Dostoevsky how much he despises the peasants who surrounded them. "*Je haïs des brigands* [I hate these robbers]," he says to Dostoevsky, words significantly spoken in French, the cosmopolitan European language par excellence that was incomprehensible to the Russian peasant class.[40]

Dostoevsky returns to his bunk and then suddenly and vividly recalls a moment from his early childhood when he was just nine years old. The remembered event had occurred in late summer as the young child

Fyodor Dostoevsky was about to leave his beloved country home to return to Moscow "to spend the whole winter in boredom over my French lessons."[41] Happily wandering on his father's estate, in sad anticipation of his imminent return to city life, the nine-year-old Fyodor suddenly hears someone shout "There's a wolf!" The young boy, terrified, is then comforted by his family's serf, the illiterate peasant Marey, whose selfless kindness, unnoticed by others, went unrewarded. Now, in prison twenty years later, Dostoevsky recalls this dramatic moment when,

> through some sort of miracle, the former hatred and anger in my heart had vanished. I went off, peering intently into the faces [*litsa*] of those I met. This disgraced peasant, with shaven head and brands on his cheek, drunk and roaring out his hoarse, drunken song—why he might also be that very same Marey; I cannot peer into his heart after all.[42]

From this moment forward during his time in the prison camp in Omsk, Dostoevsky realizes that he must encounter each of his fellow inmates as a "face" in Levinas's sense of the term—infinite, unknowable—that evokes his inescapable responsibility for the Other.[43]

What is the relation of this revelatory moment in the prison camp to the thought of Levinas? The peasant Marey exemplifies, first of all, a responsibility for the Other that ranks goodness above learning. Although he is uneducated, Marey is kind. This is in line with Levinas's insistence that it is ethics rather than knowing that is what he calls "first philosophy." Ethics precedes knowing. Secondly, Dostoevsky's recollection of the unlearned Marey's kindness urges the newly arrived prisoner Dostoevsky not to allow his preconceptions about, or his first impressions of, Russia's peasant class to determine his responses to them. Each peasant, each person, is unique. "True human subjectivity is indiscernible," Levinas observes.[44] We must not respond to the Other as a mere individual of a genus, as a replaceable part of a larger whole, a totality; there is, rather, an indiscernible "secrecy"[45] to the Other's subjectivity, a secrecy that I am commanded to respect. Preconceptions about the Other limit the Other's infinity.

The peasant Marey had taught the young Dostoevsky that, as Levinas frequently remarks, ethics is first philosophy: ethics precedes knowing. I am called out of myself by my responsibility for the Other. I cannot, moreover, peer into the Other's heart. Preconceptions about the Other limit the Other's infinity. The inmate Dostoevsky now realizes that the peasant Marey first taught him these lessons when he was a frightened young child. Recalling this moment in prison, Dostoevsky is now inspired to respond to the face of each of his fellow prisoners in a manner that anticipates the thought of Levinas, whose notion of ethical responsibility was so deeply influenced by Dostoevsky's fiction.[46]

Notes from the House of the Dead and Raskolnikov

The "Epilogue" to *Crime and Punishment* is greatly indebted to Dostoevsky's experiences in the prison in Omsk. Here the author certainly makes good on the claim he had made, in a letter he wrote to his brother Mikhail (dated February 22, 1854) upon being released from prison, that, in the wake of his four-year sentence, as a writer he now has "enough [material] for volumes and volumes."[47]

Dostoevsky was arrested in 1849 for having joined a circle of political activists with utopian ideas. He was charged with the setting up, without properly informing the government, of a printing press that distributed materials encouraging a rebellion of the serfs. Dostoevsky was, by his own account, an intellectual steeped in the secular thought of the European Enlightenment, someone who thought he knew what was best for Russia, including for Russia's peasants. When he entered Omsk Prison in western Siberia the 29-year-old Dostoevsky was profoundly alienated from his fellow inmates, as I have mentioned. Many were peasants who perceived him as aloof and arrogant—very much as Dostoevsky portrays Raskolnikov in *Crime and Punishment*. When Gorianchikov tries to assist his fellow convicts from the peasant class with their manual labor, he was "pushed aside almost with abuse."[48] One of the Polish prisoners who, like Gorianchikov (and Dostoevsky), was from the "gentlemen" class, tells Gorianchikov early on in his captivity that the other convicts "are ill-disposed to you because you are a gentleman and not like them."[49] Dostoevsky emerged from captivity four years later as a humbled, aspiring Christian whose first impressions of his fellow convicts were altered by his experience of living with them, and who had gained, in the process, an enduring longing for a fraternal intimacy with Russia's peasant class. Raskolnikov is in many ways a portrait of Dostoevsky himself before he was sentenced to prison.

In *House of the Dead*, Dostoevsky represents the inmates as respectful of Christian observance. Respect for solemn festival days like Christmas "passed indeed into a custom strictly observed among the convicts; very few caroused, all were serious." They

> tried to keep up a certain dignity. . . . It seemed as though laughter were prohibited. In fact they showed a tendency to be over-particular and irritably intolerant, and if anyone disrupted the prevailing mood, even by accident, the convicts set on him with outcries and abuse and were angry with him, as though he had shown disrespect to the holiday itself.[50]

In the epilogue to *Crime and Punishment*, as in *House of the Dead*, the inmates' hostility toward the newly arrived prisoner—Raskolnikov, in the case of *Crime and Punishment*—is based largely on social class. Raskolnikov, Dostoevsky tells the reader, "was disliked and avoided by everyone. In the end, they even began to hate him—why, he did not know . . . 'You're a gentleman [*barin*],' they said to him. 'What did you take up an axe [the instrument Raskolnikov used to bludgeon the pawnbroker and her step-sister Lizaveta] for; it's no business for a gentleman.'"[51]

In the epilogue to *Crime and Punishment*, Dostoevsky offers another reason, related to social class, for the inmates' hostility towards Raskolnikov. Raskolnikov is an intellectual, and with the opportunity to attend university and the exposure to liberal ideas comes the greater likelihood that one will drift away from the simple faith of one's ancestors, a faith largely shared by the uneducated, peasant population. During his first Easter in the prison, Dostoevsky's narrator reports, Raskolnikov went to church with the other inmates. Suddenly one day "during the second week of the Great Lent," a quarrel broke out and the inmates turned to Raskolnikov and shouted "You're godless! You don't believe in God! [*Ty bezbozhnik! Ty v boga ne veruesh'*] . . . You ought to be killed!"[52] This reaction puzzles Raskolnikov, who notes that he had never discussed matters of religious faith with the other inmates. One of the convicts then "rushed" (*brosilsia bylo*)[53] towards Raskolnikov "in a perfect frenzy" and was about to kill him before he was restrained, at the last moment, by a prison guard.

This passage from *Crime and Punishment* describing the near murder of the novel's protagonist appears to have been inspired by a passage from *House of the Dead* in which that earlier work's protagonist is nearly murdered. There is a significant verbal link between the two passages. We just observed that, in the passage from *Crime and Punishment*, one of the convicts "rushed" (*brosilsia bylo*) toward Raskolnikov. The verb *brosit'sia* ("to rush [at or towards]") appears four times in the passage from *House of the Dead*. In *House of the Dead*, the horrific convict Gazin, a huge, cruel, and hideously ugly man known for the most heinous crimes including murdering and torturing children, comes very close to killing our narrator Gorianchikov but is foiled, as were Raskolnikov's assailants, at the very last minute. Gazin was known for his violent behavior. When he got drunk, "he passed into a stage of blind fury, snatched up a knife, and rushed [*brosalsia*] at people. . . . he fell upon [*brosalsia*] anyone he met." The convicts finally found a way to protect themselves. A dozen or so would rush (*brosalis'*) at Gazin and beat him mercilessly until he was unconscious. This pattern continued for several years until the once seemingly invulnerable Gazin began to break down physically and emotionally. One day Gazin, filled with frustration and resentment after years of experiencing these terrible beatings provoked by the violence he inflicted on others, sets his sights on Gorianchikov and a few of the other "gentlemen" inmates. Irritated at seeing them enjoying their refined and costly gentlemanly ritual of drinking tea, Gazin becomes enraged and is about to bring a huge tray down on the heads of Gorianchikov and a few of the other gentlemen convicts. None of Gorianchikov's fellow inmates are willing, it first appears, to come to his aid because of their class hatred of Gorianchikov. One of the other inmates suddenly shouts to Gazin that some vodka has been stolen. Gazin, alarmed that it was perhaps his own plentiful and expensive supply of vodka that has been pilfered, rushed (*brosilsia*)[54] out of the kitchen. Gorianchikov comments that "the convicts said among themselves" that "God saved them,"[55] that is, God saved Gorianchikov and the other gentlemen prisoners.[56]

In the epilogue to *Crime and Punishment*, Dostoevsky transforms the passage from *House of the Dead*, in which the religious faith of the protagonist Gorianchikov is not primarily at issue, or is at issue only implicitly, into a strong indictment, by his fellow inmates from the peasant class, of Raskolnikov's strongly suspected atheism despite Raskolnikov's having just gone through the motions—apparently unconvincingly, from the peasants' perspective—of communal prayer with his fellow convicts. In the epilogue to *Crime and Punishment*, the particularly heated animosity of the inmates toward Raskolnikov is the result not so much of his higher social class but rather of his atheism, of the fact that he doesn't believe in God. "You're godless!" (*Ty bezbozhnik!*), the convicts shout at Raskolnikov. "You don't believe in God! [*Ty v Boga ne veruesh'*] . . . You ought to be killed!"

This charge puzzled Raskolnikov and it stung Raskolnikov's creator, who was tormented by his desire to believe, as he confessed to his close friend and correspondent Apollon Maikov in 1870 (March 25): "The main question . . . that I have been tormented by [*ia muchilsia*] . . . my whole life [*vsiu moiu zhizn'*] . . . is the existence of God."[57] The bitter truth of the imagined charge leveled against the fictional Raskolnikov by his fellow inmates is confirmed by the future author of *Crime and Punishment* and creator of the character Raskolnikov just after his release from the prison in Omsk. In a letter sent from Omsk to his friend N. D. Fonvizina and dated February 15–March 2, 1854, Dostoevsky writes:

> I can tell you about myself that I am a child of this century, a child of unbelief [*neveriia*] and of doubt [*somneniia*], I have always been and shall ever be (that I know), until they close the lid of my coffin. What terrible torment this thirst to believe [*eta zhazhda verit'*] has cost me and is still costing me, and the stronger it becomes in my soul, the stronger are the arguments against it. And, despite all this, God sends me moments of great tranquility, moments during which I love and find I am loved by others.[58]

Before pursuing these thoughts further, Dostoevsky tells his friend Fonvizina that "it is better to stop talking like this. Why is it," he continues, "that certain topics of conversation are completely banned in society and, if they are broached, someone or other gives the impression of being shocked?"

We shall pursue this shocking conversation in chapter 3 of this book. Specifically, I shall ask how Dostoevsky, in the four great novels of his maturity, confronts the issue of belief in God, especially his own avowed disbelief, alongside his sense that "God" sends him moments during which he loves and finds himself loved by others—moments in which the I is turned inside out by the Other.

The Meaning of Persecution: Dostoevsky and Levinas in Captivity

Before we pursue that conversation, however, I shall conclude this chapter with a brief comparison of the prison experiences of Levinas and Dostoevsky. Both, I have suggested, had the experience of being turned inside out in prison, of having their identity, particularly their "bourgeois" identity, deeply shaken by the experience of their incarceration. This entailed, for both Levinas and Dostoevsky, a sense of horror and of liberation. Both Levinas and Dostoevsky experienced callous, inhumane treatment by their fellow men during their captivity and both, it is worth noting here, were treated more humanely by nonhuman companions, namely by two dogs. Levinas contrasted the treatment he received from his captors and from many of the German citizens he encountered during his captivity with the warmth with which he was greeted by the dog Bobby after his arduous days cutting wood in the German forest near Bergen-Belsen. In a grimly humorous reference to Kant's categorical imperative, Levinas famously refers to Bobby as "the last Kantian in Nazi Germany."[59] The narrator of *House of the Dead* makes a similar observation. "There was only one creature in the world who loved me," Gorianchikov remarks, "who was devoted to me, who was my friend, my one friend—my faithful dog Sharik."[60]

Then there was the experience, shared by both Levinas and Dostoevsky, of the subject's being turned inside out through the ethical relation, by the sense that I am my brother's keeper, and that this is the very meaning of the I. Levinas experienced this fraternal intimacy, this call to fraternity, with his fellow Jewish prisoners. Dostoevsky writes of such moments in *House of the Dead*, but it was perhaps only later, in his reflections on the peasant Marey in his *Writer's Diary*, that Dostoevsky came decisively to see his fellow inmates from the peasant class as brothers for whom he was inescapably responsible.

Immediately following his release, Dostoevsky clearly and bitterly tells his brother Mikhail of how cruelly he was persecuted by the majority of his fellow inmates, and how alienated this made him feel. Levinas certainly experienced profound alienation during his captivity. "The Jew," he writes, "knew he was living in a world that was harsh, without tenderness, without paternity. He existed, without any human recourse."[61] In stark contrast to Dostoevsky, however, Levinas bonded with his fellow inmates in the labor camps in which he was held prisoner during the five years of his confinement. He and the other Jewish prisoners came to feel their persecution in biblical terms as a communal suffering undergone for the sake of bringing righteousness into the world. Even the totally secular Jews, who had never even thought of themselves as Jews before the war, came to experience a transformative solidarity with each other, Levinas observes, in the Nazi labor camps. In his reflections recently published in *Prison Notebooks and Other Unpublished Writings*, Levinas describes how he came to understand the persecution that he and his fellow Jewish inmates experienced in their prisoner-of-war camps in biblical terms as a mark of election, of being part of a people chosen, as it were, to be responsible for the Other, for their neighbor, to pursue good in the world, to be a light to the nations and thus persecuted—like Jesus[62]—for that very reason.[63]

In a text entitled "The Jewish Experience of the Prisoner," which Levinas delivered as a radio broadcast (of September 25, 1945) soon after his release, he speaks of how some of the religiously nonobservant Jewish prisoners were, while in captivity in Nazi Germany, "driven back to their Judaism" and then "sought refuge there." I will take the liberty of quoting from this remarkable passage, only recently published and not previously translated into English, at some length. Levinas continues:

> Jewish history, Hebrew, the Bible appeared worthy of interest and of study. And even religious services became possible.
>
> All this often with awkwardness, almost always without a coherent plan. But the imperfection of human endeavor is only as valuable as the purity of a few instants. I wish to describe some of these exceptional moments, lived during these religious services in captivity where the whole meaning, the whole content of Judaism appeared in miniature.
>
> I shall avoid adopting a facile lyricism to describe the ambiance of these services. A meeting of ten willing participants[64] in the barracks, in the midst of beds illuminated by gas lamps—when there was gas available—by acetylene lamps when there wasn't any gas. But it was necessary that the service not be too long, because the flame of the acetylene lamp goes out quickly especially in the old bicycle lights of which one made use and which were always broken. The end of the service in the dark. I will not say much about the sarcastic smiles of those who did not attend the service out of a sense of obligation to their convictions and their membership in the twentieth century. Always evening services, because at dawn it was necessary to go to work. All these evening services without a future. All the Ma'ariv [evening] services never followed by Shacharit [morning services]. All these twilight rituals.
>
> Rapid flow of ancient prayers. And here are some of the faithful who, in murmuring them half-heartedly, recover, in their souls, the meaning of these ancient formulations.
>
> We are in the period of the great German successes—France crushed, England and London being bombed, Yugoslavia and Greece destroyed, Russia invaded all the way to Moscow.—Force in its most brutal triumph, in this triumph that throws into doubt everything that one had been taught about Good and Evil, about a world governed by Mercy. Someone said: all this leads one to believe either that God isn't good or that he's not powerful.
>
> And the old liturgical words tell unlikely stories: God who loved Israel with an eternal love—the Lord who saves us from the hand of all tyrants—the power of the Pharaoh swallowed up by waves, and

the songs of the rejoicing of Israel. All these Jewish prayers, indefatigable repetition of a belief in the triumph of the weak. What to think of these outdated words when, in 1940 or 1941, one is a Jewish prisoner in Germany and when one tries to make sense of them?

With a contemptuous air to close the prayer book and to leave, restraining oneself from uttering the blasphemous remark that is hurrying to one's lips? To repeat these things without thinking about them, without believing them, with the indulgence one can allow for the ingenuousness of ancient times, to think that these things were dead and that one was without the benefit of religious teachings and without truth as one was without protection and without a future. At the bottom of the abyss, to implore the Lord like Jonas?[65] All this certainly, and by turns. But one was still able to climb, for an instant, a brief instant, up a rung and to exit from that magic circle where one was turning. One was able to find, in that love of God, a terrible confirmation in the experiences themselves of sorrow and of doubt. In the total passivity of having been abandoned, in the detachment from all connections—to feel that one is in the hands of the Lord, to be affected by his presence. On the burner of suffering to sense the flame of the divine kiss. To discover the mysterious turning around of extreme suffering into happiness. What then, ultimately, is Judaism—how does it differ from other religions that are full, as is Judaism, of moral teachings and of good precepts—these other religions having also had access to the idea of the unity of the divine principle; what is Judaism if not the experience, since Isaiah, since Job, of this possible turning around—having hope, in the depths of despair—of sorrow into happiness; the discovery in suffering itself of the signs of election. All of Christianity is already contained in this discovery which long precedes Christianity. Oh! there were instants when the perverse contentment in suffering penetrated some of us at the very moment we were becoming aware of the triumph of Force and our affirmation of the eternal love of the Lord for Israel was no longer either a lie or an anachronism.[66]

Here is a Jewish solidarity that, sixty years earlier, as we will note in chapter 4, had so threatened Dostoevsky, who will complain, in the *Writer's Diary*, of the Jews excluding "the Russians"[67] in the prison camp in Omsk, and who had a completely different experience of persecution in captivity from that of Levinas. Perhaps the most notable quality of Dostoevsky's experience in prison was one of isolation from the other prisoners, mainly of the peasant class. Dostoevsky's experience in prison was of a relentless persecution with no meaning. That meaning came later for Dostoevsky, when he imagined himself, in the wake of the recollection of his childhood encounter with the peasant Marey, as an aspiring participant in what he came to understand as the salvific and self-sacrificing mission of the Russian people (*narod*), as I will discuss in chapter 4.

Chapter 2

✦

Thinking God on the Basis of Ethics
in Levinas's Later Work

In chapter 1, I spoke of what Dostoevsky referred to as his chronic religious "unbelief," of his insatiable but forever frustrated "thirst to believe [*zhazhda verit'*]." I noted that the fundamental question that had, by his own admission, always tormented him—and that continued to torment him—was the question of whether or not God exists. "Yes, for real Russians," Alyosha Karamazov tells his brother Ivan, "the questions of God's existence and of immortality . . . come first and foremost."[1] In chapter 3, I shall argue that Dostoevsky, in the four great novels of his maturity, attempts—anticipating Levinas—to think God on the basis of ethics, outside of ontology, outside of the question of God's existence or nonexistence that so tormented him. This attempt reaches its culmination and, as it were, its destination in the trial scene toward the end of Dostoevsky's last and greatest novel, *The Brothers Karamazov*, in Ivan's offer of substitution for his innocent brother Dmitry: "Come, take me instead of him!" Here the I is individuated, singled out as responsible for the other, even for an other of whom the I is not particularly fond.

There is perhaps an irony here for believers, for Dmitry's words "Come, take me instead of him!" issue from the lips of one of Dostoevsky's most famously skeptical characters, someone who had concluded that, if God does not exist, which is distinctly possible, then everything is permitted. This moment of the transcendence of the skeptic Ivan's ego toward the Other perhaps calls into question any necessary correlation between my firm and unwavering *belief* in God, on the one hand, and my assuming of fraternal responsibility, on the other. In chapter 3, I shall look at the relation between "belief" in God and ethical responsibility in the great novels of Dostoevsky's maturity—in *Crime and Punishment*, *The Idiot*, *Demons*, and *The Brothers Karamazov*. I shall take note of how Dostoevsky, who was so skeptical regarding questions of belief, attempts in these novels to think God outside of ontology, outside of the question of God's existence or nonexistence, on the basis of ethical responsibility.

But what does Levinas mean, exactly, by thinking God outside of ontology, outside of the question of God's existence or nonexistence? What does Levinas mean by thinking God *à partir de l'éthique*, on the basis of ethics, or beginning with the ethical relation? In order to answer this question, in the current chapter I shall focus mainly on three pieces of Levinas's writings in which his explicit aim is precisely to "think God outside of onto-theo-logy."[2] I shall, in the first section of this chapter, discuss a transcription of the last set of lectures Levinas delivered as professor of philosophy at the Sorbonne in a course on "God and Onto-theo-logy." Levinas gave the first lecture of this course on Friday morning, November 7, 1975 and the last on Friday morning, May 21, 1976. These lectures were transcribed and edited by Jacques Rolland, the author of *Dostoïevski: La question de l'autre* (1985), a book based on the author's doctoral thesis written under the supervision of Levinas. In the second section of this chapter, I shall comment on passages from Levinas's crucially important essay "God and Philosophy," which was first published in spring 1975. In the fifth section of chapter 3, in which I discuss *The Brothers Karamazov*, we shall turn our attention to Levinas's second magnum opus, *Otherwise Than Being*, a haunting and challenging work that was published during this same period of the mid-1970s, which breathes this same atmosphere, and which concludes with an allusion to Levinas's notion—so important for his thinking God on the basis of ethics—of "illeity."

Before commenting on the writings of Levinas mentioned above, it will be useful to hear Levinas speak, in as clear and summary a manner as possible, about what he means by thinking God through the ethical relation. I shall begin by quoting two passages. The first is from the foreword to the first edition of Levinas's book *Of God Who Comes to Mind* (*De Dieu qui vient à l'idée*), published in 1982:

> The various texts assembled in this volume represent an investigation into the possibility—or even the fact—of understanding the word "God" as a significant word [*un mot signifiant*]. This investigation was carried out independently of the problem of the existence or non-existence of God.[3]

The second is from the preface to the second edition of this same book, published in 1986:

> This work, which attempts to find the traces of the coming of God to mind [*la venue de Dieu à l'idée*], of his descent upon our lips, and his

inscription in books, limits itself to the point at which, thanks to the upwelling [*surgissement*] of the human within being, there can be an interruption or suspension of the impenitent perseverance of being in its being, . . . of the struggle of all against all. . . . This interruption . . . is produced in the human being responding to his neighbor who, as an Other, is a stranger to him. . . . A responsibility . . . that comes to me from the face of the Other where both abandonment [*l'abandon*] and the election of his uniqueness signify simultaneously; the command of being-for-the-other or of holiness [*sainteté*] as the source of every value. . . . This imperative to love—which is also election and love reaching him who is invested by it in his uniqueness qua responsible one—is described in *Of God Who Comes to Mind* without evoking creation, omnipotence, rewards, or promises. We have been reproached for ignoring theology. . . . We think, however, that theological recuperation comes after the glimpse of holiness [*l'entrevision de la sainteté*], which is primary.[4]

In the preceding passage, Levinas clearly expresses some of what, for him, comes to mind when he hears or speaks the word "God"—meaning the God of the Bible—considered outside of the question of God's existence or nonexistence. What comes to mind, for Levinas, when he thinks God beginning with, or on the basis of, ethics—*à partir de l'éthique*—is "the upwelling [*surgissement*] of the human within being," of the absolute centrality and necessity of human agency and moral effort suddenly materializing out of the subject's immersion in an anonymous Being. The word "God" evokes, or bears witness to, a shattering interruption and a suspension of the natural order of beings seeking merely their own persistence in being, of beings seeking, above all, their own place in the sun, at the expense of other beings. This interruption evoked by the word "God," moreover, finds its locus in my response to the face of my neighbor who may well be a complete stranger to me, whom I am tempted—and possess the freedom—to disregard, even to murder, but whose uniqueness, at the same time, I feel uniquely commanded and singled out to serve, and even to love.

God and Onto-theo-logy

Thinking God on the Basis of Ethics

Let us now turn to the lecture Levinas delivered at the Sorbonne on the morning of December 5, 1975. The title of this lecture, "Penser Dieu à partir de l'éthique" ("Thinking God on the Basis of Ethics"), describes precisely the quest to which, I shall be suggesting, the four great novels of Dostoevsky's maturity bear witness.

"Penser Dieu à partir de l'éthique" is the fourth lecture in a course on the subject of "God and Onto-theo-logy." The word "onto-theo-logy" is a reference to Heidegger, specifically to Heidegger's readings of Hegel in Heidegger's essay "The Onto-Theological Constitution of Metaphysics." At the beginning of this lecture, Levinas acknowledges that it is Heidegger who broke with Plato and the Greek philosophical tradition in general, as Levinas understands that tradition, by no longer considering the question of being from a serene distance by a self-contained consciousness as "an interrogation held by man with curiosity." The question of being, for Heidegger, has not been settled. Being is itself in question. "Being," Levinas says, "is in question in man." Since being, in which man participates, is at stake, "a rupture is produced with the rationality of repose."[5]

Heidegger, for Levinas, decisively breaks with the Greek rationality of repose that produced the static ontological understanding of God as a supreme being. Levinas, too, toward the end of his lecture, will emphasize the significance of "agitation" and disquiet for his attempt to think God on the basis of ethics. Levinas shows how God has been understood as an ontological concept, and he reflects on the betrayals that this process leaves in its wake. Heidegger tried to think Being, in time, as Be-ing, that is, outside of ontology understood as the mind's pursuit of essences. Levinas wishes to think God outside of both ontology, as that word is conventionally understood, as well as "outside of onto-theo-logy" (de penser Dieu en dehors de l'onto-théo-logie). Is it possible, Levinas asks, "to think God outside of onto-theo-logy? Is it possible to formulate a model of intelligibility [un modèle d'intelligibilité] that would permit such a thinking? And more precisely," Levinas continues,

> since this is what our question shall become: on the basis of an *ethics* that would no longer be the corollary of a simple vision of the world, could we not formulate a model of intelligibility such that we could think God outside of onto-theo-logy?[6]

Husserl's phenomenology, for Levinas, never transcends immanence, for it never departs from "an aiming or intending by a vision." Even negative theology remains within the economy of intentional thinking and of ontology. The road to transcendence, for Levinas, is through the subject's being turned inside out by my obligation to the other. Responsibility for the Other "goes to the point of fission, all the way to the de-nucleation of the 'me.'"[7] Note that, in Rolland's transcription of this lecture, the word "me" (*moi*) is here written with the initial letter ("m") in the lower-case, as is the word for the "i" (*je*) who is humbled, turned inside out by the Other. Let us look at the words "I/i" (*Je/je*) and "Me/me" (*Moi/moi*) in Rolland's transcription of Levinas's lecture and the relation of these words to the ethical encounter. I (*Je/je*) is "I" in the nominative case, the I as subject. The "I" that eludes exposure to the Other is the *Je* (uppercase). This is the "I" as concept, the political rather than the ethical "I," the I that is the individual individuated insofar as I participate in a genus but am not absolutely unique. Even as it thinks of itself as an individuated "I" in a legal sense, the "i" (*je*) remains "unique" in the impossibility of its evading its responsibility to the other. The "I" (*Je*) who inhabits imperial time, a finite time composed of instants in which it instantiates itself in (political) being, is suddenly struck (*frappé*) by the inquietude of the "all of a sudden" (*tout un coup*). Note that this expression *tout un coup*, consisting of three words meaning "all of a sudden," contains the word *coup*, which means "blow," a "striking." Upon exposure to the Other— though it is "always already" so exposed—the "I" (*Je*) is dethroned and, as it were, humbled to a *je*. The "disquiet of the *all of a sudden*" is "the traumatism that agitates rest [*repos*]," the rest that is the "arresting" [or stopping: *l'arrêt*] of "time." This time of suddenness is "the beating of the Other in the Same," a "pure patience" and "a waking up [*éveil*] in regard to the neighbor, a suddenness that becomes the proximity of the neighbor."[8] This suddenness creates nonfinite, or infinite time.

What is the relation of all this to the word "God"? In this particular lecture, we get only a hint, but a significant one, that is contained within a parenthesis. We have noted that the word "blow" (*coup*) is contained in the French phrase meaning "all of a sudden" (*tout un coup*) and that the time of suddenness is, for Levinas, the time of the "beating of the Other within the Same" (*battement de l'Autre dans le Même*). Levinas writes, "Recall that in Hebrew the *blow* [*coup*] and the striking or beating [*battement*] of the *bell* [to mark time] have the same etymology: the verb 'to agitate [*pa'am*].'" We are then referred, in a note, to a verse from Judges (13:25) in which we are told, of Samson, who is about to save the persecuted Israelites: "the spirit of God began *to disturb him* [*leph'amo*] in the camp of Mahaneh-dan, between Zorah and Eshtaol."[9] A bell, when *struck* by a small hammer (the word for this tool in Hebrew is *pa'amon*), marks time. Biblical time, however, is very different from imperial time. Biblical time is created by the trauma that agitates rest, arresting imperial time. Biblical time bears witness, for Levinas, to the time of the *je* (i) as opposed to the *Je* (I); it is the time of suddenness, the time of "the beating of the Other in the

Same," the time that agitates Samson on behalf of the Israelites in the camp of Mahaneh-dan. Biblical time is more generally the arresting of Pharonic time by Mosaic time, by the time of revelation that awakens Moses, the most humble of men, to rise to his uniqueness as the one who answers the call to responsibility and who leads his people out of their slavery in Egypt, out of their slavery to imperial time in order to serve the Other.

Witnessing and Ethics

It was Levinas who made the just-cited reference to Samson. The reference to Moses was mine. Throughout this chapter on what Levinas means by thinking God on the basis of ethics, I shall continue to refer to passages from the Bible that, in my view, do precisely this, that is, "think" God on the basis of ethics, as understood by Levinas. Before we turn to a discussion of Levinas's philosophically challenging essay "God and Philosophy," I shall conclude my remarks on "God and Onto-theo-logy" with two citations from the Bible that clearly illustrate what Levinas means when he says that, for the Bible, "to know God is to do justice to the neighbor" (*connaître Dieu, c'est faire justice au prochain*).[10] These quotations appear in a chapter of *God, Death, and Time* entitled "Witnessing and Ethics," a transcription of the lecture Levinas gave at the Sorbonne as part of his course on "God and Onto-theo-logy" on Friday, April 23, 1976. The first quotation is from the prophet Jeremiah (22:15–16) who, in prophesying to Jehoiakim, king of Judah, says of Jehoiakim's father, the successful King Josiah:

> Behold, your father ate and drank, and practiced justice and righteousness—then it went well for him. If one does justice to the poor and destitute, then it is good; is this not 'knowing Me' [*ha da'at oti*]?—the word of HASHEM.[11]

The second is from the gospel of Matthew (25:31–40) in the New Testament:

> When the Son of man comes in his glory, and all the angels with him, then he will sit on his throne of glory. Before him will be gathered all the nations, and he will separate them one from another as a shepherd separates the sheep from the goats, and he will place the sheep at his right hand, but the goats at the left. Then the King will say to those at his right hand, "Come, O blessed of my Father, inherit the kingdom prepared for you from the foundation of the world; for I

was hungry and you gave me food, I was thirsty and you gave me drink, I was a stranger and you welcomed me, I was naked and you clothed me, I was sick and you visited me, I was in prison and you came to me." Then the righteous will answer him, "Lord, when did we see thee hungry and feed thee, or thirsty and give thee drink? And when did we see thee a stranger and welcome thee, or naked and clothe thee? And when did we see thee sick or in prison and visit thee?" "*Truly I say to you, as you did it to one of the least of these my brethren, you did it to me* [italics mine]."[12]

It was a special privilege to have facilitated a discussion of the preceding passage and this chapter of *God, Death, and Time* in an Inside-Out class I taught on *God, Death, and Time* and Dostoevsky's novel *The Idiot* in the Oregon State Penitentiary, a maximum-security correctional facility, in spring of 2009. "I was in prison," Jesus/God says in this passage, "and you came to me." "When did we visit you in prison?" ask those seeking to inherit the kingdom of God. "As you visited the lowliest of my brethren in prison," Jesus says, "you visited me." In this section of this book, I am attempting to connect what Levinas means by thinking God on the basis of ethics to my being turned inside out (*à l'envers*) by my responsiveness to, my responsibility for, the Other. The following remark, made by an inside student named Leslie from that class, bears witness to this very connection between the word "God" and the experience of being turned inside out by the Other within the prison environment:

> This wasn't a religion class, [but] it was a spiritual sanctuary for me. This class transformed my personal spirituality. I felt God, the spirit, the humbling force, or some higher power within human interaction. I no longer doubt a higher being because one was evoked in conversations in class.[13]

"God and Philosophy"

We turn now to Levinas's essay "God and Philosophy," published in 1975. This is Levinas's most sustained and focused meditation on what it would mean to think God on the basis of, or beginning with, ethics, outside of ontology. The essay consists of six sections: "The Priority of Philosophical Discourse, and Ontology"; "The Priority of Ontology and Immanence"; "The Idea of the Infinite"; "Divine Comedy"; "Phenomenology and Transcendence"; and "Prophetic Signification."

The Priority of Philosophical Discourse, and Ontology

In the first section, on "The Priority of Philosophical Discourse, and Ontology," Levinas begins with a quotation that he wishes to put into question: "Not to philosophize is still to philosophize." The quotation is from Aristotle's youthful text the *Protrepticus*, which has been reconstructed by scholars; the text's authorship is debated. The quotation is cited and endorsed by Derrida at the conclusion of his famous essay on Levinas entitled "Violence and Metaphysics." Aristotle's point seems to be, in accord with the Socrates of Plato, that not to think is willfully to resign oneself to languishing in the world of opinions, of *doxai*, to settle for the shadowy and self-satisfied life of the person Plato refers to as the "philodoxer"—the lover of opinions—rather than to become a philosopher, a lover of wisdom. Levinas is turning this sentiment in a slightly different direction. The quotation, for Levinas, suggests that Western philosophical discourse "compels every other discourse to justify itself before philosophy." The meaningful is that which shows itself. The philosopher must not, and cannot, think beyond (*au-delà*) the *geste d'être*, beyond the exploit or gesture or movement of being. Thought that is meaningful is thought of being, or of the exploits or adventures of being.

But here we have a problem, for Levinas, in confronting a text like the Bible and the God of whom the Bible speaks. If God is to have a meaning, in the ontological sense, this God must be placed within being's moves, within the *geste d'être*. The problem with making such a translation or transposition from Hebrew to Greek is that, while Greek thought moves within the boundaries of verisimilitude, of lifelikeness, "the God of the Bible signifies in an improbable manner [*de façon invraisemblable*] the beyond of being, or transcendence. That is, the God of the Bible signifies without analogy to an idea subject to *criteria*, without analogy to an idea exposed to the summons to show itself true or false."[14]

Let us stop to consider Levinas's adjective "*invraisemblable*," which describes the manner in which, for Levinas, the God of the Bible "signifies" or "means," has a meaning. This adjective means both "unlikely" or "improbably" as well as—taken literally—"not like the true." Why "not like the true"? Because the God of the Bible signifies in a manner that exceeds, that is different from or is irrelevant to, the ontological categories of truth or falseness, of verifiability. Hence, to ask the question of God's existence or nonexistence, and to be tormented by this question, as was Dostoevsky, is from Levinas's perspective precisely to insist on the all-inclusiveness (the *englobement*) of Western philosophical discourse and to exclude from the meaningful all forms of signification that are not philosophically verifiable.

We may try to think the transcendence of God through ontology, and when we do so we may then think of God as existing "eminently [*éminemment*] or *par excellence*." But, Levinas asks, "does the height, or the height above all height, which is thus expressed, still come under the jurisdiction of ontology?" Levinas then goes on to reflect on the meaning of these adverbs that register the transcendence conveyed by the word "God," if the God of the Bible is thought through ontology, or, we might say, if God's transcendence is translated from Hebrew into Greek, if God, that is, is said to "exist": if God is spoken in Greek, he then is conceived as existing "eminently or *par excellence*." Either of these two adverbs—"eminently" or "*par excellence*"—suggests God's existence in terms of height, in terms of "the sky stretched above our heads." As for the adjective "eminently" (*éminemment*): in Latin, the verb *emineo* means "to stick up," "to rise high above one's suroundings."[15] As for the adverb "*par excellence*": the Latin verb *excello*, which is related to the word *excellence* in the phrase *par excellence*, is likewise expressed in the terms of "the sky stretched above our heads." The secondary meaning of the verb *excello* is "to be preeminent or conspicuous, surpass, excel." Its primary meaning is "to be superior in height."[16] The verb *excello* contains the word *caelum*, meaning the sky or the heavens. The transcendence of God, in the language of ontology, is said to be or to exist "excellently," or *beyond the sky*. The meaning of the word "God" is thus, by ontology's own admission, excluded from the graspable, from being. It is "ungraspable" (*insaisissable*).

What, then, can we conclude from ontology's own admission that the God of the Bible is not thinkable, properly speaking (*n'est pas à proprement parler pensable*)? We might conclude, as has the philosopher Jeanne Delhomme, that the concept of God is one that is not only problematic. It is rather, according to Delhomme, "not a concept at all."[17] Levinas sees conceptual thought, or that which drives the need for conceptual thought, as deriving, ultimately, from the responsibility that is commanded by the transcendent God of Abraham, Isaac, and Jacob. Plato, the founder of philosophical thought in the Western tradition, anticipates Levinas's insight, if we understand this transcendent God—in nonliteral terms—as a commanding Good beyond being that, for Plato, is the ultimate source of philosophical thought, or of being itself. Delhomme, a philosophical rationalist, thus dismisses as nonsense, as meaningless, that which, for Levinas, is the very source of rationalism.

The importance of the last paragraph of the first section of "God and Philosophy"—which we shall consider imminently—cannot be over-emphasized both for its plumbing the depths of the ultimate sources of Dostoevsky's torment over the question of God's existence or non-existence, and more generally for calling into question the conventional distinction between reason and faith that has so dominated Western thought at least since the Middle Ages. As Etienne Gilson argued in his classic book *Reason and Revelation in the Middle Ages*,[18] what distinguishes the Middle Ages from earlier and later periods is the achievement, through the work of Thomas Aquinas, of what Gilson calls the harmony of reason and revelation. The modern period begins, Gilson implies, when these two realms of philosophy (beginning with the Greeks) and faith (biblical truth) come to be seen as mutually exclusive, when we are left, that is, with an unphilosophical theology and an untheological philosophy. Gilson divides his concise book into three parts, which he entitles the primacy of faith, the primacy of reason, and the harmony of reason and revelation. At one extreme of those who accept the absolute primacy of faith is Tertullian of the second century C.E. Philosophy is conceived by thinkers of this stripe as the absolute enemy of religious faith. The more balanced strain of those who adhered to the primacy of faith is represented by Augustine (fourth century) and his followers. For Augustine, religious faith in a revealed truth does not preclude the use of reason. Faith is, rather, the starting point of rational knowledge: "Believe that thou mayest understand."[19] These realms of reason and faith, for Gilson, are reconciled through the Thomistic tradition in the Middle Ages. In the Renaissance, with the rise of humanism, these two realms drift apart until, in the Enlightenment, we get the familiar separation, still prevalent today, of Athens from Jerusalem, of philosophy from faith.

Levinas's thinking the God of the Bible on the basis of ethics radically calls into question the conventionally stated antagonism between philosophy and faith. "It is not certain," Levinas writes, that, "in going beyond the terms of being [*être*] and that which is [*étant*]," which is precisely what Levinas is attempting in this particular essay, "one necessarily falls back into the discourse of opinion or of faith [*la foi*]." For Levinas, *both* "faith and opinion speak the language of being." In fact, Levinas asserts, "nothing is less opposed to ontology than the opinion of faith." Let us ponder this full sentence by Levinas, as well the previous sentence:

> In fact, while remaining outside of reason, or while wanting to be there, faith and opinion speak the language of being. Nothing is less opposed to ontology than the opinion of faith.[20]

When stating *what* I believe, that *what* is stated in the language of being, in the language of ontology. That *what* may be "outside of reason"—it may be miraculous or apparently supernatural—but it is stated, nonetheless, in the language of being.

"Faith" (*pistis*), moreover, in Platonic terms, is, like opinion (*doxa*), understood explicitly in relation to knowledge (*noesis*).[21] Faith—and this would include religious faith—is understood as a lesser form of knowledge, as is opinion. Thus faith and opinion remain squarely within ontology, are spoken in the language of being. The Hebrew word *emunah*, often translated as "faith," is related to the word *aman*, meaning "firm," and is associated, in contrast to Plato's *pistis* ("faith"), with firmness of action rather than of belief. In Exodus 14.13 the Israelites, having witnessed the miracle of the parting of the Red Sea and having just escaped the defeated Egyptians who had been so hotly pursuing them, now "had faith in (or trusted [*ya'aminu*]) God and in Moses, His servant." "Faith in Moses" has nothing to do with an act of faith in that which is beyond understanding. "Faith in Moses" has nothing to do with ontology. Nor, in this instance, does "faith in God"—which the text couples with faith in Moses, who is a human being—have to do with ontology. The text is saying that the Israelites now trust Moses, who had just led them out of slavery in Egypt, and that they now trust, as well, the words of the liberatory God Moses has continually been evoking.

The explicit aim of the essay "God and Philosophy," Levinas says, is to ask "if God cannot be uttered in a reasonable discourse that would be neither ontology nor faith [*ni ontologie, ni foi*]."[22] This is to call into question, Levinas says, the "formal opposition . . . between, on the one hand, the God of Abraham, Isaac, and Jacob, invoked without philosophy in faith and on the other the god of the philosophers."[23] It is to call into question, that is, the conventional opposition between Athens and Jerusalem, between "reason" and "faith." Must we truly choose between Athens and Jerusalem?

Is meaning (*sens*), Levinas asks, limited to being, "to the *esse* of being"? Or, rather, is philosophical meaning not perhaps already a *restriction* of meaning? "We must ask ourselves," Levinas says, if

> beyond the intelligibility and the rationalism of identity, of consciousness, of the present and of being—beyond the intelligibility of immanence—the significance, the rationality, and the rationalism of transcendence are not themselves understood.[24]

"Our question," Levinas continues, "is whether, beyond meaning, a meaning might not show itself whose priority, translated into ontological language, will be called *prior* [*préalable*] to meaning."²⁵ This "*prior* to meaning," this "beyond the intelligibility and rationalism of identity [*par delà l'intelligibilité et le rationalisme de l'identité*]," as we shall see, has everything to do with the meaning—the significance, the *sens*—of the I's being turned inside out by its exposure to the Other.

The Priority of Ontology and Immanence

The title of the first section of "God and Philosophy" is "The Priority of Philosophical Discourse and Ontology." The meaning of this title would seem to suggest, at first glance, that Levinas is asserting that, for thought, philosophical discourse and ontology come first, or that they "compel every other discourse to justify itself before philosophy."²⁶ But this would be to endorse rather than to put into question the quotation, of Aristotelian and Derridean provenance, with which this section, and in fact this essay itself, began: "Not to philosophize is still to philosophize." The first section of the essay ends with Levinas's emphatically stating that the question he is posing in the essay "God and Philosophy" is "whether, beyond being, a meaning might not show itself whose priority, translated into ontological language, will be called *prior* [*préalable*] to being."²⁷ The essay "God and Philosophy" is itself composed in the language of philosophy. It is written in Greek, the language of being which, it is true, translates and to some extent betrays the alterity of every other discourse, such as the biblical discourse that speaks the word "God." Thus philosophical discourse asserts its own priority, the priority of philosophical discourse and of ontology. But what Levinas wants to ask about here is the significance of this priority, this before, the meaning of that which comes prior (*préalable*) to being. Hence, there is a sense in which the title ("The Priority of Ontology and Immanence") of the second section of "God and Philosophy," on which I am now commenting, announces that its author will attempt to articulate, in the language of philosophy, that which is prior to ontology and immanence, *la priorité d l'ontologie et l'immanence* in precisely this sense.

The first paragraph of this section on "The Priority of Ontology and Immanence" is difficult. It becomes clearer if we recognize that, in French, the word *conscience* means both consciousness and conscience, that the word *conscience* in French has a potentially moral dimension that is not the case with the word "consciousness" in English. Phenomenologists speak of the intentionality of consciousness. Consciousness is consciousness *of* something, as Levinas says in the second paragraph of this section. But what is prior to consciousness, especially understood, as in French, as *conscience*? Being, for Levinas, is manifestation. Philosophy is "a manifestation of manifestation." "Philosophy would thus remain," Levinas says, "in its attachment to being—to the existent or to the being of the existent—an intrigue of knowledge and truth, an adventure of experience between the clear and the obscure. It is certain that this is the sense in which philosophy carries the spirituality [*la spiritualité*] of the West, wherein spirit [*l'esprit*] remained coextensive with knowledge."[28] Into this last sentence Levinas introduces the words "spirituality" and "spirit," which sound jarring when spoken in the context of philosophical discourse. The word *esprit* in French, moreover, as does the word *Geist* in German, usually refers to the analytical mind rather than, as in English, possessing the religious aura evoked by the word "spirituality." All this adds to the jarring quality of this sentence in French.

Knowledge, Levinas says, is not reflection, a word that is an optical metaphor suggesting a mere mirroring of something outside of consciousness. Knowledge (*savoir*) is somehow deeper. "Knowledge comprehends itself in its own essence, starting from consciousness (*conscience*), whose specificity spirits itself away (*s'escamote*) when we define it (i.e., knowledge, *savoir*) with the aid of the concept of knowledge (*à l'aide du concept du savoir*) which supposes it (*qui la suppose*),"[29] i.e., which we conventionally assume is implied by the word "knowledge."

What is this specificity that spirits itself away in our common assumptions of the nature of pure knowing, of *conscience*? The implication here is that consciousness is, ultimately—or rather, primordially—haunted by conscience. Here Levinas introduces the term *insomnia* as the primordial category of consciousness. "Insomnia—the vigil [*la veilée*] of awakening [*l'éveil*]—is disturbed . . . by the *Other* who cores out all that which in insomnia forms a core as the substance of the Same, as identity, as repose, as presence, as sleep. It is cored out by the Other who rends this rest."[30] Levinas is here trying to speak about insomnia in the language of philosophy, more specifically in the language of a Husserlian phenomenology that seeks to find an equivalence—an adequacy, an equality—between thinking (*noesis*) and that which is thought (*noema*). The word "insomnia," for Levinas, comes as close as a thinker can come to realizing the formal precision of a category, for insomnia is a "form not *arresting* (or fixing) its own design as a form, not condensing its own emptiness [*son proper vide*] into a [stable and unchanging] content." Insomnia is, in this sense, truly: "Non-content—Infinity."[31]

Insomnia, then, is for Levinas in his essay "God and Philosophy," the category that is located at the forever self-emptying core of consciousness, of *conscience*. In regard to our subtle and difficult task of thinking

God through the ethical relation, we cannot help but recall, in response to Levinas's meditation on the insomnia that continually haunts consciousness, the opening four verses of Psalm 121:

> A song of the ascents. I raise my eyes upon the mountains; whence will
>   come my help?
> My help is from The Unseen One, the Maker of heaven and earth.
> He will not allow your foot to falter; your Guardian will not slumber.
> Behold, He never slumbers nor sleeps, the Guardian of Israel.[32]

Is this psalm not an expression of gratitude to the Infinite, to the Unseen One, the Maker of heaven and earth who has created man, whose consciousness, cored out by responsibility for the Other, is continually and forever haunted precisely by *insomnia*?

Neither Husserl's phenomenology nor Heidegger's, for Levinas, provides us with a way out of immanence. And how can we think God, how can we think transcendence, within immanence? Immanence and consciousness are not, finally, shaken (*ébranlées*)[33] by affective states, such as anxiety, analyzed so brilliantly by Heidegger or by the axiological and practical levels of experience that Husserl apparently freed from their dependence on the theoretical level. Levinas states that he will attempt to describe "the affectivity that is transcendence . . . elsewhere [*ailleurs*]."[34]

We will not find this break with immanence and consciousness, however, in "'religious experience,' for "the 'narrative' of religious experience does not shake [*n'ébranle pas*] philosophy and, consequently, could not break the presence and the immanence of which philosophy is the emphatic accomplishment." The possibility of thinking God outside of ontology, for Levinas, means asking the broader question of whether or not discourse "can signify otherwise [*autrement*] than by signifying a theme. Does God signify as a theme of the religious discourse that names God, or as a discourse that precisely, at least at first glance, does not name him, *but says him in another way than by denomination or evocation* [italics mine]?" Is it possible to think God outside of ontology, outside of the question of God's existence or nonexistence that so tormented Dostoevsky? This brings us to the next section of Levinas's essay, "The Idea of the Infinite."

The Idea of the Infinite

Thematizing God, that is, making God the object of a discourse, albeit a discourse on "religious experience," Levinas argues, "has already spirited

away [*escamoté*] or 'missed' the very excessiveness, the very uncontain-ability of the scenario [*l'intrigue*] that ruptures the unity of the 'I think.' "
Here Levinas turns to Descartes's *Meditations*, specifically to Descartes's notion of the infinity associated with God. Descartes wishes, through his positing of the idea of infinity, to prove the existence of God by stating that only God, who is infinite, could have placed that particular idea in me. Levinas explicitly states that he is not interested in such proofs of God's existence but rather in Descartes's description of "the breakup of consciousness" that is "a sobering up [*dégrisement*] or a waking up [*réveil*] that shakes the 'dogmatic slumber' [described by Kant] that sleeps at the bottom of all consciousness resting upon the object."[35] "This idea of God surpasses every capacity, its 'objective reality' as a *cogitatum* [as something thought] causes the 'formal reality' of the *cogitatio* [i.e., the very essence of what it means to think] to break apart." The idea of God—"understood as signifying the uncontained *par excellence*"—causes the breakup of thinking both as a thinking *of*, that is, of thinking as inten-tionality; and of thinking as presence, that is, a thinking that "merely encloses" the thinker "in a presence, re-presents, brings back to presence." This is not a subject that tries to think negation as a formal category such that we might establish a negative theology by saying what God is not. It is, rather, "precisely *the idea of the Infinite*, that is, the Infinite in me."[36] And this would be the idea of the infinite in me in the two senses of the prefix "in" of the word "infinite": both as "not" finite and as "within" the finite, that is, within me.

The word "receptivity" does not do justice to the manner in which I encounter the Infinite, for this would be to posit a sovereign self that would have the choice of either welcoming or dismissing the Infinite. No, "in the idea of the Infinite is described a passivity more passive than any passivity appropriate to a consciousness"—a consciousness that, by defi-nition, seizes on objects that are adequate to it. The idea of the Infinite is rather "an awakening [*éveil*]" that suggests "the passivity of the created one." This would be a notion of a created one not necessarily in the sense of a world and a humanity literally created by the God of the Bible, but rather of a radical passivity at the heart of human subjectivity.

"The having placed [*la mise*] in us an unencompassable [*inenglobable*] idea overturns this presence to itself which is consciousness."[37] Note that Levinas here uses the past participle of the verb *mettre*. It is not "the plac-ing in us [of an unencompassable idea]," which would be *la mettante*, but rather *la mise*, the "having placed" in us an unencompassable idea, the idea of the Infinite, of God. The Infinite, or God, is thus an idea signifying with a significance prior to presence, to all presence, prior to every origin in consciousness, and thus an-archic [i.e., not having an *arche*, or origin in consciousness], accessible only in its trace. It is thus an idea signifying with a significance that is straightaway older than its exhibition. . . . What can this significance more ancient [*plus antique*] than exhibition mean? Or, more precisely, what can the antiquity of a signification mean? In exhibition, can it enter into a time other than the historical present [*le present historique*, i.e., the narrative technique that speaks of events from the past in the present tense], which already cancels the past and its dia-chrony by re-presenting it?

Events that happen at the same time are synchronous with each other. The "dia-chrony" of the past is that which, older than consciousness, resists being assembled into the present of consciousness.[38]

For Levinas, as he concludes this section of "God and Philosophy," this antiquity is found in "the trauma of awakening [*éveil*]."[39] Levinas wonders if the Infinite does not awaken "a consciousness that is not sufficiently awake. As though the idea of the Infinite in us were exigency and signification, in the sense in which, in exigency," that is, in a situation that demands something of us, "a command is signified."[40] Levinas asks if Infinity or God, which exceeds representation, might not signify—beyond or otherwise than through representation—as a moral summons such as Dostoevsky's "Each of us is responsible before the faces of everyone for everything, but I more than all the others."

Divine Comedy

Let us go directly to the following difficult sentence: "The difference between the Infinite and the finite is a non-indifference of the Infinite with regard to the finite, and is the secret of subjectivity" (*La différence de l'Infini et du fini, est une non-indifférence de l'Infini à l'endroit du fini et le secret de la subjectivité*).[41] What, precisely, does the "non-indifference of the Infinite with regard to the finite" mean? The Infinite, Levinas is saying, is absolutely integral to thought. It is not loftily unconcerned with the finite, like the gods of Epicurean provenance. The Infinite devastates thought, it is true, but it also calls, elicits thought. By a "having put it [i.e., thought] in its place, the Infinite puts thought in place. It wakes thought up."[42]

In what sense is "the negativity of the *In-* of the Infinite" a "divine comedy"? Levinas is speaking here of the desire for the Good which, unlike need, is a desire that is never satisfied, a desire for what Plato's Socrates, who evokes the comic genius of Aristophanes in the *Symposium*, calls, in the *Republic* (509c), the Good "beyond being." The word "God" comes to mind when we register how "the goodness of the Good—of the Good that neither sleeps or slumbers—inclines the movement it calls forth to turn it away from the Good and orient it toward the other, and only thus toward the Good." By virtue of its very intangibility, its transcendence, "the Desirable separates itself from the relationship with the Desire that it calls forth and, by this separation or holiness, remains a third person,"[43] an *il*, hence Levinas's coinage, to which we have previously referred, of the word *illeity*, a commanding illeity that, for Levinas, appears to issue from an *il* (he) that lies at the core of the *tu* (thou).

For Levinas, I do not encounter God directly, but only through my responsibility for the Other. Rather than saying "I believe in God," the I, in approaching the other, bears witness to the infinite, to "illeity," or, if you will, to "God," though we must remember that, in the Hebrew Bible, the word "God" is never actually pronounced or written. I do not confront God directly, or see God face-to-face. I confront God, through illeity, as Michael Morgan writes, "as a trace or residue, as having passed by, and the locus of that having-passed-by and of that trace is the face of the other person."[44] As Levinas writes in his essay "Signification and Sense" ("La Signification et la sens" [1964]), the "revealed God of our Judeo-Christian spirituality preserves all the infinity of his absence" and "shows himself only in his trace, as in chapter 33 of Exodus." "You will see My back ['*achorai*]," God tells Moses in this passage, "but My face may not been seen" (33.23). God's "glory" (33.18) consists in Moses's seeing "all God's goodness" passing or, rather, *having passed*, before him. To go toward God, Levinas writes, "is not to follow this trace" as if the trace were a sign or symbol of the entity or being "God." It is, rather, "to go towards the Others who stand in the trace of illeity."[45]

In *Ethics and Infinity*, Levinas gives an example of what he means by illeity—or almost gives such an example, which I will take the liberty to provide. "I am going to relate to you," Levinas tells his interlocutor Philippe Nemo,

> a peculiar feature of Jewish mysticism. In certain very old prayers, fixed by ancient authorities, the faithful one begins by saying to God "thou" and finishes the proposition thus begun by saying "he," as if, in the course of this approach of the "thou" its transcendence into "he" supervened.[46]

What prayers does Levinas have in mind? Levinas may well have been thinking of a passage from Rav Chaim of Volozhin's *Nefesh Hachaim*.[47] It is one of the most common formulas of prayer in the Jewish liturgy: *Baruch attah adonay eloheynu melech ha'olam asher kideshanu bemitzvotav vetzivanu*. . . . ("Blessed art Thou, Veiled One [a translation of the four letters, without vowel markings, of the so-called unpronounceable tetragrammaton, called in Jewish tradition the "yod-hē-vav-hē" and prounced "*adonay*"], our God, King of the universe, who has made us holy with your *mitzvot* [commandments], and commanded us . . .."). As Levinas remarks, the faithful one begins by calling God "thou" (*attah*), and then finishes by referring to God as "he" who has already commanded us: the words *asher kideshanu vetzivanu* mean "[He] who has made us holy and who has commanded us." The prayer begins as an address in the second-person singular ("Blessed art thou") and then the loyal or faithful one (*le fidèle*) suddenly shifts to the third-person singular (perfect tense) and addresses God as "[he] who has sanctified us and commanded us." What does this change of person from "thou" to "he"—the very kind of stylistic device that Longinus refers to as one of the sources of the sublime[48]—suggest, or gesture toward? This Longinian rhetorical gesture suggests that, in the context of this particular prayer, it is only through responding to an ethical command, that is, to what "he"/*il* has commanded of me morally, that I approach God. Taking responsibility for the Other is precisely how I approach God. There is, in fact, no other approach.

Illeity bears witness to "an extraordinary turning around of the desirability of the Desirable," commanding me, paradoxically, to desire "the undesirable proximity of the others."[49] In this ethical turnabout, "God is pulled out of objectivity, out of presence and out of being. He is neither object"—something to be known, or something or someone in whom I can believe—"nor interlocutor," someone I address as Thou. "His absolute remoteness, his transcendence, turns into my responsibility—the non-erotic *par excellence*—for the other." God is "other than the other, . . . other with an alterity prior to the alterity of the other, prior to the ethical obligation to the other and different from every neighbor, transcendent to the point of absence." But God's absence from presence hardly means that the word "God" is without meaning. Hence, Levinas says, it was necessary for him in the essay "God and Philosophy" to restore this extraordinary word to the meaning of every narrative in which ethics emerges, to this narrative which is a "divine comedy without which" the word "God" "could not have arisen" (*à la comedie divine sans laquelle ce mot n'aurait pu surgir*).[50]

Phenomenology and Transcendence

Here Levinas calls into question, once again, the sufficiency of the notion of "religious experience." Religion, for Levinas, precedes experience, "religious" or otherwise. The latent birth of religion is "in the other . . . prior to 'religious experience' that speaks of revelation in terms of the disclosure of being." Cain famously asks God (Genesis 4:9), "Am I my brother's keeper?" Is biological human fraternity sufficient cause for me to care for my brother Abel? Before God has been "thematized" as an entity, a being in whom I can either believe or not believe, I must first be hollowed out by the other, must first hear his cries "cried out toward God." "My responsibility . . . is a hearing or an understanding of this cry. It is an awakening." An awakening to responsibility. Cain's question is a serious one, for "responsibility does not come from fraternity," that is, from the mere biological fact of fraternity. Just because Abel is Cain's brother doesn't mean that he is responsible for him. True fraternity consists in hearing and obeying the command of responsibility issuing from "him," from the *il* of *illeity*, from God as father of the human family. "It is fraternity" in this sense "that gives responsibility for the other"—for my brother—"its name, prior to my freedom."[51] True fraternity is responsibility for the other prior to my freedom.

In section 16 of "God and Philosophy" Levinas explicitly interprets *The Brothers Karamazov* as Dostoevsky's thinking God through the ethical relation. Here Levinas again cites the words "Each of us is guilty before everyone, for everyone and for everything, and I more than the others" (*Chacun de nous est coupable devant tous pour tous et pour tout, et moi plus que les autres*).[52] He relates these words to two phrases from the Hebrew Bible, the first uttered by Abraham and the second by Moses.

The first is from the remarkable passage in Genesis in which Abraham argues with God about his intention to destroy utterly the cities of Sodom and Gomorrah. Abraham, horrified by the prospect of the death of innocents, asks God (Genesis 18:23–25), "Will you really wipe out the innocent with the guilty? . . . Far be it for You to do such a thing, to put to death the innocent with the guilty . . . Will not the Judge of all the earth do Justice?"[53] Then, two verses later, comes Abraham's "I am but dust and ashes,"[54] cited by Levinas in "God and Philosophy." Abraham's moral audacity in questioning God is, in truth, performed in all humility, and goes so far, in this regard, as to appropriate the language of sacrifice. Levinas understands Abraham's "I am dust and ashes" as a "consummation of a holocaust [*consummation de holocaust*], a burnt offering, "a consummation for the other whose very light glimmers and illuminates

out of this ardor, without the cinders of this consummation being able to
make themselves into the kernel of a being that is in-itself and for-itself,
and without the I opposing to the other any form that might protect it or
bring it to a measure [*ou lui apporte une mesure*]."[55] The second is from
Exodus 16:7. Moses, known as the humblest of men, is here minimizing
his own importance, and his brother Aaron's, in comparison with God.
Moses asks, "What are we?" Rashi understands this phrase as meaning
"of what significance are we?"[56]

   "What is signified by this summons," Levinas asks,

> in which the subject is cored out as if enucleated, and receives no form
> capable of assuming it? What do these atomic metaphors [i.e., the
> subject that "cores itself out as if enucleated" (*se dénoyaute comme
> dénucléé*)] signify, if not an I [*moi*] torn from the concept of the Ego
> [*Moi*] and from the content of obligations for which the concept
> rigorously furnishes the measure and the rule? What do these meta-
> phors signify if not an I . . . that one does not designate but which
> says, 'here I am.' 'Each of us is guilty before everyone, for everyone
> and for everything, and I more than the others,' says Dostoevsky in
> *The Brothers Karamazov*. . . . This is an I who says 'I,' and not one
> who . . . individuates the concept or the genus." This is not the recur-
> rence of consciousness but rather the "the recurrence of awakening
> [*reveil*], which one can describe as the shiver [*frisson*] of incarnation,
> through which *giving* takes on meaning, as the original dative of the
> *for the other*, in which the subject becomes heart [*coeur*] and sensitiv-
> ity [*sensibilité*] and hands that give."[57]

This "I," this subject does not prove the existence of the Infinite but rather
bears witness to it.
   This awakening of the subject "is a surprise for the respondent himself. . . . The openness of the I exposed to the other is the bursting open
[*l'éclatement*] or the having been turned inside-out [*la mise à l'envers*] of
interiority. Sincerity is the name of this extraversion . . . I am the witnessing, or the trace . . . of the Infinite."[58] In the *Republic* of Plato, the corrupt
Gyges owns a ring that makes him invisible. He rapes and plunders without being seen, and is thus able to maintain his reputation as a good man.
When I say "here I am"—*me voici* (in French)—the infinite is not "in
front of me" ('*devant*' *moi*). It is, rather, "I who express it . . . in giving a
sign . . . of the 'for-the-other,'" by saying "here I am [*me voici*]. . . . A marvelous accusative: here I am under your gaze,"[59] that is, you can see me, a
phrase that reflects the etymology of the word *voici* in French. As Bettina

Bergo comments, the phrase *me voici* preserves "the accusative form *me*, which English translates as 'here I am.' The preposition *voici* amalgamates 'to see' or *voir* in the form *vois* and the preposition *ci*, or here. *Voici* is thus 'you see me here.' "[60] Here I am, under your gaze, obliged to you, your servant. You see me here, and what you see is the sincere expression of me. I am not a Gyges, deceiving you, trying to do you harm while protected by my secret of invisibility. I am not playing a role. No, here I am, as the Bible puts it, "in the name of God" (1 Samuel 17:45). "The sentence in which God comes to be involved in words," Levinas writes, "is not 'I believe in God.' The religious discourse prior to all religious discourse is not dialogue." Rather, it is the "here I am" said by the I turned inside out by the Other. The " 'here I am,' said to the neighbor to whom I am given over, and in which I announce peace, that is my responsibility for the other." Levinas then goes on to quote—just before he begins the final section, on "Prophetic Signification," of "God and Philosophy"—a passage from the prophet Isaiah (57:19): "In making language flower upon their lips. . . . Peace, peace to him who is far off, and to him who is near, says the Eternal."

Prophetic Signification

The previous section of "God and Philosophy" ends with a reference to one of the prophets, Isaiah. The next and concluding section focuses on prophecy. Readers will be disappointed and confused, however, if they assume that Levinas, by prophecy, means the capacity to predict the future. Prophecy is, rather, for Levinas, the saying of "here I am" before the face of the neighbor, of the Other. "The Infinite transcends itself in the finite," in me, "without exposing itself to me" as a theme. "The Infinite *signifies* in the sense in which one says, *to signify an order* [*signifier un ordre* (i.e., "to serve a notice")]."[61] The Infinite serves me notice. Levinas refers here to a passage from the prophet Amos, quoting the second part of the verse (3:8) and alluding to the first: "A lion has roared; who will not fear? The Lord HASHEM/ELOHIM has spoken; who will not prophesy?" Amos "compares the prophetic reaction to the passivity of the fear that seizes him who hears the roaring of wild animals." I respond to the order as a pure witnessing before I comprehend it. I am inspired in the sense that "I make myself the author of what I hear." I am the vehicle for an anachronistic truth, for what Plato calls the Good beyond being, which is more venerable, older than being and presence.

Levinas begins the last section of "God and Philosophy" with a reference to Plato's "Good beyond being," to which I have just alluded. Plato's

"Good beyond being," Levinas says, "is an idea that guarantees the philosophical dignity [*la dignité philosophique*] of an enterprise in which
the significance of meaning [*la significance du sens*] separates from the
manifestation or presence of being. But one can only wonder if Western
philosophy has been faithful to this Platonism."[62] The dignity of philosophy consists in my acknowledging, with Plato, that the very existence
and essence of what is known or knowable derives from the Good, and
that "the Good is still beyond being, exceeding it in dignity [*presbeia*,
meaning in *dignity*, in the sense of "seniority" or "venerability"] and in
power" [509b]. The clarity of the visible, of what is illuminated in the
synchronic discourse of philosophy, owes its being to what is, as it were,
beyond—and before—being, namely to the venerability of the Good,
which commands me to say "here I am" before the face of my neighbor,
as Socrates, in the midst of the corruption of fifth-century Athens, says
"here I am" to the Athenians seeking his guidance in their own pursuit
of the Good amidst that corruption. Socrates is the prisoner who, having
turned around—or having been turned inside out—in Plato's cave, makes
the descent back into the cave to serve others.

"The intelligibility of transcendence is not ontological,"[63] Levinas
insists. Or, to put this slightly differently, the transcendence of the forms,
in the Platonic sense—in the ontological sense—derives from a previous
transcendence, a having been turned inside out by my responsibility for
the other in front of me. "The transcendence of God"—of the Infinite,
of what Plato calls the Good "beyond Being"—"can neither be said nor
thought in terms of being," Levinas insists. But this doesn't exclude the
possibility that the word "God" is a significant word, a word that regis-
ters, in fact, "the rupture between philosophical intelligibility and what is
beyond being, or the contradiction that there would be in com-prehending
the infinite." That the transcendence of God can neither be thought nor
said in terms of being, that is, of ontology, does not mean that the word
"God" boils down to "simple thoughts about a being in decline"; or to
something conceptually so vague as to be unworthy of thought; or—with
a nod here perhaps to the deconstructions of Derrida, with whose citing
of the Aristotelian "Not to philosophize is still to philosophize" Levinas's
essay began—to mere wordplay. [64]

Levinas concludes "God and Philosophy" by stating that, in our time,
"a presumption of ideology weighs upon philosophy."[65] This is a reference
to Marxism and to Marxist ideology, which is suspicious of the indiffer-
ence of philosophical inquiry toward the glaring social inequalities so
evident throughout the world. Levinas hears, in this presumption, "a
bearing witness to responsibility. The presumption begins in prophecy,"

as Levinas understands prophecy, and as he has been explaining it in this section of "God and Philosophy." Not to philosophize would therefore not be still to philosophize, but rather "to bear witness"—before beginning to philosophize in propositions, in the language of disclosure—"in interjections and in cries."[66] God is not, for Levinas, "a merely precarious certitude [*certitude simplement précaire*],"[67] with all the precariousness suggested by Dostoevsky's desperate, and finally unquenchable, "thirst to believe" (*zhazhda verit'*), but rather "the signification of an order given to subjectivity before any statement: a pure one-for-the-other [*pur l'un-pour-l'autre*]."[68] We moderns, who so highly prize our freedom—in the sense of our own autonomy—above all else might well view the ethical sensibility, as Levinas describes it, as a deprivation of freedom, "unless this would be but the trauma of a fission of oneself come to pass in a venture"—to evoke the language of the Bible—"risked with God or through God [*une aventure courue avec Dieu ou par Dieu*]." "Transcendence," Levinas writes, "owes it to itself to interrupt its own demonstration," which, as pure "monstration,"[69] as pure "showing" or "exhibition," even in the text of the Bible itself, must be brought back to its ethical meaning. God must be thought, that is, beginning with ethical obligation. In the next chapter, we will explore how Dostoevsky, in the four great novels of his maturity, attempts to do precisely this.

Chapter 3

Thinking God on the Basis of Ethics in Dostoevsky's Major Novels

Godlessness, Belief, and Love in *Crime and Punishment*

The question of God's existence or nonexistence, and the relation of this question to ethical responsibility, preoccupies Dostoevsky in the great novels of his maturity—in *Crime and Punishment* (1866), *The Idiot* (1868), *Demons* (1871), and *The Brothers Karamazov* (1879). In *Crime and Punishment*, Raskolnikov commits his murder of the old pawnbroker under the spell of a kind of totalizing Hegelian atheism.[1] He sees his victim not as a human being but rather as a somehow necessary sacrifice in his deluded quest to help humankind advance to a new stage in world history. Dostoevsky portrays Raskolnikov as a proud and often arrogant atheist who, only at the very end of the novel, begins to accept responsibility for his crime through the selfless love gratuitously offered to him by Sonya, who is a Christian. Sonya's love for Raskolnikov, and her forgiveness, allow the arrogant murderer to accept and to face himself and to take responsibility for his crime.

In Raskolnikov's first interview with the police investigator Porfiry Petrovich in part 3, chapter 3 of *Crime and Punishment*, Dostoevsky calls his protagonist's faith into question. Raskolnikov asserts that he is a believer, but his manner of speaking belies the content of his words. Porfiry Petrovich, to the astonishment of Raskolnikov, has read Raskolnikov's article about the extraordinary man who, in working toward the betterment of mankind in general, may even find it necessary to "step over" (*pereshagnut'*)[2] "a dead body," to "step . . . over blood" in order to advance mankind towards "a goal [*k tseli*]."[3] Do you believe," Porfiry Petrovich asks Raskolnikov, in the "New Jerusalem"[4] promised in the book of Revelation (21:1–3)? "I believe [*Veruiu*],"[5] Raskolnikov answers firmly, though in answering the question he continually looks at the ground rather than at the face of his interlocutor. Perhaps because Porfiry Petrovich imagines that Raskolnikov may understand this "New Jerusalem" in a secular sense—that is, as the utopian socialists' immanent heaven on earth rather than the transcendent *eschaton* of Christian theology—the investigator then asks Raskolnikov, point-blank, "do you also believe in God?" "I believe," Raskolnikov "repeated [*povtoril*],"[6] giving the reader the impression, by means of the verb "repeated," that there is something rote, something perhaps not quite heartfelt in Raskolnikov's response. Then Porfiry Petrovich asks Raskolnikov, "do you believe in the raising of Lazarus?"—and, by implication, in the possibility of resurrection? "I be-believe [*Ve-veruiu*],"[7] Raskolnikov replies, his stutter giving the speaker away as a shaky believer at best, though Raskolnikov (questionably) insists, in answer to Porfiry Petrovich's next question, that he believes "literally [*bukval'no*]."[8] For Porfiry Petrovich, and perhaps for Dostoevsky as well, Raskolnikov's suspected nonbelief clearly increases the likelihood that he is the murderer of the aged pawnbroker Alyona Petrovna and her younger half-sister, Lizaveta.

So far, then, Dostoevsky appears to be suggesting that Christian belief and ethical responsibility go hand in hand: the embracing of Christian belief, for Dostoevsky at this stage in his spiritual and creative journey as a novelist, is an antidote for pride. But even as early as *Crime and Punishment*, Dostoevsky questions any easy association of ethics with Christian *belief*. Or, more precisely, Dostoevsky appears to rank the experience of being turned inside out by the other as more significant and, as it were, holier, than an avowed expression of *belief* in God. An openness to the possibility of being turned inside out by the other, we might say, bears witness to God in a way that the assertion of mere belief does not.

We do not believe Raskolnikov when he assures Porfiry Petrovich that he not only believes in God, but that he also believes—and believes literally—in Christ's raising of Lazarus. Jacques Rolland, who transcribed Levinas's lectures at the Sorbonne that are contained in the book *God, Death, and Time* and who is also the author of *Dostoïevski: La question de l'Autre*, remarks that Dostoevsky, in *Crime and Punishment*, writes the time of his narrative as the time of "the beating of the Other-within-the Same."[9] Raskolnikov may be a religious skeptic, but there is no doubt that he has an alert moral sense, a deep and abiding moral conscience.

In part 6 of the novel, the murderer Raskolnikov is at a crossroads. He is wracked by guilt, by his conscience. There are only two ways out: he will either kill himself or confess his guilt to the authorities. His sister Dunya and his lover Sonya both fear that Raskolnikov will choose suicide. Raskolnikov contemplates suicide, but decides against it. He tells Dunya that he "wanted to end" his life by throwing himself into the Neva River, but he couldn't, finally, go through with it, to which Dunya responds:

> "Thank God! We were afraid of just that, Sofya Semyonovna and I! So you still believe in life—thank God, thank God!" . . .
>   Raskolnikov grinned bitterly.
>   "I didn't believe, but just now, with Mother, I wept as we embraced each other. I don't believe, but I asked her to pray for me. God knows how these things will work out, Dunechka, I don't understand any of it."[10]

This passage is interesting for the way it ponders and plays with the notion of belief, and with the word "God." For Dunya, in her concern for her brother's fragile mental state and the terrifying specter of his possible suicide, what matters is not so much her brother's belief in God as his belief in life. Sonya and Dunya are both believing Christians, and Sonya is particularly devout. Dunya, in response to her discovery, to her great relief, that Rodya has chosen *not* to take his own life, says to her brother, "So you still believe. . . ." We expect that Dunya's next words will be "in God." We expect her to say, that is, "So, you still believe *in God*." But what she says, instead, is "So you still believe in life" (*v zhizn'*).[11] Rodya then replies as if he had in fact heard Dunya say, "So you believe *in God*," for he responds, "I didn't believe" (*Ia ne veroval*).[12] But Rodya, when contemplating his suicide and deciding not to kill himself, *did* believe in life; if he didn't, he would have killed himself, as he was planning to do. When Rodya says "I didn't believe," then, he appears to mean that he didn't believe *in God*, for he immediately goes on to say, "I don't believe [*ia ne veruiu*],[13] but I asked her to pray for me," that is, in my recent meeting with my mother, I asked her to pray for me even though I don't believe in God. Immediately upon asserting that he doesn't believe in God, Rodya paradoxically invokes God's name: "God knows [*Bog znaet*] how these things work, Dunechka, I don't understand any of it."[14] Rodya says he doesn't believe in God, but he nonetheless invokes God's name.

The ending of *Crime and Punishment* has been faulted for the forced quality of Raskolnikov's conversion to Christianity. Yet even here we witness more a shift in Raskolnikov's feelings rather than in his beliefs. Has Raskolnikov, in fact, been "converted"? Or does he, rather, experience a transcendence of his ego that is, finally, turned inside out by his love for Sonya, by his realization that "he loved her infinitely" (*beskonechno*)?[15]

Dostoevsky writes that Raskolnikov was now "risen" (*voskres*), it is true, but it is not the case that he suddenly now "believes" in the immortality of the soul and in the afterlife. Dostoevsky's emphasis is upon life, not the afterlife. "Instead of dialectics," Dostoevsky writes of Raskolnikov's newly attained spiritual state, "there was now life [*zhizn'*]."[16] Raskolnikov has a copy of the Gospel under his pillow, the very same text from which Sonya had earlier in the novel read to him about the raising of Lazarus from the dead. Raskolnikov entertains the possibility that Sonya's "convictions" (*ubezhdeniia*)[17] are now his own. They may or may not be. But that is not the point. What matters to Raskolnikov is that he now senses that he shares Sonya's "feelings" (*chuvstva*) and "aspirations" (*stremleniia*).[18] Now that Raskolnikov has been emptied of his ego, "[it] had even seemed to him . . . as if all the convicts, his former enemies, already looked at him differently."[19]

Raskolnikov's "godlessness" had been registered by the majority of the inmates as an arrogant refusal to humble himself and to share, with the other inmates with whom he prayed during Lent, in a humble acceptance of his own flawed humanity, of the wrongs that he, like they, had committed against others. This arrogance had enraged them against him. That rage has now dissipated. The painful and seemingly intractable rift between Dostoevsky and the vast majority of his fellow convicts in the prison camp at Omsk is, at least in the author's imagination, finally being healed, thirteen years after Dostoevsky's release, by Sonya's love in the "Epilogue" to *Crime and Punishment*.

Belief in *The Idiot*

Is there a relation between belief in God and moral goodness? As conventionally understood, the belief in a just and punishing God serves to rein in man's murderous impulses. A person is less likely to harm others if the consequence is severe divine punishment. Dostoevsky himself at moments makes precisely this case. In *The Idiot* and *Demons*, however, he considers the possibility that belief in God, and particularly in a forgiving Christian God, may actually offer the perpetrator cover for criminal acts. I will kill, but before I do, I will pray for God's forgiveness. Belief thus grants me cover. I can believe in God and still do evil. This appears to be the modus operandi of the criminal Fedka in *Demons* who, after he murders Marya, Lebyadkin, and a housekeeper, berates Stavrogin for failing "to believe in God himself, the true creator."[20] We can find Fedka's progenitor in a chapter in *The Idiot*.

Let us turn to part 2, chapter 4 of *The Idiot*. Prince Myshkin is visiting Rogozhin, his romantic rival for the affections of Nastasya Fillipovna.

Myshkin correctly senses that Nastasya's decision to return to Rogozhin cannot end well. Just before leaving Rogozhin's gloomy house, Myshkin sees hanging on the wall a copy of Holbein's portrait of the dead, unresurrected Christ that we mentioned in our introduction. The two discuss the painting briefly, and then Rogozhin suddenly asks Myshkin, "I've long wanted to ask you something, Lev Nikolaich: do you believe in God or not?" Clearly, Rogozhin sees a connection between Holbein's painting and this question. "I love looking at that painting," Rogozhin tells Myshkin. Myshkin is surprised by Rogozhin's remark. "At that painting!" he tells Rogozhin. "A man could even lose his faith from that painting."[21] "Lose it he does," Rogozhin agrees. Rogozhin is a man who has clearly lost his faith. He observes to Myshkin that many people today no longer believe in God, and that we Russians have gone further than most in their atheism. The Prince is about to bid Rogozhin farewell when he appears inspired to respond to Rogozhin's question about "belief." Rather than answer directly with a yes-or-no answer, Myshkin relates "four different encounters" that he had had in two days of the previous week.

First, Myshkin describes a conversation that he had on a train with an avowed atheist who was uncommonly courteous and, though a very learned man, treated the spottily educated Myshkin as an absolute equal without a trace of condescension. While this man "doesn't believe in God," Myshkin notes, "it was as if that was not what he was talking about all the while." And this is true as well, Myshkin notes to Rogozhin, of many of the unbelievers he has met as well as many books that argue for atheism: "however many unbelievers I've met, however many books I've read on the subject [of atheism], it has always seemed to me that they were not at all about that," that is, about atheism, about nonbelief. Myshkin's interlocutor was clearly a good man who treated the Prince with respect. His avowed atheism went hand-in-hand with ethical behavior. In this case, the matter of belief is irrelevant. It is one's ethical comportment that counts, it is—to evoke Levinas's vocabulary—the saying rather than the said that counts, one's comportment toward the Other rather than the formal correctness of one's propositional statements about one's belief or lack of belief in the existence of God.

Second, Myshkin tells the story of a recent murder that occurred in a hotel at which he was staying. Two peasants on friendly terms were sharing a room. One of them became enamored of the other's silver watch and, though he had lived an honest and crime-free life up to this point, he cautiously approached his friend "from behind, took aim, raised his eyes to heaven, crossed himself and, after praying bitterly to himself:

'Lord, forgive me for Christ's sake!'—killed his friend with one blow, like a sheep, and took his watch."[22] Rogozhin sums up the paradoxes conveyed by Myshkin's response so far to Rogozhin's question about whether or not he, Myshkin, believes in God: "The one [who is courteous to his neighbor] doesn't believe in God at all, and the other believes so much that he even stabs people with a prayer."[23] Once again, the point of Myshkin's example appears to be that it is one's ethical comportment that counts rather than one's avowed statements of belief in God.

Myshkin's third example is that of a drunken soldier who recently cheated the Prince by selling him a tin cross that the soldier had claimed was silver. Rather than condemn the "Christ-seller," Myshkin says he suddenly became conscious of a vaguely articulated special feeling for Russia that leads him to refrain from passing judgment on the drunken soldier who had duped him. This refraining from judgment appears to be connected with Myshkin's attempt to respond to Rogozhin's question to Myshkin about his belief in God. To be forgiving, to refrain from harsh judgment, appears, for Myshkin, to be the equivalent of belief in God.

Myshkin's final example in response to Rogozhin's question is his encountering a young nursing peasant mother an hour after his having been duped by the drunken soldier. The Prince sees the young mother cross herself after noticing that her six-week-old baby smiled at her for the first time. When a mother notices her baby's first smile, she tells the Prince, it's "the same as God" rejoicing "each time he looks down from heaven and sees a sinner standing before him and praying with all his heart."[24] God rejoices over a repentant sinner as a father rejoices over his own child—or as a peasant mother rejoices over her baby's first smile. And now Myshkin answers Rogozhin's question directly, though with a rather vague religious emotiveness: "the essence of religious feeling doesn't fit in with any reasoning, with any crimes and trespasses, or with any atheisms; there's something else here that's not that, and it will eternally be not that; there's something in it that atheisms will eternally glance off, and they will eternally be talking *not about that*. But the main thing is that one can observe it sooner and more clearly in a Russian heart, and that is my conclusion!"[25] God is the God of love, of forgiveness—not of judgment. And this loving-kindness is somehow present most of all, or most clearly, in a Russian heart. The relation between Russianness and the question of belief in God will be developed by Dostoevsky in his portrayal of the Slavophile Shatov in his next great novel, *Demons*. There Shatov tells Stavrogin that he believes in the messianic mission of the Russian people. "But in God? In God?" Shatov asks. His belief in God, Shatov answers, is a work-in-progress: "I . . . I will believe in God [*Ia . . . ia budu verovat' v*

Boga]," Shatov defensively responds to Stavrogin's insistent interrogation about the Slavophile's faith.[26]

Myshkin and Rogozhin then exchange crosses in an uneven exchange that recalls a moment in Homer's *Iliad*, a favorite text of Dostoevsky's, when Glaucus—in an act of heroic generosity, of a selfless giving to the Other in a warrior culture that prizes, above all, the glory gained from a violent triumphing over the Other—exchanges his arms of gold for Sarpedon's brass arms.[27] So the violent Rogozhin becomes Myshkin's brother by exchanging his gold cross for Myshkin's tin one, and by offering, at the chapter's end, to give Nastasya Fillipovna to Myshkin: "Take her, then, if it's fate! She's yours! I give her up to you! . . . Remember Rogozhin!"[28]

The Idiot: God, Justice, and Other Others

Throughout the *Idiot*, Dostoevsky refers to a painting by Hans Holbein that depicts Christ recently descended from the cross (*The Body of the Dead Christ in the Tomb*, 1521–22). Christ's stiffened body has a bluish tinge. The painting has the shape of a coffin, with very little air or space around it, or around the body of Jesus. Here is a Christ who hardly seems to be a candidate for resurrection. The painting stunned Dostoevsky, who encountered it in Basel in August 1867, one month before he began writing *The Idiot*. As the demonic Rogozhin remarks in *The Idiot*, the experience of viewing this painting, a copy of which hung in his house, could well make you lose your faith. Dostoevsky's novel asks its readers: if we entertain the distinct possibility that Christ died on the cross and was not resurrected, is goodness, without the expectation of any reward, possible or even efficacious?

Given the novel's tragic ending, Dostoevsky appears to answer this question in the negative. No, goodness is not necessarily even desirable, Dostoevsky is perhaps suggesting, for the perfectly good man, Prince Myshkin, makes a royal mess of things. He first agrees to marry the beautiful and socially prominent Aglaya Ivanovna Epanchina. It seems an unlikely match, given the Prince's social awkwardness and eccentric nature, but the Prince goes forward with his plan until he sees the anguished face of the fallen beauty Nastasya Filippovna, who he now realizes is much needier, much more desperate than the emotionally sturdier Aglaya. As Val Vinokur brilliantly argues, the Prince is torn between two faces, two others for whom he feels responsible, without possessing the capacity to pursue the justice required in comparing faces, in comparing incomparables.[29] The Prince pities Nastasya more than he does

Aglaya, and on this basis spontaneously, even impetuously, chooses to go to Nastasya. Aglaya is humiliated, and the Prince's rival for the affections of Nastasya, the mad and violent Rogozhin—in whose home a copy of the Holbein portrait hangs—murders Nastasya out of jealousy, or out of a mad possessiveness. The novel ends with the Prince, out of his wits, comforting the distraught murderer Rogozhin, passing "his trembling hand over . . . [Rogozhin's] hair and cheeks, as if caressing and soothing him."[30] Like that of his Cervantine prototype Don Quixote, Prince Myshkin's emotive idealism leaves moral wreckage in its wake.

My aim in this chapter is to show how Dostoevsky in his major fiction, in anticipation of Levinas, thinks God outside of ontology, outside of the question of God's existence or nonexistence, outside of the question of faith. Prince Myshkin embodies this responsibility to the Other. He consistently empties himself before others. He consistently sees the face of the Other and thus bears witness to God in his seeing, in others, the image of God and in responding to them with compassion and without preconceptions.

But the God of the Hebrew Bible is not just the God of compassion. He is also the God of justice. Ethics refers to my untransferable responsibility for the Other in front of me. Nobody can take my place. Ethics, understood in this sense, is commanded by God. I am commanded to see, in the face of the Other, the image of God. I am commanded to respond to the Other with *chesed* and with *rachamim*, with loving-kindness and with mercy.

As Levinas always reminds us, however, there aren't just two people in the world, I and the Other in front of me. We are

> at least three. Two plus a third. If I heed the second person to the end, if I accede absolutely to his request, I risk, by this very fact, doing a disservice to the third one, who is also my other. But if I listen to the third, I run the risk of wronging the second one. This is where the State steps in. The State begins as soon as three are present. It is inevitable. Because no one should be neglected, yet it is impossible to establish with the multiplicity of humanity a relation of unique to unique, of face to face. One steps out of the register of charity between individuals to enter the political. Charity pursues its fulfillment in a demand for justice. It takes a referee, laws, institutions, an authority: hence the State, with its tyrannical authority.[31]

There is the third party, the other other, and all the other others. I am commanded to be responsible both for the other in front of me as well as for the other others and, thus, to pursue justice. But justice often has a guilty conscience, for justice may even require a betrayal or deception of the other in front of me, as Jacob deceived his brother Esau. Having just fled from his nightmare of a father-in-law Laban in Genesis 32, Jacob is now facing the terrifying prospect of being hunted down by his estranged, impulsive, and vengeful brother Esau, who is accompanied by four hundred men. Jacob is on the run because, at his mother Rebecca's urging, he had left his father's house in order to avoid the anticipated revenge of Esau, who lost both his birthright and his father's blessing to Jacob through Jacob's deceit—albeit a deceit that is in keeping with God's will.

Just before the two brothers meet face-to-face, Jacob comes face-to-face with, and wrestles with—with whom, exactly? The biblical text refers to Jacob's antagonist first as "a man" and then, twice, as *Elohim*, "God." The two wrestle all night long. When Jacob's antagonist perceives that he cannot overcome Jacob, he strikes the socket of Jacob's hip, dislocating it. But Jacob will not let go until his antagonist agrees to bless him. Jacob's antagonist asks, "What is your name?" "*Ya'akov*," Jacob replies. Jacob's antagonist then says, "No longer will it be said that your name is *Ya'akov*, but Israel, for you have struggled [*sarita*] with God [*El*] and with men and you have prevailed" (Genesis 32:29). Jacob's new name "Israel," moreover, at last disburdens the patriarch of the etymological link between the name Jacob (*Ya'akov*) and the Hebrew word for deceit (*'akvah*). "No longer will it be said that your name is Jacob [*lo Ya'akov*]," God tells the newly named patriarch Israel. Rashi comments: "No longer will it be said that the blessings came to you through *treachery* [*be'akvah*] and deceit, but rather through *authority* [*biserarah*], and in full view."[32] Jacob asks his antagonist to reveal his name. He does not answer. Or, rather, his answer is an action: he blesses Jacob. Jacob then names the place of their encounter Peniel because, Jacob says, he has just seen God (*Elohim*) face-to-face (*panim el-panim*), and yet his life was spared.

God, then, is Jacob's antagonist, who leaves Jacob blessed but limping at the beginning of a new day. But what, precisely, does God signify here? Part of the answer is revealed in the extraordinary scene that follows. Esau, whom Jacob sees coming toward him in the distance, approaches Jacob, embraces him, and the two then weep together. A grateful and relieved Jacob insists, despite Esau's hesitations, that Esau accept the gifts Jacob has brought with him for the brother he had harmed for, Jacob says, "seeing your face is like seeing the face of God" (Genesis 33:10). Jacob sees, in his brother's face, the face of God. God is transcendent, beyond the world, not visible but, as Levinas reminds us, this invisible God leaves his trace in the human face, to which I feel myself compelled to respond, for whom I am responsible. Esau, at this moment, senses this responsibility for his brother Jacob, despite his well-founded and long-simmering grievance again him. Esau is overcome with mercy for his brother Jacob, and Jacob sees God's presence in his brother Esau's remarkable display of mercy rather than vengeance.

Let us now return to the earlier scene of Jacob wrestling with God. Before the face of the Other, I say *hineni*, "Here I am," ready to serve. "But we are never, I and the other, alone in the world," as Levinas remarks. "There is always a third," the other other. I am responsible for this third party, as well as for the other in front of me. I am commanded to make the world a more just place, to pursue justice: justice, justice we shall pursue.[33] But sometimes that seeking of justice, commanded by God, may painfully require that I betray the other facing me, as Jacob betrayed and tricked Esau, because Jacob—urged on by his inspired mother Rivkah—intuited that if Esau were to inherit the rights of the first born and rule over Jacob and the Jewish people, this would bring untold suffering to the other others subject to Esau's rule. Jacob understood that he was the responsible one, that he was commanded to assume responsibility for the continuation of the lineage of Abraham, to create a people commanded to pursue justice, to redeem the world.

Ethics: my untransferable responsibility for the other in front of me. Nobody can take my place. Ethics, understood in this sense, is commanded by God. I am commanded to see, in the face of the Other, the image of God. I am commanded to respond to the other with *chesed* and with *rachamim*, with loving-kindness and with mercy.

Justice: I am also commanded to be responsible for the other others and to pursue justice. But justice often has a guilty conscience, for justice may require a betrayal or deception of the other in front of me. This betrayal in the name of justice leaves me limping, like Jacob after his wrestling match. Before he is reunited with his wronged brother, Jacob wrestles with God, with his guilty conscience. Jacob has already received his father Isaac's blessing, but he needs to be sure that he has God's blessing, that God is the God not only of mercy, but of justice as well. Jacob's limp bears the trace of God's presence dwelling in him, bearing witness to his inability to come to any easy truce with his betrayal of his brother, no matter how noble or how just the cause of that betrayal. God is the God of both mercy and justice, but with a sense of justice that must, however painfully, maintain its connection with mercy.

God is the God of both mercy and justice. This is how Levinas understands the following verse from Isaiah (57:19): "I create the speech of the lips: 'Peace, peace, for the far and near,' said God." Levinas cites this verse in *Otherwise Than Being*, although he reverses the order of the

Hebrew: "Peace, peace," Levinas writes, "to the neighbor and to the one far-off."[34] I owe everything, according to Levinas, to the Other in front of me, to the neighbor. Illeity so commands me, singles me out as the responsible one. My relationship to the Other is an asymmetrical one. "I substitute myself" for the Other, "whereas no one can replace me," for "the substitution of the one for the other does not signify the substitution of the other for the one."[35] When the third person appears, for Levinas, there is a betrayal (*trahison*) of my relation to illeity, to the *il* (the "he") that commands me to respond to the Other in front of me. But with the appearance of the third party there is also, at the same time, a new and positive relationship established with illeity, as I am now myself potentially a third party, a member of a society moving toward justice. "It is only thanks to God [*grâce à Dieu*]," Levinas writes—that is, it is only in the trace of illeity—"that I am approached as an other by the others. . . . 'Thanks to God' I am another for the others."[36]

The God of the Bible is the God of both mercy and of justice. In *The Idiot*, Dostoevsky portrays the failure of pure mercy without justice. In his next major novel, *Demons*, Dostoevsky portrays the catastrophic failure, without mercy at its core, of the revolutionary impulse to create an egalitarian and just society.

Belief in *Demons*

"The main question . . . that I have been tormented by [*ia muchilsia*] . . . my whole life [*vsiu moiu zhizn'*] . . . is the existence of God," Dostoevsky writes to Maikov in 1870 (March 25).[37] The following year Dostoevsky begins *Demons*. In this novel Dostoevsky creates the character Kirillov, who precisely echoes Dostoevsky's own confession to his friend Maikov when Kirillov says that "God has tormented me all my life [*Menia Bog vsiu zhizn' muchil*]."[38] Note the repetition, in this sentence from *Demons*, of the verb *muchit'* (to torment). In Kirillov, Dostoevsky creates a character who, despite his own moral goodness, is so tormented by the question of God's existence that he absurdly commits suicide in order to prove, to himself and to others, that he does *not* believe. "It is my duty to believe that I do not believe," Kirillov asserts. And then, just before he goes through with killing himself, he works himself up into a frenzy and shouts, "I believe! I believe! [*Veruiu! Veruiu!*]"[39] Kirillov is here enunciating his belief, his credo, that he does not believe.[40]

In *Demons*, Dostoevsky goes so far as to suggest that the structure of belief or of conviction itself, and not just religious conviction or belief, may inhibit ethical responsibility, may inhibit the I from being turned inside out by the Other. Shatov, the victim of the murder that is at the center of the novel, is one of the novel's most sympathetic characters and he is, moreover, a Slavophile who embodies many of Dostoevsky's own most cherished beliefs. But even Shatov, despite his sympathetic nature, is blinded—as he himself comes to realize—by his beliefs or convictions. When Shatov is desperately searching for a midwife for his ex-wife Marie's baby, who is about to be born, he seeks out the help of Arina Prokhorovna, who is a member of the radical political circle against whom Shatov has now turned. Arina Prokhorovna, the wife of the revolutionary Virginsky, agrees to come and help as a midwife, whether she is paid or not. Shatov's response illustrates a transcendence of his own ego toward the Other, that is, toward the alterity of Madame Virginsky: "So there's magnanimity in these people, too! . . . Convictions [*Ubezhdeniia*] and the man [or, more precisely, "human being," *chelovek*]—it seems they're two different things in many ways. Maybe in many ways I'm guilty before them . . . We're all guilty/responsible [*vinovaty*], we're all guilty/responsible and . . . if only we were all convinced [*ubedilis'*] of this!"[41] We all must be convinced, have the conviction (*ubedilis'*), Shatov suddenly realizes, that convictions (*ubezhdeniia*) are themselves dangerous to hold, for convictions inhibit the transcendence of the ego toward the other; they may inhibit and constrict, in other words, one's very humanity.

Dostoevsky was tormented by the question of whether or not God in fact exists, and he was deeply concerned, as we have noted, about the ethical implications of the answer to this question. If God does not exist, Dostoevsky worried, then, in the phrase of Ivan Karamazov, it seemed very possible, even likely, that "everything was permitted." Despite Kirillov's determination not to believe in God, Kirillov's goodness, as Levinas would say, nonetheless bears witness to God, for Kirillov consistently says "Here I am" before the face of the Other. In the character Kirillov in *Demons*, Dostoevsky creates a character who is determined to sever any possible connection between the question of the existence or nonexistence of God, on the one hand, and ethical obligation, on the other, but whose actions bear witness to the traces of this very God, understood in Levinas's sense, in whom he is determined not to believe. Ethics, responsibility for the Other, haunts the very passage in which Kirillov is attempting to sever the relation between ethics and God.[42]

In the chapter "Night" from part 2 of *Demons*, the novel's protagonist, Stavrogin, visits his former disciples, Kirillov and Shatov—disciples from two very different stages in the development of Stavrogin's thought. Let us focus on Stavrogin's dialogue with Kirillov and defer our discussion of Stavrogin's dialogue with Shatov until chapter 4. Stavrogin has heard that Kirillov is planning to shoot himself. Perhaps that is the very reason for his visit for, it turns out, Stavrogin himself had contemplated suicide, though for very different reasons, as the reader will discover. Kirillov, who is determined not to believe in God, nonetheless paradoxically lives on Bogoyavlensky Street—the street of the miraculous appearance (*iavlenii*) of God (*Boga*), or "Epiphany Street." Stavrogin, about to leave his estate to travel to "Epiphany Street" to see Kirillov and Shatov, is bid farewell by Alexei Yegorych, "an old servant" who had formerly taken care of Stavrogin "and used to dandle him in his arms, a serious and stern man, who liked hearing and reading about things divine. . . . 'God bless you, sir,' " the servant says, " 'but only in the event that you are setting out upon good deeds [*dobrykh del*].' "[43]

Stavrogin now arrives at the house on Epiphany Street. Shatov opens the gate for Stavrogin, who coldly walks past him toward Kirillov's wing of the house. We see an old woman holding a vulnerable, one-and-a-half-year-old baby who had just been crying, tears fresh on its face. The absence of the child's mother is obvious. Joy is brought into this apparently unfortunate infant's life by Kirillov, who is playing ball with him. The reader, like the baby, immediately senses Kirillov's kindness, his empathy, his ability to relate to children. When Stavrogin enters the room, in contrast, "the baby, seeing him, clutched at the old woman and dissolved in a long, infantile cry; she carried it out at once."[44] Stavrogin's presence, apparently, has a very different effect on the infant. His dialogue with Kirillov will suggest why, though Dostoevsky's original readers were deprived of the reason when the censors banned the chapter "At Tikhon's" that is now included as an appendix to the novel.

"I, of course, understand shooting oneself," Stavrogin comments. He continues:

> "I myself have sometimes imagined, . . . if one did some villainy or, worse, some shame, that is, disgrace, only very mean and . . . ludicrous, so that people would remember it for a thousand years and spit on it for a thousand years, and suddenly comes the thought: 'One blow in the temple, and there will be nothing [*nichego*].' What do I care then about people and how they'll be spitting for a thousand years, right?"[45]

Stavrogin has a very different reason than Kirillov for why he would want to shoot himself. Stavrogin wishes to eradicate his sense of shame for a crime that he, perhaps, committed (the reader doesn't know this, which

Dostoevsky meant to reveal in the finally censored chapter "At Tikhon's") and that he expects, were the truth revealed, would make him the object of public disgust and condemnation. But what if you committed this crime on the moon and, because of it, earned the near-eternal disdain of the inhabitants of the moon—and then you found yourself on the earth, far from the site of your crime. Would the crime matter?

Stavrogin is haunted by his guilty conscience. The matter of conscience doesn't concern Kirillov. He is, after all, a good man. He helps others. But he sees no relation between ethical responsibility, time, and God. Kirillov wishes to arrive, now, at a moment of ecstasy, of ecstatic connection with all things. Kirillov tells Stavrogin that he believes not in the "future eternal" life but rather "in the here eternal" (*v zdeshniuiu vechnuiu* [237]).[46] After Adam and Eve eat of the forbidden fruit of the tree of knowledge in the Garden of Eden, they become like God in the sense that they know good and evil, including the difference between good and evil. Unlike God, however, they are mortal—though they attempted, before they were exiled from the garden, to eat of the tree of eternal life. But they were unsuccessful in this attempt. The Bible sees time as the dimension in which a human being, in his brief life, has the opportunity to elevate himself, to meet his obligation to be his brother's keeper.

Stavrogin, despite his criminality, or perhaps because of it, senses a connection between time and the other. Kirillov wishes to achieve a state of absolute happiness now. Stavrogin, however, is skeptical about Kirillov's quest. "It's hardly possible in our time," he tells Kirillov. Only at the Apocalypse, Stavrogin comments, will time be no more. Kirillov agrees: "When all mankind attains happiness," Kirillov comments, "time will be no more, because there's no need." The implication here is that human happiness—the messianic era, if you will—will come about as a result of man's pursuing justice. When man has done all he can in this regard, time will be no more, for time—which is the time of redemption—will not be necessary. But Kirillov wishes to transcend time and to attain happiness now. Ethics, however, would vanish in the process. "Everything is good," Kirillov insists, in the wake of a recent ecstatic vision. He tells Stavrogin that he has recently achieved such a state of ecstasy—in fact earlier that day, at precisely "two thirty-seven," at which time he stopped his clock. He was ecstatically happy. Time stopped.

Stavrogin, strangely—for Stavrogin is hardly a model of ethical uprightness—bears witness to ethical responsibility by questioning Kirillov about the ethical consequences of his insistence that everything is good. "And if someone dies of hunger," Stavrogin asks, "or someone offends and dishonors a girl—is that good?" To which Kirillov answers,

"Good. And if someone's head gets smashed in for the child's sake, that's good, too; and if it doesn't get smashed in, that's good, too. Everything is good, everything." Kirillov's ecstatic vision severs the relation between ethics, on the one hand, and religiosity or spirituality, on the other. Kirillov feels a sense of gratitude, of oneness with the universe. He says he prays "to everything," including to the spider crawling on the wall. Kirillov's prayerfulness strikes the atheist Stavrogin as a prelude to some imminent declaration, by Kirillov, of his belief in God. Stavrogin had taught Kirillov not to believe. Kirillov now appears to Stavrogin as someone who is on the brink of regaining his belief, although Kirillov assures Stavrogin, "It's not that." Kirillov continues: "You've inverted my thought. A drawing-room joke. Remember what you've meant in my life, Stavrogin."

What is the meaning of Kirillov's accusing Stavrogin of "inverting" his, that is, Kirillov's, thought? And what is his "drawing-room [or 'worldly,' 'secular'] joke" (*svetskaia shutka*)?[47] Stavrogin is accusing Kirillov of a retrograde belief in God, of a retreat from the atheism that Stavrogin himself had taught Kirillov: "Remember what you've meant in my life," Kirillov reminds Stavrogin. You taught me atheism. I am not retreating from that atheism. I still believe that I do not believe. My ecstatic vision is not related to belief in God. You are inverting my thought, as if I had begun with belief and then proceeded to a reverence for all things. No, I begin with ecstasy, with a deep gratitude for being, which you, in your cynical worldliness, summarily dismiss as a mere "joke." If you deduce from that gratitude for being that I now believe in God, or am heading in that direction, that's an inversion of the process I'm describing. Kirillov senses a oneness with all things, a cosmic pantheism, but this doesn't mean that he "believes in God." He didn't start with belief. He started with a feeling of oneness with all things. Kirillov cannot bring himself to believe, but he can testify to the reality of the experience of oneness with all things, which he intuits as spiritual and, at the same time, as not dependent on belief in God. The "man-God"—and not the "God-man"— "who teaches that all are good," Kirillov insists, "will end the world." Why not the "God-man"? Because this is Christ, in whom, if one calls oneself a Christian, one must believe. The man-God, in contrast, is the man who, through an act of will, *becomes* God. Dostoevsky is alert to the paradox that the man who cannot bring himself to believe in God nonetheless can bring himself to believe that he *is* God. And, at the same time, this good man—this nonbeliever who nonetheless believes that he can himself become God—wishes to sever the link between spirituality and ethics, between ethics and God.

Kirillov is obsessed, as was Dostoevsky himself, with the question of God's existence or nonexistence. "Of course there is no God," Eric Voegelin once remarked, "but we must believe in him."[48] We must believe in him, from Voegelin's perspective, apparently because a "belief" in God is necessary, or certainly very helpful, for the moral life. Kirillov appears to agree with Voegelin. "God is necessary," Kirillov tells Stavrogin, "and therefore must exist. . . . But I know that he does not and cannot exist. . . . Don't you understand," he tells Stavrogin, "that a man with these two thoughts cannot go on living?" Voegelin, who was able to understand "God" as an index, or symbol, of what the great thinker called a "pole of existential tension,"[49] was able to go on living while still holding on to these two thoughts, namely that "God is [morally] necessary," on the one hand, and that he does not and cannot exist, at least in a literal sense, on the other. For Voegelin, the "symbol" God remains within ontology, or what Voegelin refers to, following Plato, as *noesis*. Levinas, in contrast, tries to think God, on the basis of ethics, outside of ontology, outside of the question of God's existence or nonexistence, outside of "belief" or "faith"—outside of Plato's *pistis*, a term that is drawn from the vocabulary of ontology, of relative degrees of the fullness of being and knowing.

Kirillov may not be able to prove, through reasoning, that God does not exist, but he is determined to prove, by example, that he does *not* believe. Just before his suicide, Kirillov explains that, by killing himself, he will both signal to others that there is no God, because he will have shown that he has no fear of God, and he will then, paradoxically, himself "become God."[50] "It is my duty," he says, "to proclaim self-will, it is my duty to believe that I do not believe . . . I believe! I believe [that I do not believe]!" Kirillov is a good man who cannot bring himself to believe in God. The absurdity of the good man Kirillov's obsessive determination to prove that he is not a believer suggests that Dostoevsky is pondering, in this inventive and exploratory major novel that he wrote before *The Brothers Karamazov*, the possibility of thinking God outside of ontology, outside of the question of God's existence or nonexistence, on the basis of ethics. This, we shall argue, is precisely what Dostoevsky attempts in his last and greatest novel.

"Come, take me instead of him": Responsibility as Transcendence in *The Brothers Karamazov*

In *The Brothers Karamazov*, Dostoevsky tries to think God outside of the ontological question that so tormented Kirillov. He tries to think God, on the basis of ethics, as conscience—or, more precisely, on the basis of what Levinas calls "illeity." In order for us to further our understanding of what Levinas means by illeity and its relation to the word "God," let us begin our discussion of Dostoevsky's last and greatest novel by focusing on a passage from Levinas's last magnum opus, *Otherwise Than Being*. We shall turn to the section entitled "Witness and Language" in the book's final chapter. The passage is part of Levinas's radical and very original reinterpretation of the word "God" and of the infinity traditionally associated with God.

In Levinas's late work, as we have shown, the philosopher boldly attempts to think God, as he puts it (minus the preposition "of"), beginning with, and on the basis of, the ethical relation. Obedience to God, for Levinas, translates into responsibility for the Other, into Father Zosima's statement, in *The Brothers Karamazov*, that "each of us is guilty [or responsible] before everyone, for everyone and everything, and I more than all the others" (*Vsiakii iz nas pred vsemi vo vsem vinovat, a ia bolee vsekh*).[51] In this statement of Dostoevsky, the I is defined and singled out in its responsibility for the other. Levinas cites this quotation in the very section of *Otherwise Than Being* that we are about to discuss. Dostoevsky worries that his own belief in God and in the immortality of the soul is not sufficiently free of doubt. Levinas, in contrast, attempts to remove the word "God" from the realm of ontology and belief. True "consciousness," for Levinas, is "conscience," which, as we have already observed, is the same word in French: "*la conscience*" is both "consciousness" and "conscience."

"The word God," Levinas writes in the very next section of *Otherwise Than Being*, "is still absent from the phrase in which God is for the first time involved in words."[52] The characters portrayed in the Hebrew Bible do not say "I *believe* in God." Rather, by undergoing a fission of what Levinas refers to as their "interior secrecy" (*secret intérieur*),[53] they are turned inside out through their encounter with the Other and thus, as it were, *bear witness* to God, or to the infinite. Responsibility, for Levinas, bears witness to the infinite, to that which cannot be contained or represented, through my saying "Here I am" before the face of the Other, who is infinite and for whom I am infinitely responsible. God's very absence, his "absolute remoteness, his transcendence, turns into my responsibility . . . for the other."[54]

The following passage from *Otherwise Than Being* will take us directly into those portions of the text of Dostoevsky's novel that I now wish to discuss. In the ethical relation, Levinas writes, the infinite commands me, ruptures what he calls my interior secrecy:

76   Chapter 3

Interiority is not a secret place somewhere in me. It is that reversal
in which the eminently exterior, precisely in virtue of this eminent
exteriority, this impossibility of being contained and consequently
entering into a theme, . . . concerns me and defines me and orders me
by my own voice. The commandment is stated through the mouth of
him it commands, the infinitely exterior becomes an interior voice,
but a voice testifying to the fission of interior secrecy, signaling to the
Other. Sign or gesture of the giving that lies at the very heart of what
and how signification truly means. Crooked road. Claudel chose as
an epigraph for his *Satin Slipper* a Portuguese proverb that can be
understood in the sense I have just put forth: "God writes straight
with crooked lines."[55]

The witness does not say, "I believe in God," which would limit the infinite by attempting to contain it in a theme.

The tormented, usually skeptical religious thinker Ivan Karamazov on
more than one occasion in the novel asserts that he believes in God.[56] In
trying to explain his views on theology to his pious brother Alyosha in the
chapter entitled "Rebellion" (*Brothers Karamazov* 2.5.4), Ivan explicitly
says, "I believe" (*ia veruiu*) in God.[57] In the previous chapter, Ivan had
insisted, despite the atheistic remarks he acknowledges he had previously
made in Alyosha's company, that he believes in God, though he cannot
accept the world that God has created, a world in which the innocent suffer. While insisting that he is a believer, however, in this very same chapter
he bristles at the expectation that he should be his brother's keeper. "Am
I my brother Dmitry's keeper or something?" Ivan snaps "irritably"
(*razdrazhitel'no*), clearly repeating Cain's fatal question (Genesis 4:9), the
question that is the paradigmatic evasion of the very ethical responsibility that the God of the Bible commands. "Well, damn it all," Ivan says, "I
can't stay here to be their [i.e., my brothers'] keeper."[58]

Ivan makes these remarks to his brother Alyosha in the chapter entitled
"The Brothers Get Acquainted" (book 5, chapter 3). Two chapters later,
at the conclusion of the "Grand Inquisitor" chapter, Ivan, just before he
and Alyosha part, repeats his refusal to be his brother Dmitry's keeper.
"And with regard to brother Dmitry," Ivan "suddenly" tells Alyosha "irritably" (*razdrazhitel'no*), "I ask you particularly, do not ever even mention
him to me again."[59] Dostoevsky draws the reader's attention to the irritation Ivan feels as a result of his betraying his obligation—impossible to
truly ignore—to be his brother Dmitry's keeper. Ivan's irritation bears
witness to his responsibility for Dmitry. He is free to ignore it or embrace
it. He chooses to ignore it here, to his moral peril.

In his prose "poem" on the Grand Inquisitor, which he narrates for Alyosha in chapter 5 of book 5, Ivan explains that, for the Grand Inquisitor, the "freedom" to choose the way of Christ is simply too difficult and uncertain for the vast majority of people. Only a very few would willingly choose to follow Christ without "the reward of heaven and eternity."[60] Hence, the Grand Inquisitor controls the masses by means of miracles, mysteries, and authority. At the same time, however, the Grand Inquisitor deprives human beings of their very humanity, deprives them of the freedom of choosing to say "Here I am!," of saying "Each of us is responsible, before the faces of everyone and for everything, but I more than all the others." Or, as Dostoevsky had stated this same thought, in more explicitly Christian language in *Winter Notes on Summer Impressions* (1863), "To *voluntarily* lay down one's life for the sake of all, to go to the cross or to the stake for the sake of all, can be done only in the light of the strongest development of the personality."[61] It is, as Dostoevsky writes in a letter of 1876, to "deprive man of . . . *individuality, self-sacrifice and the sacrifice of one's goods for one's neighbor*, in short the ideal of life would be taken away."[62] Freedom, for Dostoevsky—as for Levinas—is not, finally, about free "thinking" but about free "doing," freely responding to the call to be a responsible I, to be "my brother's keeper." Ivan worries about "justice" in the abstract, justice for the other others, justice in the political sense; but he betrays ethics, betrays his responsibility to the other in front of him, betrays his responsibility for his brother Dmitry until the trial scene, to which we shall turn our attention very soon, when he will say, "Come, take me instead of him!"

Ivan insists to Alyosha in these chapters that he believes in God. This God in whom Ivan believes appears to be the God of the philosophers rather than the God of Abraham, Isaac, and Jacob. Ivan's God is the God of free thinking rather than of free and righteous doing. Ivan insists that he will not renounce his formulation that "everything is permitted." Alyosha remains committed, at the conclusion of the Grand Inquisitor chapter, to being his brother Ivan's keeper. I won't renounce my formulation that everything is permitted, Ivan tells Alyosha, and he then asks his brother if he, Alyosha, will then in turn renounce him, Ivan, for not renouncing his formulation that "everything is permitted." Ivan then says goodbye to his brother and leaves "without looking back." In contrast, after waiting a little, Alyosha, rather than leaving and not looking back, "looks after his brother" (*gliadia vsled bratu*)[63]—looks after him, that is, in the sense of looking out for him, of being his brother Ivan's keeper. As Alyosha looks at and after at his departing brother, he notices that "Ivan swayed as he walked and that his right shoulder looked lower than his left," which he "had never noticed before." Here we have the parting of two Alexeis with two very different conceptions of God. One, Alexei/ Alyosha, is reminiscent of Saint Alexei, "the man of God,"[64] and the other is Ivan/Alexander the Great, the Greek conqueror and student of Aristotle whose head, as Plutarch writes, was inclined "a little on one side towards his left shoulder."[65]

While Ivan insists to Alyosha that he *believes* in God, his actions, thus far in the novel, do not, as it were, *bear witness* to the bibilical God, for the witness says, "Here I am" before the face of the Other; or, in the words of Dostoevsky, "Each of us is responsible, before the faces of everyone, for everything; but I more than all the others." The witness, through his or her voice, testifies to the dissolution of the self that, like the self of Shakespeare's Prince Hamlet, is closed up into itself and that, like the self of Shakespeare's *King Lear* at the end of that later play, is transformed into a self that has been turned inside out (*à l'envers*)[66] by its responsiveness to, its responsibility for, the Other. Consciousness becomes conscience. Is this not precisely what happens in the testimony of three key witnesses in the trial of Dmitry Karamazov? Let us listen to the testimony of Ivan, then of Katya, and finally of Dmitry Karamazov himself.

We shall begin with chapter 5, entitled "A Sudden Catastrophe," of the novel's final book—book 12, "A Miscarriage of Justice" (or, more literally, "A Legal Error"). Ivan enters the courtroom to testify at his brother Dmitry's trial. Ivan's manner strikes the novel's narrator as strange and we, as readers, prepare ourselves for the unexpected. Ivan is about to leave the courtroom when he stops while suddenly pondering (*obdumav*) something and then turns back around and stays.[67] The usually brainy and relentlessly philosophical Ivan oddly likens himself to a "peasant girl"[68] who, at her wedding, is determined to do precisely as she pleases. Thus Dostoevsky prepares us for an unlikely peasant-like straightforwardness in Ivan, a departure from his usual intricacy of mind. Ivan then presents the court with the money that Smerdyakov had stolen from Fyodor who, Ivan shockingly announces to those present, was murdered not by Dmitry but by the "lackey" Smerdyakov. "I got this money," Ivan tells the court,

> from Smerdyakov, from the murderer, yesterday. It was he, not my brother, who killed our father. He murdered him and I incited him to do it.[69]

Before Ivan's third and final interview with Smerdyakov, to which we will return at the conclusion of this section of our analysis, Ivan had cruelly knocked down a drunken peasant in the snow and left him, for all intents and purposes, for dead. The peasant was singing to himself the following song:

> Ah, Vanka's gone to Petersburg,
> I won't wait till he comes back.[70]

"Vanka" is a nickname for "Ivan," who left town—though for Moscow rather than Petersburg—at precisely the moment when he sensed, correctly, that his father might well be murdered, thus emboldening his disciple Smerdyakov to commit the crime. Because Ivan feels responsible for that crime, in large part because of his shameful disappearance to Moscow, he is haunted by and sings that song in court now. Immediately after reciting the line "Vanka's gone to Petersburg," he says, in reference to his brother Dmitry: "Come, take me instead of him! [*Nu, berite zhe menia vmesto nego*]."[71] Ivan is experiencing a rupture of his interior secrecy. The obsessively cogitating Hamlet has astoundingly if very briefly become the loving and maternal Lear of the last scene of Shakespeare's play.[72] Ivan is being ordered, by his own voice, to substitute himself for his unjustly charged brother Dmitry, to be his brother's keeper.

Ivan's defiant rejection of the world created by God, in whom he had just claimed to believe, is fueled, in large part, by his outrage, shared by Dostoevsky himself, against a world in which innocent children suffer, and are even tortured. It is surely incumbent upon me as a moral being to express such outrage but not, Dostoevsky is suggesting in his portrayal of Ivan's character, at the expense of evading my own personal responsibility for alleviating another's unjust suffering. Ivan, at long last, becomes a responsible subject here, singled out, in the accusative—"me [*menia*]"—as a responsible I: "Come, take me instead of him!" "*Me voici!*" The brilliant theological thinker Ivan, a witness at his brother's trial, is here bearing witness—and thus retracting, by example, his earlier dismissal of this command—to the injunction that he must indeed be his brother's keeper. Crooked road!

Ivan's "Come, take me instead of him!" bears witness, in Levinas's terms, to the "fission" of Ivan's "interior secrecy," transforming that secrecy, at this very moment, into an interior voice that testifies to Ivan's responsibility for the Other, for his brother Dmitry, whom he doesn't like but for whom he is responsible. As Levinas remarks in "God and Philosophy," illeity is manifested in the way in which "the Infinite, or . . . God, . . . from the heart of its very desirability," turns me toward "the undesirable proximity of the others."[73] Levinas associates this "extraordinary turning around" (*retournement extra-ordinaire*) with illeity. Here the reader witnesses the awakening of Ivan's true self "sobered up," as Levinas puts it in his essay "God and Philosophy," "from the ecstasy of intentionality," from Ivan's theories about a world in which the innocent suffer, theories that served to justify his own evasions of responsibility.[74] This return (*renvoi*) of consciousness to the Other, for Levinas, is an awakening (*éveil*), an "awakening to proximity, which is responsibility for the neighbor to the point of substitution for him."[75] Come, take me instead of him!

Let us continue to turn to "God and Philosophy" for its relevance to this extraordinary scene in which Ivan, through his actions, answers Cain's question "Am I my brother's keeper?" in the affirmative. We recall that, in his *Winter Notes on Summer Impressions*, Dostoevsky observed that true "fraternity" was absent in bourgeois, enlightened Europe. In "God and Philosophy," in a section (15) of this text just preceding a direct reference to his mantra from *The Brothers Karamazov* ("Each of us is responsible before everyone for everything, but I more than all the others"), Levinas alludes specifically to the biblical Cain. Levinas wishes to make the point that "biological human fraternity, considered with sober, Cain-like coldness, is not a sufficient reason that I be responsible for a separated being [i.e., for the other, who is separate from me]."[76] Fraternity is not a matter of biology. If it were, then Cain would never have asked God if he, Cain, were indeed his brother's keeper. It would have gone without saying, or without asking, that he was.

Cain is biologically Abel's brother, but he betrays fraternity in a deeper, truer sense of the word, a sense of the word deeply connected with the meaning of another word, that is, the word "God." Genesis 4:9 reads, "And God said to Cain," 'Where is Abel your brother?'" It is in response to God's asking Cain, in Genesis 4:9, "Where is Abel your brother?" that Abel says "I do not know. Am I my brother's keeper [*Ha shomer achi anochi*]?" We conventionally translate the unpronounceable four-letter Hebrew word that appears toward the beginning of Genesis 4:9 ("And God said to Cain") as "God," but it is truly untranslatable. The word signifies, as Levinas might say, in a manner outside of ontology, beyond being. It is Cain's conscience that is speaking to him here in the biblical text, or, better yet, it is what Levinas calls "illeity," a "he-ness" or a third-ness issuing neither from the "I" nor from the Other. It is a command that humbles and singles me out as responsible.

"Sober, Cain-like coldness," Levinas continues in the passage just referred to in "God and Philosophy," "consists in reflecting on responsibility from the standpoint of freedom or according to a contract. Yet responsibility for the other comes from what is prior to my freedom."[77]

Earlier in *The Brothers Karamazov*, Ivan had rejected the Grand Inquisitor largely on the grounds that his actions are an assault on his freedom, on my freedom. The eternal life promised by the Grand Inquisitor, in Christ's name, is a reward—but truly a mere ruse—that is designed to keep the faithful in line and to deprive them of their freedom. Neither the Inquisitor, nor Ivan in revolting against him, however, says anything about the subject's responsibility for the other. Neither says anything about Dostoevsky's insistence, throughout the novel, that "I am responsible more than all the others." Levinas continues:

> Before the neighbor I "compear" [*comparais*] rather than appear [*apparais*]. I respond from the first to a summons. Already the stony core of my substance is hollowed out. But the responsibility to which I am exposed in such a passivity does not seize hold of me as if I were an interchangeable thing, for no one here may substitute himself for me. In appealing to me as someone accused who cannot challenge the accusation, responsibility binds me as irreplaceable and unique.[78]

Before the neighbor I "compear" (*je comparais*) rather than appear (*plutôt que je n'apparais*). The verb *comparaître* means to appear—just as Ivan is doing in Dostoevsky's narrative at this very moment—before a court, to answer a summons. In concluding this section of "God and Philosophy," Levinas writes, "Responsibility does not come from fraternity; fraternity is what we call responsibility for the other prior to my freedom."[79] It is this notion of fraternity that Ivan's "Come, take me instead of him!" precisely signifies at this crucial moment in Dostoevsky's novel. Ivan is now more than Dmitry's mere biological brother. He is, rather, fraternal in precisely Levinas's sense.

Once Ivan testifies in this extraordinary way, declaring Dmitry's innocence and strangely but understandably acknowledging his own part in—his own responsibility for—his father's murder, Katerina Ivanovna feels compelled to retract her previously expressed defense of Dmitry's innocence. What are her motives? On the one hand, by revealing and suddenly introducing as evidence a powerfully incriminating document written by Dmitry, Katya is taking revenge on Dmitry for his leaving her for Grushenka. In this letter that a drunken Dmitry wrote to Katya, Dmitry says of his father, "I shall kill him as soon as Ivan has gone away."[80] Is Katya's revealing this letter at this particularly charged moment another instance of her haughty nature, of her need always to be in control and of her fear of allowing herself to be vulnerable? Perhaps not. Perhaps what we are witnessing instead is a "fission" of Katya's ego in a bold gesture coming from who knows where, from Levinas's "Je ne sais d'où."[81] Katya, who had "just before, in her maidenly modesty before all these people, telling of Mitya's generous conduct, in the hope of softening his fate a little," now once again

> sacrificed herself but this time it was for another [za drugogo], and per-
> haps only now—perhaps only at this moment—she felt and knew how
> dear [dorog] that other [drugoi chelovek] was to her! She had sacrificed
> herself in terror for him . . . to save his good name, his reputation![82]

Finally, and perhaps even more remarkably in its anticipation of Levinas's description of the "infinitely exterior" becoming an "interior voice" that signals to the Other, we shall consider Dmitry's immediate response to the guilty verdict. "I swear by God and the dreadful Day of Judgment," Dmitry declares, "I am not guilty of my father's blood!" Dmitry continues:

> "Katya, I forgive you. Brothers, friends, have pity on the other [the
> word for 'the other' here is druguiu, marked as feminine and thus
> meaning 'the other woman']!"
> He could not go on, and broke into a terrible sobbing wail that
> was heard all over the court in a voice not his own, in a new, surpris-
> ing voice that suddenly emerged from God knows where [Bog znaet
> otkuda].[83]

Here we have an extraordinary example of what Levinas means when, in *Otherwise Than Being*, he says that "the commandment [to say "Here I am" before the face of the Other] is stated through the mouth of him it commands, the infinitely exterior becomes an interior voice, but a voice testifying to the fission of an interior secrecy, signaling to the Other."[84] The jury has found Dmitry "guilty" (*vinoven*).[85] Dmitry then declares that he is innocent of the crime of parricide: he truly is not guilty in the technical, legal sense of the word. But the adjective *vinoven*, or *vinovat*, can be taken in both a legal, technical sense and also in a moral and ethical sense. It is the latter that Dostoevsky has in mind when he has Father Zosima's brother Markel, and later Zosima himself, express what the novel's translator Ralph E. Matlaw refers to as "the leading idea of the novel" that "we are all responsible for everyone and everything."[86] "It would not have done," Matlaw insists, "to translate the word 'responsible' [*vinovat*] as 'guilty,' for that would be to limit the meaning and introduce an unwarranted legal note."[87]

Dmitry is not guilty (*vinovat*) in the technical, legal sense of the word, as he correctly insists. But he is *vinovat* in the ethical sense of the word, and that assumption of responsibility is expressed "in a new, surprising voice that suddenly emerged from God knows where [*Bog znaet otkuda*]."[88] Dmitry speaks in this new voice that emits "a terrible sobbing wail" just after, upon hearing the verdict, he immediately forgives Katya and urges those present, whom he lovingly describes as "brothers" and "friends," to "have pity on the other [*druguiu*]!" *Druguiu* can be translated as "the other"; because the ending of this noun marks it as feminine, however, it means "the other *woman*," that is, Grushenka who, as Dmitry's beloved, will suffer and share with Dmitry the terrible consequences of this miscarriage of justice, as Dmitry is headed for prison to serve time in Siberia for a crime he did not commit.

Dmitry's new voice has suddenly emerged, Dostoevsky writes, "from God knows where" (*Bog znaet otkuda*), a phrase that uncannily anticipates Levinas's stating, in *Otherwise Than Being*, that the commandment to say "Here I am" before the face of the Other comes from "Je ne sais d'où," from "I know not where."[89] Levinas gives the name "illeity" to the source of this command which, "beyond representation, affects me unbeknownst to myself, 'slipping into me like a thief.'"[90] The word "illeity" is derived from the Latin *ille*, meaning "that" or "he." As opposed to the Latin word *hic* ("this"), *ille* means "[t]he other, more remote, person or thing."[91] The word "illeity" signifies that the command that I say "Here I am!" before the face of the Other is sensed by the "I" as a supervening "that-ness" or "he-ness,"[92] a "thirdness"[93] that is separate from self and Other. It comes neither from the self nor from the Other, is neither the "I" nor the "you." The word "conscience" suggests a moral force that is too purely interior. The word "illeity" more accurately preserves the sense of how the moral command seems to come from some place outside the self, from the exterior. One could refer to "illeity" by means of the word "God," but for Levinas that would be to "tame the subversiveness worked by illeity" and would pose the danger of turning "God" into a being, while what Levinas wishes to convey is that the word "God" signifies a beyond being, an otherwise than being that "gets its meaning from the witness borne, which thematization certainly betrays in theology, which introduces it into the system of a language, into the order of the Said."[94]

In Ivan's third and final interview with Smerdyakov, who absorbed Ivan's teaching that "everything is permitted," there is another passage that remarkably anticipates Levinas's notion of "illeity." It is during this interview that Ivan comes to recognize, beyond a shadow of a doubt, his role in his father's murder. Smerdyakov reminds Ivan that, by leaving for

Moscow at precisely the most critical time, Ivan betrayed his responsibility for his father and thereby signaled, to Smerdyakov, that he would not stand in the murderer's way. Ivan had, at the time, referred to himself as a "scoundrel" (*podlets*)[95] on account of this betrayal. Levinas, as I have mentioned, speaks of illeity as a "thirdness": illeity, he says, signifies "in the third person."[96] In their last interview, Ivan reacts with horror to Smerdyakov's confession that it was he, Smerdyakov, who killed Fyodor, but that he was a mere instrument following what he took to be Ivan's orders. Shocked, Ivan imagines that the Smerdyakov who is making such chilling assertions is a dream or a phantom. Smerdyakov responds:

> "There's no phantom here, but only two and one other. No doubt he is here, that third, between us."
>
> "Who is here? What third person?" Ivan Fyodorovich cried in alarm, looking about him, his eyes hastily searching in every corner.
>
> "That third is God Himself, sir, Providence, Sir. He is the third beside us now. Only don't look for him, you won't find him."[97]

"'Who is here? What third person?' Ivan Fyodorovich cried in alarm." Dostoevsky's use of the patronymic "Fyodorovich"—meaning "son of Fyodor"—here perhaps betrays Ivan's guilty conscience. Dostoevsky refers to Ivan as "son of Fyodor" at precisely the moment when Ivan admits to being haunted by an invisible, absent something that Smerdyakov identifies as a "third" beside them. This third person signifies Ivan's betrayal of the command—issuing from Levinas's "Je ne sais d'où" or from Dostoevsky's "God knows where"—that he assume responsibility for his father.[98]

Demons: Responsibility Resisted and Tragically Deferred

Myshkin feels responsible for everyone and everything. After explaining to Evgeny Pavlovich, toward the end of the novel, how torn he feels between the two beckoning faces of Aglaya and Nastasya, he says: "Oh, yes, I'm to blame [*ia vinovat*]! Most likely I'm to blame for everything [*vo vsem*]! I still don't know precisely for what, but I'm to blame [*ia vinovat*]!"[99] At the center of the novel, we thus have a character who feels responsible for everyone and for everything. In *Demons*, in contrast, we have at its centerless center a character, Stavrogin, who is pathologically cold and impassive, and a whole host of characters who either refuse responsibility altogether, or who respond too late to evade moral catastrophe.

Demons is, for the most part, a remarkably centrifugal work of fiction. As the narrative unfolds, the reader continually experiences the disorienting effects of responsibility betrayed or deferred. Chaos—nothing, *nihil*, "the absolute emptiness that one can imagine before creation"[100]—reigns. This is what Levinas refers to as the experience of the "*il y a*," the "there is." *Dans le vide absolu, qu'on peut imaginer, d'avant la création—il y a*.[101] Who is who? What is what? Where are we? What is happening? Why? What does it all mean? And then catastrophe: fire, murder, more murder, death, desperate last efforts at responsibility dodged, betrayed. And behind it all?

In this chapter, I am suggesting how Dostoevsky, in the four great novels of his maturity, is—in anticipation of Levinas, whose thought he so deeply influenced—trying to think God outside of ontology, on the basis of ethics, on the basis of responsibility for the other. "Before creation" means, for Levinas, before "the upwelling of the human within being,"[102] before the human subject comes to imagine himself or herself as a "created" being, that is, as commanded to be good, rather than purely autonomous and unconditionally free. The *il y a* recalls the Bible's "waste and void" (*tohu vavohu*, Genesis 1:2), the astonishingly palpable emptiness that precedes creation. Rashi sees the opening of the Bible as articulating not a cosmology about the literally true beginning of the world but rather as bearing witness to the emergence of the light of righteousness that Levinas tries to capture in his articulation of the "awakening" of the responsible subject whose idea of the Infinite, innate in me—"born and produced with me from the time I was created" (in the words of Descartes)—suggests, for Levinas, "the passivity of the created one."[103]

As the novel moves toward its conclusion, and in particular toward the suppressed chapter that became the famous appendix "At Tikhon's," we sense the narrative moving in a centripetal direction. Behind it all is not, finally, a secret society, but a secret life, a "rigorously private domain of a closed interiority," a "secrecy which holds to the responsibility for the Other," but to a secrecy unable to break free—by saying "Here I am" before the face of the Other—of its prideful solitude. The novel's protagonist, it turns out, is haunted, tormented by the young face and tiny little fist of a terribly vulnerable and fatally harmed Other. Nikolai [Tsar Nikolai?] Vsevolodovich ["Son of the Ruler of All"] Stavrogin ["cross-bearer"?] is everything.[104] Nikolai Vsevolodovich, the "Son of the Ruler of All," is always in control, or is seemingly so, and is idolized by several key characters in the novel who, fearful of transcending their own frail egos, fearful of their own vulnerability, of having their own sense of identity called into question by a risky responsibility for the Other, instead attempt to shore up their identities by true belief in the Son of the Ruler of All, in an anti-Christ.

A confession, contained in a suppressed chapter that didn't appear in Dostoevsky's original text, explains that, at the core of its charismatic but continually masked protagonist's soul, there lurks a dark and finally fatal secret, a burdensome cross that he bears to the bitter end.

Stavrogin's shameful secret, which is at the core of the novel, recalls Totsky's less meticulously closeted but still shameful secret in Dostoevsky's earlier novel, the *Idiot*. The earlier novel's tragic ending has its ultimate source in the nobleman Totsky's sexual abuse of the beautiful young Nastasya Filippovna, his once adolescent charge, whom he later wishes to marry off as the novel begins and as the worldly Totsky seeks a socially more acceptable match for himself. Nastasya's lack of self-esteem, indeed her self-loathing, issues from this abuse and its aftermath. Nastasya's self-loathing prevents her from imagining herself as a fit lover for the morally pure Prince Myshkin, and fatally draws her to the violent and abusive Rogozhin.

The Belated Fissure of Secrecy in *Demons*

The fissure of interior secrecy in *The Brothers Karamazov*, as we have seen, turns Ivan, Katya, and Dmitry inside out. This is precisely what does not occur, or what occurs too late, in *Demons*. We shall focus here on the horrific scene of Shatov's murder in the chapter entitled "A Toilsome Night" (part 3, chapter 6.1). Pyotr Stepanovich Verkhovensky, a self-described "crook"[105] posing as a socialist, is planning on imminently murdering Shatov on the grounds that the Slavophile, who is now determined to leave the group, is prepared to denounce them to the authorities. Verkhovensky employs the rhetoric of a politics cut off from ethics to persuade the others to go through with this gruesome task. We must execute Shatov, Verkhovensky urges them, for "the common cause."[106] It is your "duty" and "responsibility"[107] to do so, he tells them.

Virginsky, however, whose wife had just assisted in bringing Shatov's son into the world, feels commanded to do otherwise. "I protest . . . I protest with all my strength,"[108] he declares, but in vain. Two of the conspirators seize Shatov in the darkness. Three lanterns, held by the conspirators, suddenly light up the scene, apparently—"it is said"—allowing Shatov to see his executioner, and for his executioner to see Shatov's face. "Shatov suddenly cried out a brief and desperate cry; but he was not to cry out again." Pyotr Stepanovich presses his revolver to Shatov's forehead and, at point-blank range, pulls the trigger. Just after the murder, and after stones are tied onto Shatov's body so that it would sink to the bottom of Skoreshniki Pond, "a strange thing [*odna strannost'*] suddenly [*vdrug*] happened, which was totally unexpected [*sovershenno neozhidannaia*] and surprised [*udivivshaia*] almost everyone."[109] What was this "strange thing," this totally unexpected thing, that suddenly transpired? We are reminded here of Levinas's discussion in his lecture on "Thinking God on the Basis of Ethics," which we noted earlier in the previous chapter, of the "all of a sudden" that happens upon the subject who wakes up and, in this time of suddenness, bears witness to "the beating of the Other in the same." At this moment in Dostoevsky's narrative, two of the conspirators are suddenly turned inside out by the Other, by the now dead Shatov, in whose murder they have participated.

At a moment like this, the instinct for self-preservation would urge caution and quiet. The group, above all, would want to keep their crime hidden. But precisely the opposite happens with regard to Virginsky and Lyamshin. They undergo a strange and totally unexpected transcendence of their own egos toward the Other, the suddenness of the Other beating in the same. First, Virginsky "cried ruefully [*gorestno*, 'in a sad or piteous manner'] at the top of his voice, 'This is not it, this is not it! This is not it at all' (*Eto ne to! Net, sovsem ne to!*)."[110] A political movement begun in the spirit of freedom and of socialist principles of sharing the fruits of capital equally among all classes has resulted in the senseless murder of a sympathetic, if dogmatic, young father who has just assumed responsibility for the birth of a son who, he knew, was fathered by someone else—in fact, by his former mentor Stavrogin, who had betrayed him. So here we have, first, Virginsky, who is very possibly attracting attention to the crime that was just committed by shouting these words as loudly as he can. And then another accomplice—this time a willing one, Lyamshin—rushes at Virginsky from behind in order, the reader thinks, to silence him. But then Lyamshin himself lets out "some sort of incredible shriek." The narrator continues: "There are strong moments of fear when a man will suddenly cry out in a voice not his own, but such as one could not even have supposed him to have before then, and the effect is sometimes even quite frightful." Lyamshin is here turned inside out by the Other, as Dmitry will be turned inside out in his concern for Grushenka just after the guilty verdict is announced at his trial toward the end of Dostoevsky's last novel, *The Brothers Karamazov*. Lyamshin, "squeezing Virginsky from behind harder and harder with his arms, in a convulsive fit, . . . went on shrieking without stop or pause, his eyes goggling at them all, and his mouth opened exceedingly wide. . . . Virginsky got so scared that he cried out like a madman himself. " Lyamshin then rushes at Pyotr Stepanovich, who is unable to silence Lyamshin's deafening scream, despite Verkhovensky's threatening him with his revolver. Only when Erkel, another accomplice, stuffs a piece of cloth in Lyamshin's mouth does he stop screaming. "This is very strange [*Eto ochen' stranno*]," Pyotr Stepanovich said. "I had quite a different idea of him." Verkhovensky did not count on the heretofore meek, if vain, Lyamshin—the despised Jew who desperately wanted to be accepted as part of the revolutionary cabal—undergoing so evident a rupture of his ego, so evident a beating of the Other in the same. He did not imagine that Lyamshin could so clearly bear witness to the infinite in him.[111]

What is the relation between Lyamshin's scream, his subsequent confession to the police, including his revealing "the innermost secrets"[112]concerning the group of terrorists of which he had been part, and his Jewishness? Goldstein makes a good case for reading Lymanshin-as-snitch as an antisemitic smear that reveals the Jew's cowardly and self-serving nature.[113] But Lyamshin's desire to come clean could also reveal a soul that, having been turned inside out by the horror of his having betrayed the commandment not to kill—a horror so memorably and graphically depicted by his extraordinary scream just after the murder of Shatov—then becomes determined to be as absolutely truthful as possible about the crimes and deceit of the revolutionary group in which he himself had so fully participated. Is Dostoevsky here depicting the Jew, outside of the question of ontology or of doctrinal belief in God, as ethical witness par excellence? Does the Jewish fireman in the famous—and famously cryptic—passage from *Crime and Punishment* (the end of part 6, chapter 6), likewise, bear witness to the commandment not to kill, which would include not killing oneself, as Svidrigailov goes on to do, with the Jew as witness, despite his attempts at discouraging Svidrigailov by telling him, several times, that "dzis is not dze place"?[114]

Demons: Inside-Out, Responsibility, and the Dalai Lama

"The secret of man," Václav Havel notes, "is the secret of his responsibility."[115] This secret is more of a secret, more fundamentally a secret, than the secret of Stavrogin's abuse of a young girl, which haunted his conscience and about which we do not learn until the end of the novel in an appendix that was never included in the editions of the novel published in Dostoevsky's lifetime. The secret of responsibility, however, is a secret that is continually denied by many characters in the novel, most glaringly by the cynical, amoral Pyotr Stepanovich Verkhovensky. After facilitating a heinous crime for which he takes no responsibility, Pyotr Stepanovich tells the novel's protagonist, Stavrogin, "of course, none of us is responsible for anything, and you first of all [*nikto iz nas ni v chem ne vinovat, i prezhde vsekh vy*], because it's such a conjunction . . . a coincidence of events . . . in short, legally it cannot involve you . . . and I'm not responsible [*ia . . . ne vinoven*] . . . either" (part 3, chapter 2:2). Verkhovensky's "none of us is responsible for anything [*nikto iz nas ni v chem ne vinovat*], and you first of all [*i prezhde vsekh vy*]" will be refuted, in *The Brothers Karamazov*, by the sentence, first uttered by Father Zosima's brother Markel, that "each of us—before [the faces of] everyone and for everything—is responsible [*Vsiakii iz nas pred vsemi vo vsem vinovat*], but I more than all the others [*a ia bolee vsekh*]." Verkhovensky refuses this responsibility, and he does so, in large part, by idol worship—by idolizing Stavrogin, who possesses a strange charisma that had captivated many of those around him, including Kirillov and Shatov, all of whom betrayed the secret of their own responsibility through idolizing Stavrogin. Verkhovensky is a genius at manipulating those around him, consistently betraying the secret of his responsibility that is replaced by a relentless pursuit of a nihilist path inspired by Stavrogin. "You are my idol! [*Vy moi idol*]," Verkhovensky tells Stavrogin. He continues:

> You insult no one, yet everyone hates you; you have the air of being everyone's equal, yet everyone is afraid of you—this is good. . . . You're a terrible aristocrat. An aristocrat, when he goes among democrats, is captivating! You are precisely what's needed. I need precisely such a man as you. I know no one but you. You are a leader, you are a sun, and I am your worm . . .[116]

Verkhovensky's idolizing of Stavrogin, his shame before Stavrogin, obscures the greater shame that results in his continual betrayal of the secret of his own responsibility. This truth was brought home to me in an Inside-Out class I taught in spring 2013, in which we read *Demons* and *Ethics and Infinity* by Levinas. During that academic quarter, the Fourteenth Dalai Lama came to the University of Oregon to give a talk held in the sports arena at the university. My Inside-Out students were invited to ask the Dalai Lama a question. The question was prerecorded and broadcast for the Dalai Lama, following his talk, on the Jumbotrons—the huge television screens—installed in the state-of-the-art Matthew Knight Arena on the University of Oregon campus.

My class was inspired by this opportunity to ask the Dalai Lama a question. Just before his visit, we met in groups for an hour in our classroom on the fourth floor of the Oregon State Penitentiary to come up with possible questions, which I then submitted to the committee that vetted the questions for the Dalai Lama. The committee, consisting of a number of faculty and others who were knowledgeable about Buddhism, chose the following question, which was composed by an inside student named Jeff: "If you had one thing to say to the next Dalai Lama, what would that be?" I was very pleased to be able to tell Jeff, when the class met the following week, that his question had been chosen and that Elizabeth, Jeff's classmate on the outside, had been to the television studio and recorded his question for the Dalai Lama. The stage had been set for a very interesting encounter, and a fascinating Inside-Out class, in which we would have the privilege of discussing the Dalai Lama's response to Jeff's question.

The day of the Dalai Lama's talk and visit arrived. It was His Holiness's first visit to Eugene and the campus was alive with excitement. I had excellent seats in the arena, only fifty or a hundred feet from the platform on which the Dalai Lama, having now entered the arena to a cheering crowd, was standing and bowing to the audience with his hands clasped together palm to palm in front of his face, as if in prayer, turning and bowing in respectful recognition of his wildly appreciative audience. His Holiness gave an inspiring speech about compassion. Then came the time for the question-and-answer period. All eyes in the arena were now on the huge set of Jumbotrons. I had been asked to submit a question of my own, which was the first one posed to the Dalai Lama. "Does Buddhism," I asked His Holiness, "have a special role to play today in discouraging acts of violence in the name of religion?" The Dalai Lama responded to my question respectfully and at some length. He gave a satisfying answer. Then the televised image of my student Elizabeth, who was sitting just a few seats away from me in the arena, appeared on the screen, being watched by the nearly fifteen thousand people in attendance in the arena, as well as by many, many more via streaming video. I watched Elizabeth watch herself asking the question to the Dalai Lama that had been prerecorded. As Elizabeth's teacher, I was proud of her poise in front of what she knew would be a huge crowd and in front of the Dalai Lama himself. I was feeling very grateful that I had helped to facilitate a connection between my students and His Holiness on this very special occasion, which my students, I was sure, would not forget. Elizabeth said,

> Hello, my name is Elizabeth. I am a student in an Inside-Out class being taught this quarter in the Oregon State Penitentiary in Salem. We are studying ethics and literature. I am asking this question on behalf of my classmate Jeff, who is an inmate in the institution and thus unable to be with me in the television studio today. Jeff asks, "If you could say one thing to the next Dalai Lama, what would that be?"

His Holiness listened to the question, which his translator, sitting by his side, clarified to him. After a few moments of silence, His Holiness said, in his deep, husky voice, "I don't know!" Another pause. His Holiness chuckled to himself and then remarked, "Foolish question! Next question."

There was an abrupt change in the atmosphere in the arena. Some in the audience, myself among them, seemed almost to be gasping for air. We were confused, disappointed, even stunned by the response of His Holiness. During his address on compassion, the Dalai Lama had stumbled a bit, before a mostly liberal and politically correct Eugene crowd, when he remarked that, should the next or a future Dalai Lama be a woman, she would certainly be better looking than the current one. But mainly His Holiness had the crowd with him. Now, however, he had managed, with a single dismissive gesture that hardly seemed compassionate, to have alienated many in his audience.

What, I asked myself and my students, is the teaching here? What might this teaching have to do with Dostoevsky's portrait of Stavrogin in *Demons* and its relation to the author's later assertion, in *The Brothers Karamazov*, that "each of us, before everyone and for everything, is responsible—but I am more than all the others," an assertion that Pyotr Stepanovich, in *Demons*, pointedly and explicitly rejects, the rejection of which brings moral chaos, murder, and wanton destruction in its wake?

I was deeply disappointed in the Dalai Lama's response. As a teacher, I felt responsible for putting my students in the position of being dismissed and even humiliated, in a large and very visible public forum, by one of the world's most celebrated spiritual teachers. I also felt personally disappointed in what I perceived was the harshness of the Dalai Lama's answer, in the lack of compassion and even of respect that it appeared to convey. I remember feeling, as the Dalai Lama uttered his response, that I so wished His Holiness had responded more appropriately. Like many of the people with whom I later spoke who had been in the audience in the arena, I was having a difficult time accepting the fact that the Dalai Lama may have simply been impatient, snappy, and less than compassionate. I wanted to learn, for myself and on behalf of my students, precisely why the Dalai

Lama considered Jeff's question "foolish." I therefore wrote to the Dalai Lama's personal secretary in Dharamsala, Chhime R. Chhoekyapa, who courteously and promptly responded that there were three reasons for the seemingly curt response of His Holinesss to Jeff's question. First, Chhime said, the matter of who will be the next Dalai Lama is politically very complex and sensitive given China's insistence that it has sole authority to choose the next Dalai Lama. Second, there is the issue of reincarnation. Both the current Dalai Lama and the next Dalai Lama are and will be, technically speaking, reincarnations of the previous Dalai Lamas. When he is speaking in the West, Chhime explained, His Holiness is reluctant to speak about reincarnation because he does not wish to create the impression that he is preoccupied with unrealistic and mystical ideas at the expense of common sense and of a radical acceptance of what is. This is related to Chhime's third point. The Dalai Lama, he explained, does not wish to engage in unfounded speculation about what might happen in a possible future. He is concerned with living realistically in the present. Chhime then assured me that the Dalai Lama's response was not intended in any way to hurt or reprimand the person who posed the question.

I was very grateful for this thoughtful response from the personal secretary to the Dalai Lama. Chhime's explanation of the reasons behind the Dalai Lama's response to my student Jeff's question, however, remains in the very realm of speculation in which the Dalai Lama refuses to indulge. What did my disappointment with the Dalai Lama's response, I then asked myself, have to do with *me*? Had I perhaps turned the Dalai Lama into an idol? Was I, like Pyotr Stepanovich with regard to Stavrogin in Dostoevsky's novel *Demons*, engaging in idolatry? The reality is that I am responsible for the Other, regardless of how the Dalai Lama comports himself, just as, for Dostoevsky, Pyotr Stepanovich is responsible for the Other, regardless of what Stavrogin says or does. The Dalai Lama is just a simple monk, as His Holiness frequently insists—as he insisted, in fact, during the very address he gave in the arena in Eugene and as Chhime R. Chhoekyapa, the personal secretary to the Dalai Lama, mentioned in his letter to me. The Dalai Lama is not "the sun" and I am not his "worm." I am responsible for the other. "Each of us is responsible, before the faces of everyone and before everything—but I more than all the others." As the Dalai Lama himself remarked in his Nobel Lecture of December 11, 1989, "Responsibility does not only lie with the leaders of our countries or with those who have been appointed or elected to do a particular job. It lies with each of us individually."[117]

Chapter 4

Dostoevsky's Antisemitism and the Torment of Belief

We come now to the vexed and unpleasant question of Dostoevsky's hostility toward Jews and Judaism, which I shall consider in the context of the great novelist's own struggles with religious belief. It is worth remarking at the outset that Levinas, whose thoughts about responsibility owe so much to Dostoevsky, and particularly to *The Brothers Karamazov*, never himself noted this particular dimension of Dostoevsky's thought and character. Perhaps Levinas had come to accept expressions of anti-Jewish sentiment from the majority population of non-Jews in cultures dominated by Christianity as simply par for the course.

Let us begin with Joseph Frank's essay "Dostoevsky and Anti-Semitism," a lucid survey of Dostoevsky's attitudes toward Jews and Judaism.[1] I will first offer a summary of Frank's assessment, and then discuss where his analysis, in my view, is not sufficiently critical of Dostoevsky's attitudes.

Frank begins his essay with the following lofty statement, uttered by Prince Myshkin in *The Idiot*, as expressing the author's "highest positive ideal."[2] "Compassion," Myshkin muses, is "the chief and perhaps the only law of human existence."[3] Frank muses over Dostoevsky's "intense sensitivity to human suffering," on the one hand and, on the other, his "adamant refusal, at least after a certain point in his career, to extend such sensitivity to the Jews."[4] Frank finds no egregious examples of antisemitism in Dostoevsky's early work. He argues that Dostoevsky and his brother Mikhail, in their journal *Time*, "strongly supported the cause of greater tolerance" of Jews. Frank finds little overt antisemitism in Dostoevsky's great novels of the 1860s and the early 1870s, that is, in *Crime and Punishment* (1866), *The Idiot* (1868), and *Demons* (1871), nor, for the most part, in *The Brothers Karamazov*, the complete version of which was published in 1881, the year of Dostoevsky's death.

There is, however, according to Frank, one particularly troublingly antisemitic passage in the last and greatest of Dostoevsky's novels. Liza Khokhlakova, an emotionally mercurial and physically disabled young woman who is in love with Alyosha, asks him, "Is it true that at Passover [or Easter; the Russian word is *Paskha*, which means both Passover and Easter] the Yids steal children and kill them?"[5] "Yids" is an accurate translation of the Russian *zhidy*; the word *evrei* would have been a more respectful way for Lizaveta to refer to Jews. The usually merciful, gentle, and forgiving Alyosha shockingly refuses to quell this rumor. Where we would hope to hear a firm "no" to the warped Lizaveta's question about the absurd age-old charge of "blood libel" that has cost so many innocent Jewish lives, the usually ethically scrupulous Alyosha utters a timid "I don't know" (*Ne znaiu*).[6] Lizaveta asks this question in the context of her telling Alyosha that she had been reading a book, in Frank's words, "about the torture of a Christian child by a Jew."[7]

It was in the 1870s, Frank suggests, "that Dostoevsky's concern with the Jewish question took on a new intensity and a new animosity."[8] Frank attributes this new intensity and animosity to Dostoevsky's conviction that Russia's Jews were economically exploiting the peasant population and that Jewish nationhood, which had endured for millennia, encouraged the Jews willfully to estrange themselves from others "in a belief," Dostoevsky writes, "that Jehovah will one day gather them together in Jerusalem . . . and will use his sword to bring down all the other peoples to sit at their feet."[9] In his famous Pushkin speech, which he delivered in 1879, Dostoevsky declares that Russia will bring about "the universal brotherhood of all peoples" and he then goes on, ominously, to limit this seemingly universalist redemption of humankind to "all the tribes of the great Aryan race [*so vsemi plemenami velikogo ariiskogo roda*],"[10] thus clearly excluding the Jews, according to Frank's understanding of Dostoevsky's use of the adjective "Aryan" here.

Frank ends his essay by speaking of how Dostoevsky's messianism has been linked, by scholars such as Aileen Kelly, "to his anti-Semitism," that Dostoevsky "saw Russia as taking up the role of the 'God-bearing' people, which the Jews had proclaimed for themselves, and that he thus regarded them as rivals who had to be denigrated and disgraced."[11] I would like to suggest another rationale for Dostoevsky's antisemitism, a rationale that is linked to Dostoevsky's reflections on the relation of ethics to the question of God's existence or nonexistence.

Before doing so, however, I feel obliged to question Frank's characterization of Dostoevsky's allegedly unproblematic attitudes toward the Jews before the last decade or so of the author's life, when the novelist made so many clearly hateful comments about Jews and Judaism.

Frank finds no egregious examples of antisemitism in Dostoevsky's early work. I am not so sure. Isai Fomich Bumshtein, a strikingly memorable character in *House of the Dead*, is the earliest and perhaps most exhaustive portrait of a Jew in Dostoevsky's fiction.[12] The narrator of *House of the Dead*, it is true, expresses affection for Isai Fomich, the prison's only Jewish inmate. "We were great friends [*My s nim byli bol'shie druz'ia*]," he says.[13] But the portrait itself is a caricature, a stereotype. Bumshtein is a jeweler who is also, "of course [*razumeetsia*]," a "usurer [*rostovshchik*]" who "supplied the whole prison with money at a percentage."[14] Bumshtein is consistently referred to, both by the narrator and the other inmates, by the clearly more derogatory (*zhid*, meaning "Yid") of the two most common Russian words (*zhid* and the more respectful *evrei*) for "Jew." The narrator calls Bumshtein "vain and boastful" and is irritated by the Jew's unwillingness to celebrate Christmas. On Christmas day, the narrator informs the reader, Isai Fomich lights "his candle with an obstinate and supercilious air and set to work, evidently wanting to show that the holiday meant nothing to him."[15]

Perhaps the most offensive section of Dostoevsky's portrait is the narrator's description of Bumshtein observing the Jewish Sabbath in prison on Friday evenings. Alexander Petrovich ridicules Isai Fomich for so self-consciously performing a religious ritual and ostentatiously "playing a part"[16] in front of his fellow convicts. Dostoevsky is here not just lampooning a particular character whom he portrays as a vain performer rather than a humble servant of God. He lampoons and demeans, as well, the Jewish rituals themselves. Jews traditionally don tefillin before they pray. Tefillin consist of two leather straps, to each of which is attached a small box containing sacred verses. One strap is wrapped around the left arm and the other around the forehead, with a small box protruding in the center of the strap that is wrapped around the forehead. The narrator of *House of the Dead* calls the phylacteries that are strapped around the arm "manacles" or "handcuffs" (*naruchniki*), the leather strap around the head a "bandage" (*perevliazkoi*), and the protruding box "a ridiculous [*smeshnoi*] horn sprouting out of his [Isai Fomich's] forehead."[17] Also characterized as "ridiculous" (*smeshnoi*) is the tune—the "shrill little chant"—that was "the only tune that Isai Fomitch hummed all the years he was in prison."[18] This tune is sung to the words of one of the high points of the traditional Jewish service that commemorates the miracle of God's parting of the Red Sea during the exodus from Egypt and the sudden salvation, against all odds, of the Jewish people, a band of just released slaves who were being hotly pursued by the powerful Pharaoh and his army.

Religious Jews, in communal prayer in the synagogue, will often rock back and forth as they pray. Dostoevsky's narrator refers to these movements that sometimes accentuate davening, that is, Jewish prayer, as "wild and absurd [*smeshnye*] gesticulations."[19] Suffice it to say that Dostoevsky's narrator is hardly respectful of Jewish prayer. Nor did Dostoevsky even care to be accurate in his representation of Jewish prayer. Tefillin are wrapped around only one arm, not two, as the narrator reports. They are never worn in the evening (after sundown) and never on the Sabbath. The narrator describes Isai Fomich putting on his prayer shawl. After lighting his two (Sabbath) candles, Bumshtein "began putting on his vestment" which was "a parti-coloured shawl of woolen material."[20] Unless a Jew happens to be leading a religious service, prayer shawls are worn after sunset only once a year, on the eve of Yom Kippur.

There were other non-Christians in the prison, notably a number of Muslims, about whom Dostoevsky has only good things to say. The brothers of the narrator's beloved Muslim friend Aley respond to the narrator, in the chapter in which the reader is first introduced to Isai Fomich, "with a dignified and gracious, that is, a typically Mussulman, smile (which I love so much, and love especially for its dignity)."[21] Dostoevsky's narrator reserves his ridicule solely for Jewish observance.[22]

In Dostoevsky's demeaning portrait of Isai Fomich's ritual act of prayer on the evening of the Jewish Sabbath, we see nothing less than its author's betrayal of God understood on the basis of ethics. We see at work here Dostoevsky the satirist, the vulgar rather than the divine comedian. The word "God," as Levinas says in his essay "God and Philosophy," traces its meaning to its implication "in every ethical intrigue, to the divine comedy without which this word could not have arisen. A comedy taking place in the ambiguity between temple and theater, but wherein the laughter sticks in your throat [*vous reste dans la gorge*] at the approach of the neighbor, that is, of his face or his abandonment [*délaissement*]."[23] Let us attempt to explicate this last sentence from "God and Philosophy." The word "God" participates in the ambiguity between temple and theater. The word "temple" suggests a religious context, a spiritual context, in which God commands me to love my neighbor, to be responsible for the Other. "Theater" suggests representation and thus language in its mode of representation, of exhibition. When we utter the word "God" we think of this word as referring to an entity, something represented to the consciousness, something that exists, something adequate to the understanding that thinks it. The word "God," Levinas is saying here, is found in the ambiguity between ethics or spirit, on the one hand, and representation, on the other: the word "God" signifies between the temple and the theater. The word truly signifies in regard to the approach of the neighbor, with his destitute face which commands my responsibility.

The laughter Dostoevsky attempts to evoke through his vulgar comedy, through his caricature of the solitary Jew praying on the evening of the Sabbath in *House of the Dead*, "sticks in your throat" especially today, after we have experienced the aftermath of such laughter—after the Shoah.

Let us return to Joseph Frank's discussion of Dostoevsky's antisemitism. Frank argues that Dostoevsky and his brother Mikhail, in their journal *Time*, "strongly supported the cause of greater tolerance" of Jews. Frank finds little overt antisemitism in Dostoevsky's great novels of the 1860s, that is, in *Crime and Punishment, The Idiot, Demons*, and *The Brothers Karamazov*, save for the troubling scene in his last novel in which Alyosha refuses to dismiss as a hateful lie the infamous charge of Jewish blood libel. Again, Frank's assessment is too kind to Dostoevsky. There are ugly references to Jews in *Crime and Punishment* as well as in *Demons*. In fact, virtually every reference to Jews in these novels is unpleasant. Leonid Tsypkin's assessment of Dostoevsky's antisemitism is closer to the mark. Tsypkin was a Jewish writer of the Soviet period who loved Dostoevsky in spite of the great writer's pervasive antisemitism. In his innovative and moving novel *Summer in Baden-Baden*, Tsypkin puzzles over his attraction to the virulently antisemitic Dostoevsky:

> [I]t struck me as being strange to the point of implausibility that a man so sensitive in his novels to the sufferings of others, this jealous defender of the insulted and the injured who fervently and even frenetically preached the right to exist of every earthly creature and sang a passionate hymn to each little leaf and every blade of grass—that this man should not have come up with even a single word in the defence or justification of a people persecuted over several thousands of years—could he have been so blind?—or was he perhaps blinded by hatred?[24]

Frank, as we have discussed, finds the most unforgiving example of Dostoevsky's antisemitism in his portrayal of his hero Alyosha Karamazov's unwillingness, in *The Brothers Karamazov*, to put to rest the rumors, referred to by Liza Kokhlakova, about the Jews murdering Christian babies on Easter or Passover, with the understanding that the Jews would use the blood of these babies to make matzo. It is, however, not just Dostoevsky's insidious allusion to the infamous "blood libel"— disappointingly left unrefuted by Alyosha—that is disturbing about this passage. But it is also the perversity, admittedly uttered by a perverse character, of Dostoevsky's description of Liza's having just read, in a book that she shows to Alyosha, "about some trial somewhere, and that a Jew first cut off all the fingers of a four-year-old boy, and then crucified him on the wall, nailed him with nails and crucified him, and then said at his trial that the boy died quickly, in four hours. Quickly! He said the boy was moaning, that he kept on moaning, and he stood admiring it."[25] In *Summer in Baden-Baden*, Tsypkin draws his readers' attention to this passage from *The Brothers Karamazov* when he writes of his dismay at Dostoevsky's depiction of "the Jew who crucified the Christian child and then cut off its finger, relishing the child's agony."[26]

Frank, as we have noted, cites the following lofty statement, uttered by Prince Myshkin in Dostoevsky's novel *The Idiot*, as expressing the author's "highest positive ideal." "Compassion," Myshkin asserts, is "the chief and perhaps the only law of human existence."[27] It is precisely compassion, however, that Dostoevsky refuses to see in the Jewish character, at least in his late reflections in *A Writer's Diary*. If you were to "ask the native [Russian] population in our border areas," Dostoevsky asks, "what is it that drives the Jew and what is it that has driven him for so many centuries? You will always get the same answer: *mercilessness*."[28] Frank muses over Dostoevsky's "intense sensitivity to human suffering," on the one hand and, on the other, his "adamant refusal, at least after a certain point in his career, to extend such sensitivity to the Jews."[29] Frank is here virtually repeating the cadence and sentiment of the passage we just cited from Leonid Tsypkin's *Summer in Baden-Baden*.

Tsypkin's impression of Dostoevsky's lifelong antisemitism is, in my view, closer to the truth than the account offered by Professor Frank. Dostoevsky's antipathy toward Jews and Judaism was most acute in the final decade of the novelist's life, it is true, but his attitudes toward Jews and Judaism as expressed in his fiction in the previous decade, beginning with the publication of *Notes from the House of the Dead* in 1861, were hostile. In *Summer in Baden-Baden*, Tsypkin, a Jew, imagines himself visiting an elderly friend, Gil'da (Gilya) Yakovlevna, with whom he would always stay when he was in Leningrad. Gilya had lived for many years with a Jewish doctor of German descent named Moisey (Mozya) Ernstovich. Gilya keeps Mozya's/Moisey's/Moshe's old edition of Dostoevsky's complete works on her shelves. Gilya greets Tsypkin and asks him, as she always did, "Are you still so keen on Dostoevsky? [*Ty vse eshche uvlekaesh'sia Dostoevskim?*]"[30] Before receiving an answer to this question, Gilya urges Tsypkin not to mention his love of Dostoevsky when they go to visit the Brodskys, a religiously observant Jewish couple.

Before he goes to bed that evening, Tsypkin takes a volume off the shelf from the deceased Mozya's collected works of Dostoevsky. He comes upon Dostoevsky's article, which he apparently had not read before, from *A Writer's Diary* "for 1877 or 1878" on "The Jewish Question." This article, written just a few years before Dostoevsky's death, hardly surprises Tsypkin as evidence of a new and ominous turn in Dostoevsky's attitude toward the Jews, as Joseph Frank's essay would have us believe. Tsypkin sees it, rather, as part and parcel of a lifelong antipathy. "I should not have been surprised to discover" this article, Tsypkin writes, because Dostoevsky

> was bound after all somewhere or other to have gathered together in one place all those "Jews, Jewesses, Jew-boys and Yids" with which he so liberally besprinkled the pages of his novels—now as the poseur Lyamshin squealing with terror in *Demons*, now as the arrogant and at the same time cowardly Isai Fomich in *Notes from the House of the Dead* who did not scruple to lend money at enormous interest to his fellow-convicts, now as the fireman in *Crime and Punishment* with that 'everlasting grief, so sourly imprinted on all members of the tribe of Judah without exception,' and with his laughable way of pronouncing Russian which is reproduced in the novel with such particular and fastidious pleasure, now as the Jew who crucified the Christian child and then cut off its finger, relishing the child's agony (Liza Khokhlakova's story in *The Brothers Karamazov*)—but most often he would depict them as nameless money-lenders, tight-fisted tradesmen or petty thieves who are not even fully portrayed but simply mentioned as little Jews or some other term implying the lowest and basest qualities of the human character—no, there was nothing surprising about the fact that the author of these novels should somewhere or other have finally expressed his views on this subject, have finally expressed his theory—although in fact there was no special theory—only fairly hackneyed arguments and myths (myths which have not lost their currency to this very day, incidentally).[31]

No "special theory," perhaps, but then how does one square the antipathy so consistently expressed toward Jews and the Jewish people throughout Dostoevsky's fiction with a curious and seemingly contradictory passage, in praise of the Jews, from *A Writer's Diary*, that Tsypkin does not mention?

I refer here to the following passage about "the Jew" in *A Writer's Diary* in which Dostoevsky uses the more respectful word *evrei*: "It's an odd thing, indeed! [*Da i strannoe delo!*] A Jew without God is somehow unthinkable [*evrei bez boga kak-to nemyslim*]; one can't even imagine a Jew without God [*evreia bez boga i predstavit' nel'zia*]. Moreover, I do not believe in the existence of atheists [*bezbozhnikov*] even among the educated Jews: they are all of the same substance!"[32] A "godless person" (*bezbozhnik*), as we noted in chapter 1, is precisely what Raskolnikov's fellow prisoners, in the epilogue to *Crime and Punishment*, angrily call the aloof young murderer. Raskolnikov's "godlessness," according to them, is what most alienates them from the better educated and more gentlemanly Raskolnikov. The peasant convicts, like the Jews, feel a closeness to God denied the arrogant Raskolnikov. Dostoevsky as a prisoner felt that same alienation from most of his fellow inmates. Dostoevsky resented the peasants' persecution of him and no doubt envied their solidarity with each other, just as he perhaps envied Jewish solidarity and the closeness to God that, he imagined, accompanied this solidarity.

For Dostoevsky in *A Writer's Diary*, moreover, it is the Jews who have mistreated the "Russians" rather than the other way around. The "Russian," according to Dostoevsky, "is much, much less to blame" for the problematic relations between "Russians" and "Jews" living in Russia than the "Jews" themselves. "Self-importance and arrogance," Dostoevsky arrogantly claims, "are traits of the Jewish character that are very painful for us Russians."[33] The touchy and irritable Dostoevsky asserts that no one is "more ready" than the Jew "to take offence."[34] Brotherhood, Dostoevsky claims, "*is needed on both sides*. Let the Jew himself show the Russian even a little brotherly feeling so as to encourage him."[35] Dostoevsky clearly feels excluded by the Jews! He in fact explicitly says so in the letter he wrote to Arkady Grigorevich Kovner, a Russian Jew who had written to Dostoevsky to chastise the novelist for his "hatred for the 'Yid,'" which, Kovner maintained, "manifests itself in almost every issue of your *Diary*."[36] "During the 50 years of my life," Dostoevsky responds to Kovner, "I have found that Jews, whether good or bad, won't even sit down at the same table with a Russian, while a Russian feels no hesitation about sitting down with a Jew. So who hates whom? Who is intolerant towards whom?"[37] The "touchy" Dostoevsky goes on to observe that "all Jews" are "touchy . . . when it comes to things Jewish."[38] It is perhaps not so surprising that, when the touchy Dostoevsky, toward the end of Tsypkin's novel *Summer in Baden-Baden*, looks in the mirror, he is shocked to see the image of the touchy Jew so prominently featured in *Notes from the House of the Dead*, Isai Fomich Bumshtein! Dostoevsky as Isai Fomich Bumshtein? But perhaps there is something beyond mere self-loathing in Tsypkin's imagining Dostoevsky imagining himself as a despised Jew. What are the implications of Dostoevsky's insisting, in *A Writer's Diary*, that he can't imagine the existence of atheists, of "godless ones," even among secular Jews?

Dostoevsky goes very far in his last and greatest novel, *The Brothers Karamazov*, the complete version of which was published in the year of the author's death, toward equating God with conscience, toward thinking God on the basis of ethics. *The Brothers Karamazov* inspired and profoundly influenced the thought of Emmanuel Levinas, the aim of whose late work was, in large part, to recover the word "God" in a secular age by thinking God outside of the ontological tradition, by thinking God *à partir de l'éthique*—by thinking God beginning from, or on the basis of, ethical responsibility. Dostoevsky did not, perhaps could not, go quite this far in thinking God outside of ontology—outside of what Levinas calls "thematization." For Levinas, I can say " 'Here I am, in the name of God,' without referring myself directly to his presence. 'Here I am,' just that! The word God is still absent from the phrase in which it is for the first time involved in words." For Levinas, I am true to the meaning of the word "God," as it first becomes involved in words in the Hebrew Bible, by saying "Here I am" before the face of the Other rather than by stating, " 'I believe in God [*Je crois en Dieu*].' "[39]

For Dostoevsky, in contrast, a doctrinal adherence to a belief in God and in immortality remained crucial. At the end of March 1878, less than a year before he began publishing *The Brothers Karamazov* serially in *The Russian Messenger*, Dostoevsky advises the mother of an eight-year-old boy to "acquaint" her son "with the Gospels, teach him to believe in God, strictly, according to the Law. This is a sine qua non, because, without that, he cannot become a good person."[40] The importance of a strict adherence to doctrinal truth seems to be the point, in part, of the novel's conclusion, which asserts the certainty of immortality. Alyosha and the friends of the young boy Ilyusha have gathered around the stone that marks the boy's sadly brief life and recent death. Kolya, the boy who serves as Ivan's atheist double in the novel, asks Alyosha, in the wake of Ilyusha's death, if "we shall all rise again from the dead and see each other again, all, Ilyushechka too?" Alyosha replies, "Certainly [*Nepremenno*] we shall all rise again, certainly [*nepremenno*] we shall see each other and gladly, joyfully will tell each other all that has happened. . . ."[41]

Kolya the erstwhile atheist has now come fully around and, as the novel concludes, shouts a loud "Hurrah for Karamazov!" and "once more all the boys joined in his exclamation."[42] Dostoevsky here, through Alyosha, appears to be asserting a literal belief in the resurrection. "Certainly" (*Nepremenno*), Alyosha asserts, we shall all be resurrected and we shall all "certainly" (*nepremenno*) see each other again. Here we have a very different response to the meaning of resurrection than that of Tolstoy who, in conversation with his friend the philologist I. M. Ivakin, remarked at virtually the same moment (1881): "What is it to me if [Christ] is resurrected? If he was resurrected, then God bless him! The questions important to me are: What should I do? How should I live?"[43]

I do not wish to underestimate or discount the reasons just discussed for Dostoevsky's antisemitism: his suspicion of, or rather his pathological convictions about, alleged Jewish materialism and greed that, he asserted, were responsible for the exploitation of Russia's venerable and vulnerable peasant class who had only recently been freed from centuries of serfdom; and the Jewish sense of nationhood that resisted assimilation into the unfolding of what Dostoevsky saw as the Russian national myth.

But there is yet another aspect of his relationship to Judaism that Dostoevsky, the obsessive and perhaps always insecure spiritual seeker, might well have found particularly threatening. I shall draw inspiration here from Franz Rosenzweig's *The Star of Redemption*, first published in 1921, just forty years after Dostoevsky's death. In *The Star*, Rosenzweig makes some brilliant comparisons between Judaism and Christianity, the religion to which he very nearly converted and for which he maintained a lifelong sense of admiration. I wish to focus here very briefly on Rosenzweig's analysis of the place of "belief" in Judaism and Christianity. For Rosenzweig, "belief" is crucial in the case of Christianity, "in which a community founded on dogma gives itself reality."[44] In order to assure its reality and continuity, "Christianity must proselytize . . . Only he belongs to Christianity who knows his own life to be on the way which leads from Christ come to Christ coming."[45]

The belief of a Christian, Rosenzweig continues,

> is belief as the content of a testimony [*eines Zeugnisses*]. It is belief in something. That is exactly opposite of the belief of the Jew. His belief is not the content of a testimony, but rather the product of a reproduction [*einer Zeugung*]. The Jew, engendered a Jew, attests his belief by continuing to procreate the Jewish people. His belief is not in something: he is himself the belief. He is believing with an immediacy which no Christian dogmatist can ever attain for himself. This belief cares little for its dogmatic fixation: it has existence and this is worth more than words.[46]

Christian belief, Rosenzweig later asserts, "is dogmatic in the highest sense, and must be so."[47]

For Rosenzweig, Judaism and Christianity are two related but different and equally valid spiritual paths. For Dostoevsky, in contrast, Judaism is a threat to the utopian future which, in his eschatological fervor, he imagined for Russia alone. But perhaps Dostoevsky resented the Jews as well and perhaps most unforgivably for what he might have perceived to be their unearned closeness to the eternal, to God. The Jew's belief, for Rosenzweig, "is not in something; he is himself the belief. He is believing with an immediacy which no Christian dogmatist can ever attain for himself." Dostoevsky makes a similar claim, as we have noted, in discussing "The Jewish Question" in *A Writer's Diary*. "It's impossible," Dostoevsky observes, "even to imagine a Jew [*evreia*] without God; moreover," Dostoevsky continues, "I don't believe that there are godless people [*bezbozhnikov*] even among educated Jews: they are all of the same essence."[48]

Levinas makes a similar claim about the Jew and belief in the following anecdote that he tells about the famous political philosopher Hannah Arendt:

> Hannah Arendt, not long before she died, told the following story on French radio. Once when she was a child in her native Königsberg, one day she said to the rabbi who was teaching her religion: "You know, I have lost my faith." And the rabbi replied, "Who is asking you for it?"

Commenting on this story, Levinas remarks,

> What matters is not "faith" but "doing." Doing, which means moral behavior, of course, but also the performance of ritual. Moreover, are believing and doing different things? What does believing mean? What is faith made of? Words, ideas? Convictions? What do we believe with? With the whole body! With all our bones! (Psalms 35:10). What the rabbi meant was: "Doing good is the act of belief itself."[49]

But doing good is not good enough, according to Rosenzweig's analysis, for the Christian dogmatist. Nor was it good enough for Dostoevsky, who was tormented, precisely as was his character Kirillov in *Demons*, by the question of God's existence. The belief in God that Dostoevsky struggled with great and punishing difficulty to attain is, according to Franz Rosenzweig and to Dostoevsky in *A Writer's Diary*, of less concern to the Jew whose closeness to God is not dependent on belief. The question of belief or of faith is, for Levinas, a matter less of faith than of faithfulness to a tradition that commands the faithful to be and to do good and to perform religious rituals that train the sensibilities of the faithful to pursue goodness in the world. For the Christian dogmatist, on the other hand, faith or belief is crucial.

In *Crime and Punishment*, Dostoevsky even likens the unbelieving murderer Raskolnikov to the Jews who, in the fourth Gospel—the Gospel according to John—crucify Jesus precisely as a result of their lack of "simplistic belief" in Jesus as the son of God, a lack of belief which the tormented, aspiring believer Dostoevsky himself shared. "It is clear that I do not believe in Christ," Dostoevsky writes in a notebook entry made in the last year of his life, "and preach Him like a child."[50]

Raskolnikov is consumed with guilt following his murder of the old pawnbroker and her half sister, Lizaveta. He finds himself seeking out Sonya Marmeladova for reasons about which he himself is not yet entirely clear. He surely senses, in her, a salvific presence. On the one hand, he is troubled by Sonya's capacity—to her own detriment—for self-sacrifice. She has debased herself and undergone terrible suffering by becoming a prostitute so that she can provide for her alcoholic father's wife Katerina Ivanovna and the couple's two young children. Raskolnikov suggests to Sonya that, despite Sonya's desperate efforts to provide for the family, her young stepsister Polya is bound to follow in Sonya's footsteps. No, Sonya objects, "God won't allow such horror." Raskolnikov answers, "But maybe there isn't any God [*mozhet, i Boga-to sovsem net*]."[51] We learn in this passage that Sonya used to read aloud from the New Testament to the same Lizaveta whom Rasknolnikov murdered. Lizaveta was, like Sonya but certainly unlike the nonbelieving murderer Raskolnikov, a "holy fool," a *iurodivaia*. Lizaveta and Sonya were both believers. Raskolnikov wants Sonya to read to him, but Sonya asks, "What is it to you? You don't believe [*ne veruete*], do you?"[52] Rasknolnikov insists that Sonya read from the New Testament, and she hesitatingly does so, from John 11. The text tells the story of Jesus's raising of Mary's brother Lazarus from the dead. It also speaks of how the Jews, who at first did not believe that Jesus was either the son of God or the Messiah, had been stoning Jesus. Some Jews comforted Mary on her loss, though they too did not believe until Jesus performed, before their eyes, the miracle of raising Lazarus from the dead. Dostoevsky's Sonya focuses on the moment when the Jews pass from a state of nonbelief to belief. Sonya reads verses 32–37, culminating in the incredulity of the Jews as expressed in verse 37.

In these verses, which Sonya reads aloud to Raskolnikov from a copy of the New Testament translated into Russian, Jesus approaches Mary, who is weeping. Mary asks Jesus where her brother Lazarus can be found. Jesus weeps in response to the weeping Mary, and the Jews—apparently moved by Jesus's display of compassion—comment on how much Jesus loved Lazarus. "Jesus wept. Then said the Jews, Behold how much he [Jesus] loved him [Lazarus]. But some of them said, Could not this man, who opened the eyes of the blind, have brought it about that this man in particular should not have died?" We note that, in the text from John, this last verse, beginning with the word "But" ("*A*" in Russian), is an expression of a lack of faith, a lack of belief, on the part of the Jews, in Jesus's divine powers, specifically in his ability to work miracles. Why could not this man, who had performed the miracle of curing the blind, have saved Mary's brother Lazarus from dying? Dostoevsky writes:

> At this last verse, "Could not this man, which opened the eyes of the blind . . ." she had lowered her voice, conveying ardently and passionately the doubt [*somnenie*], the reproach, and the verbal abuse of the unbelieving [*neveruiushchikh*], blind Jews [*iudeev*], who in another moment, as if thunderstruck, would fall down, weep, and believe [*uveruiut*] . . . "And *he, he* who is also blinded and unbelieving [*neveruiushchii*], he, too, will believe [*uveruet*]—yes, yes! Right now, this minute," she dreamed, and she was trembling with joyful expectation.[53]

Sonya, despite her profession, is morally virtuous and self-sacrificing. She singles herself out by her responsibility for others. When Raskolnikov asks her what is preventing her from killing herself as a consequence of the degraded existence she has assumed, she responds, "But what would become of them?" that is, of the beloved members of her family that she is keeping alive through her shameful profession. It is as if her extraordinary compassion derives from her "belief" in God and particularly, of course, in Jesus's miraculous powers. Sonya's hope is that her reading the passage to Raskolnikov will transform him into a believer. The Jews, like the murderer Raskolnikov, are portrayed here as nonbelievers, until they are convinced to *believe* by the miracle of Jesus's resurrection of Lazarus from the dead. The Christian, it appears, requires belief. The Jews, until they in effect become Christians, are nonbelievers.

The Jew may be a nonbeliever (until it is clearly proven otherwise) in Jesus's resurrection of Lazarus, but at the same time, for Dostoevsky, "A Jew without God is somehow unthinkable." Dostoevsky's hostility toward Jews is the result perhaps not only of their immemorial notion of nationhood that stands in competition with, and refuses to be assimilated into, Dostoevsky's messianic notion of a Christian Orthodox Russia whose selflessness will serve as a model to the nations. But Dostoevsky's hostility is perhaps the result, as well, of his sensing, in Judaism as opposed to in Christianity, a relative lack of concern with adherence to correct belief as the royal road toward closeness with God, the Jews' very lack of concern

with doctrinal certainty about the existence of God to which the Slavophile Shatov aspires in *Demons*.

Shatov, in a conversation with his former mentor Stavrogin in *Demons*,
asserts that "the only god-bearing nation is the Russian nation." Stavrogin then asks Shatov, "I simply want to know: do you yourself believe in
God or not?" Shatov answers, "I believe in Russia, I believe in her Orthodoxy . . . I believe in the body of Christ . . . I believe that the new coming
will take place in Russia . . . I believe . . . ." "But in God? In God?" Stavrogin asks again, insistently. Shatov answers: "I . . . I will believe in God."[54]
Shatov is angry that Stavrogin has forced him to confront, and to reveal,
his own embarrassing uncertainty about his belief in God, so angry that
it was "as if he wanted to burn" Stavrogin "with his eyes." "But I didn't
tell you," he rather desperately asserts, that "I don't believe at all!" Russia will be a model to the nations of selfless giving and will thus take up
the messianic mantle that the Jews, through their worldliness, allegedly
betrayed: "The Jews lived only to wait for the true God," Shatov asserts,
"and left [or 'gave over'] the true God to the world [*miru*]."[55]

There is something distinctly Jewish about this primacy of doing over
believing, of understanding messianic deliverance as the I—or the "*Moi*,"
in the accusative case—saying "Here I am!" (*Me voici!*) before the face
of the Other in the very "world" of which Shatov so dismissively speaks.
This is how Levinas, in a commentary on the meaning of the messianic
age in the Talmudic tractate *Sanhedrin*, understands Rav Nachman
when he remarks (*Sanhedrin* 98b4): "If he [the Messiah] is of those living
[today], then he is Me [*c'est alors Moi*]."[56] The primacy of doing good
over believing is, for Hannah Arendt's rabbi as well as for Levinas, the
truly royal road toward closeness to "God." Shatov truly believes in this
royal road, in the goodness of this road, but he is still harboring a hope
that, once Russia arrives at its destination, he will then believe in God in
an uncomplicated, doctrinally certain manner. Perhaps Dostoevsky, like
Shatov, cannot silence within his own psyche the insistent voice of Stavrogin buttonholing him with the question: "I simply wanted to know: do
you yourself believe in God, or not?"[57]

As an example of what he takes to be Dostoevsky's "almost pathological revulsion" for Judaism, David I. Goldstein discusses a passage from
a letter Dostoevsky wrote, from Wiesbaden (Germany), to his wife Anna
Grigor'evna in which he abjectly apologizes for his gambling addiction.
After a particular gambling disaster, Dostoevsky, wracked with shame
and guilt, rushes to the house of a priest in order to confess to him. This
in itself is remarkable, given Dostoevsky's, and his wife's, antipathy
towards Catholicism. Dostevsky loses his way, only to spot—as a kind of

"oasis"—what he imagines is a Russian church, which terrifyingly turns out to be a synagogue, or, as Dostoevsky puts it, a "Yid" (*zhidovskaia*) church:

> By half past nine I had lost everything and I fled like a madman. I felt so miserable that I rushed to see the priest (don't get upset, I did *not* see him, no, I did *not*, nor do I intend to!). But I lost my way in this town and when I reached a church, which I took for a Russian church, they told me that it was not Russian but Yid. It was as if someone had poured cold water over me. I ran back home. And now it is midnight and I am sitting and writing to you. (And I won't go to see the priest, I won't go, I swear I won't!) [58]

Perhaps this passage reveals not so much, or not simply, a pathological revulsion toward Judaism, as Goldstein understandably suggests, but rather the sense that, as a non-Jew, the desperately needy Dostoevsky here feels excluded and rejected at the very moment that he is thirsting for acceptance to the point that he had even been willing to debase himself by confessing his sin of gambling to a Roman Catholic priest, which he knew his wife would find intolerable.

In his *Notebooks*, Dostoevsky defends himself against those critics who imagine that he has "an *uneducated* and retrograde faith in God." Quite to the contrary, Dostoevsky insists, his secularly inclined critics "have never conceived so powerful a rejection of God as exists in the Inquisitor and the preceding chapter [of *The Brothers Karamazov*]." [59] Throughout all of enlightened, secular Europe, Dostoevsky writes, "there *has not been* and does not exist so powerful an *expression* [of ideas] from the atheistic point of view as mine. . . . My *hosannah* has passed through a great *furnace of doubt*." [60] Dostoevsky's antisemitism perhaps bears witness to the fact that he never quite passed all the way through that furnace, that he kept feeling its heat, which stoked his resentment of the Jews who were, Dostoevsky felt, far surer than he—in his agonizing struggles with religious belief—about their closeness to the eternal.

Chapter 5

✦

"The Death of a Certain God Inhabiting the World behind the Scenes"

Loss and Hope in *Otherwise Than Being* and Vasily Grossman's *Life and Fate*

Gogol, Tolstoy, Chekhov and Korolenko appear to have instilled in Russians an almost religious reverence for the printed word.[1]

—Vasily Grossman

The Death of a Certain God Inhabiting the World behind the Scenes

Levinas's non-ontological way of thinking God on the basis of ethics and outside of the framework of belief was deeply influenced, as we have shown, by his reading of Dostoevsky, and particularly by *The Brothers Karamazov*—even if Dostoevsky himself was tormented by an ultimately unquenchable "thirst to believe" [*zhazhda verit'*] in God. A non-ontological way of thinking God on the basis of ethics, we have suggested, is true to an understanding of the significance—of the very way of signifying—of the God of the Bible, and not just the Hebrew Bible, as Levinas suggests in his reading of Matthew 25:31–40 in his lecture on "Witnessing and Ethics" that we discussed in chapter 2. In Judaism in particular, however, in contrast to dogmatic Christianity,[2] we have argued, "belief" is generally understood as being far less important—if it is important or even required at all—than a dedication to the continual effort to be good and to do good in the world, to love one's neighbor as if the loving of one's neighbor were precisely what it means to be a self.[3]

Levinas's way of thinking God on the basis of ethics, we have stressed, was deeply influenced by Dostoevsky. "*I am responsible,*" Levinas says, "and may not be concerned about whether the other is responsible for me. The human, in the highest, strictest sense of the word is without reciprocity. I didn't discover that, Dostoevsky did."[4] Levinas's thinking God through the ethical relation was indebted to Dostoevsky, an aspiring Christian with a desperate and finally unquenchable thirst to believe. If Levinas's thinking God through ethics was inspired by Dostoevsky, it was affirmed by his reading of the great Soviet-era novel *Life and Fate* by Vasily Grossman, a secular Jew who was, by his own admission, a nonbeliever (*neveruiushchii*).[5] *Life and Fate* preoccupied Levinas in the last decade and a half of his life.[6]

I begin these reflections on loss and hope with an acknowledgment of two momentous losses registered by Emmanuel Levinas in his second and last magnum opus, *Otherwise Than Being, or Beyond Essence*. The first acknowledgment inaugurates the book, the second concludes it. The two are intimately connected. Let us begin with the dedication of the book:

> To the memory of those who were closest among the six million assassinated by the National Socialists, and of the millions on millions of all confessions and all nations, victims of the same hatred of the other man, the same anti-semitism.[7]

Levinas then names, in the discrete letters of the Hebrew alphabet, those irreplaceable others closest to him who were victims of the Nazi horror: his father, mother, brothers, father-in-law, and mother-in-law.

Levinas concludes his great book with the following paragraph, consisting of a single, breathless sentence:

> In this work which does not seek to restore any ruined concept, the destitution and desituating of the subject do not remain without signification: after the death of a certain god inhabiting the world behind the scenes, the substitution of the hostage discovers the trace, the unpronounceable inscription, of what, always already past, always "he," does not enter into any present, to which are suited not the nouns designating beings, or the verbs in which their essence resounds, but that which, as a pronoun, marks with its seal all that a noun/name can convey.[8]

What is acknowledged as lost here, and what hope might be engendered in the wake of that loss? And what is the relation, if any, between this concluding sentence–paragraph and the book's dedication?

What is lost is the belief "in a certain god [*un certain dieu*] inhabiting the world behind the scenes." The god declared dead by Nietzsche is indeed dead. This is both the particular god whom Nietzsche pronounced dead—a "certain" god in this sense—and also a god in whom one could believe with certainty: "un dieu certain" as well as "un certain dieu." An undeniable and untransferable sense of being held hostage by the other is precisely that which, for Levinas, replaces or substitutes for this now dead, certain god. As a subject, I sense this trace, impossible to write or even to enunciate, in the pronoun "he" or "it" (*il*), as the subversive force of "illeity," which Levinas describes earlier in *Otherwise Than Being*, and which we sought to elucidate in chapters 2 and 3.

We will repeat here what we understand by Levinasian "illeity." Levinas gives the name "illeity" to the source of the ethical command which, "beyond representation, affects me unbeknownst to myself, 'slipping into me like a thief.' "[9] The word "illeity" signifies that the command that I say "Here I am!" before the face of the Other is sensed by the "I" as a supervening "that-ness" or "he-ness," a "thirdness" that is separate from self and Other. It comes neither from the self nor from the Other, is neither "I" nor "you"/"thou." One could refer to "illeity" by the word "God," but for Levinas that would be to "tame the subversiveness worked by illeity"[10] and would turn God into a being, while what Levinas wishes to convey is that the word "God" signifies a beyond being, an otherwise than being that "gets its meaning from the witness borne, which thematization certainly betrays in theology."[11] Theology names God as a being, turns illeity into a theme or a proposition.

The Shoah, for Levinas, signaled the definitive end of theodicy, of the attempt to explain evil as somehow part of a divine plan. The Shoah meant the end of happy endings, the end of a providential view of history. Six million innocents were murdered. The word "holocaust," which literally means "a burnt offering" and thus a sacrifice, regretfully suggests, when referring to the six million who perished at the hands of the National Socialists, that these deaths were part of a divine plan that is beyond our understanding. The word "Shoah," meaning "catastrophe," in its bluntness, is far more respectful of the unique and irreplaceable specificity of those who were murdered. And here we have a link between the conclusion of *Otherwise Than Being* and its dedication. The unspeakable loss of human lives that is the Shoah bears witness to the loss of a certain god inhabiting the world behind the scenes, of a providential God pulling the strings. But in the wake of this loss there is born, or revived, a hope in the continued manifestation of acts of human goodness.

And here we have a link between Levinas's last great philosophical work, *Otherwise Than Being*, and the literary work that obsessed Levinas during the last fifteen or so years of his life, Vasily Grossman's *Life and Fate*. Our contention is that, in the wake of the devastation of the Shoah and the Second World War, it is precisely their shared hope in the possibility of a continuing manifestation of acts of human goodness that unites the observant, orthodox Jew Emmanuel Levinas and the secular, nonbelieving Jew, Vasily Grossman. Both Levinas and Grossman manage to think God on the basis of ethics.

Thinking God on the Basis of Ethics in *Life and Fate*

Je dirai non, mio padre, je dirai non!

Vasily Grossman's massive novel *Life and Fate*, a Chekhovian epic modeled in many ways on Tolstoy's *War and Peace*, is often regarded as the greatest novel of the Soviet era. Grossman juxtaposes narrative accounts of the Battle of Stalingrad during the Second World War with scenes from everyday life in Soviet Russia, and he reflects on the relation between the two. In my commentary on Grossman's great novel and the moral hope it inspires in the wake of profound loss, I will focus on the characters Ikonnikov and Viktor Shtrum, the nuclear physicist who is the novel's protagonist, who discovers his Judaism in the course of the novel, and who is based on Grossman himself.

In *Life and Fate*, Vasily Grossman explores and critiques the theology of an Italian Roman Catholic priest named Gardi, who is a prisoner in the camp.[12] We turn now to an extraordinary passage in *Life and Fate*, indeed to one of the most extraordinary passages in modern literature. We are in a Nazi concentration camp in German-occupied Ukraine with a character named Ikonnikov, a genuine holy fool, a *iurodivyi* in the highest spiritual sense of this Russian word, at a critical moment in his own tortured but magnificent spiritual journey.

It is Ikonnikov, "the preacher of senseless kindness,"[13] who, for Levinas, speaks the novel's essential truth. "The essential thing in this book," Levinas says, "is simply what the character Ikonnikov says—'There is neither God nor the Good, but there is goodness'—which is also my thesis."[14] We first meet Ikonnikov early on in the novel. He comes from a long line of priests. Hence the significance of his name, which is suggestive of the Russian religious symbol par excellence, the icon. Ikonnikov had, in his early years, been a devotee of Tolstoy's Christian-inspired pacificism, later embraced by Mahatma Gandhi. He then came to believe in the promise of the Russian Revolution to "bring about the Kingdom of Heaven on earth,"[15] but after witnessing Stalin's brutal persecution and murder of the kulaks (the wealthier peasants), "he began preaching the Gospel and praying to God to take pity on the dying."[16] Ikonnikov was first sent to prison and then, as a result of the traumas he had experienced, was placed for a year in the prison's psychiatric hospital. The traumas experienced by Ikonnikov included witnessing an emaciated peasant woman, starving as a result of Stalin's collectivization campaign, who "had just eaten her two children."[17] After the war began and the Nazis invaded Belarus and Ukraine, Ikonnikov desperately entreated others to save the Jews and made efforts, despite the dangers to his personal safety, to save Jewish lives. Ikonnikov's witnessing of what Father Patrick Desbois refers to as "the Holocaust by Bullets"[18] caused Ikonnikov to lose his faith in God. After witnessing the murder of twenty thousand Jews—"women, children, and old men"—in a single day, Ikonnikov concludes "that God could not allow such a thing and that therefore he did not exist."[19] "The essential thing" about *Life and Fate*, Levinas writes, as we noted earlier, "is simply what the character Ikonnikov says: 'There is neither God nor the Good, but there is goodness'—which is my thesis."[20]

This remark, uttered by an observant Jew and a philosopher, may well strike the reader as shocking at first glance, for in a single sentence Levinas appears to be asserting the nonexistence of both the God of the Bible and the Good of Plato. Upon reflection, however, the sentence may appear less surprising if we recall the title of Levinas's last magnum opus, *Autrement qu'être ou au-delà de l'essence* (*Otherwise Than Being, or Beyond Essence*). For Levinas, God does not appear and thus has nothing to do with the word "is," with ontology. God signifies in a manner *autrement qu'être*, otherwise than being. I can say "'Here I am, in the name of God,' without referring myself directly to his [i.e., God's] presence. 'Here I am,' just that! The word God is still absent from the phrase in which it is for the first time involved in words." For Levinas, I am true to the meaning of the word "God," as it first becomes involved in words in the Hebrew Bible, when I say "Here I am" before the face of the Other rather than by stating "'I believe in God [*Je crois en Dieu*].'"[21] And it was no less a philosopher than Plato who insisted that the Good was "beyond being" (*epeikeina tês ousias*, *Republic* 508e–509a), beyond essence. Indeed, the phrase *au-delà de l'essence* in the title of Levinas's last great book is a literal translation of Plato's "beyond being" (*epeikeina tês ousias*). Hence, technically speaking, for Levinas, there "is" neither God nor the Good, for both are beyond, or signify in a manner otherwise than, being.[22]

Ikonnikov, as a result of the great cruelty he personally witnessed, ceased to believe in God. He also ceased to believe in the Good, for he became convinced that great violence was being pursued in the name of an abstract notion of the Good, whether by Marxists or by Nazis. Unspeakable harm to others, he says, was the result of Stalin's collectivization campaign, a campaign that "was carried out in the name of Good,"[23] Ikonnikov tells the Marxist Mostovskoy, a fellow inmate in a Nazi prison camp in the Ukraine. "I don't believe in your 'Good,' " he tells Mostovskoy. "I believe in human kindness."[24] Ikonnikov professed, rather, "an 'absurd' theory of morality that—in his own words—'transcended class.' " "You ask Hitler," Ikonnikov tells Mostovskoy, "and he'll tell you that even this camp was set up in the name of Good."[25] In rejecting an "existing" God who slumbers in the midst of great evil; and in rejecting, as well, the pursuit of an abstract notion of the Good that is in fact a cover for violence against others, Grossman is here thinking God on the basis of ethics in precisely Levinas's sense. In a remarkable passage from the essay "God and Philosophy" which we discussed in chapter 2, Levinas says that "the goodness of the Good—of the Good that neither sleeps nor slumbers—inclines the movement it calls forth to turn it away from the Good and orient toward the other, and only thus toward the Good."[26] Levinas wrote these words a decade before he encountered Grossman's great novel. It is no wonder that Levinas was so inspired and preoccupied by Grossman's great text.

Let us now turn to the passage from Grossman's novel upon which we shall comment in detail. Ikonnikov, who is a prisoner in the camp, has just realized that the work his Nazi captors have ordered him to do is none other than to dig the foundations of a gas chamber. Ikonnikov appears to want to make a kind of preemptive confession to an Italian Roman Catholic priest named Gardi, also a prisoner in the camp, who is lying in the bed above him. Ikonnikov grasps the priest's bare foot and, in anguish, shares with him the shocking truth, which Ikonnikov has just discovered, that they are all building an extermination camp—that the prisoners are in fact engaged in digging the foundations of a gas chamber for the Nazi authorities. There are two other characters who appear in this passage, both Communists, though from feuding branches of the Party: a former Menshevik named Chernetsov, who has one eye and who, when he speaks and looks at his interlocutor, usually covers his open socket with his hand; and Mikhail Sidorovich Mostovskoy, an old Bolshevik:

Chernetsov's blind, bloody pit stared point-blank at Mostovskoy.

Ikonnikov reached up and tugged at the bare foot of the priest sitting on the second tier of boards; in broken French, German, and Italian he began to ask:

"*Que dois-je faire, mio padre? Nous travaillons dans una Vernichtungslager.*"

Gardi's coal-black eyes looked around and scrutinized people's faces.

"*Tout le monde travaille là-bas. Et moi je travaille là-bas. Nous sommes des esclaves,*" he said slowly. "*Dieu nous pardonnera.*"

"*C'est son métier,*" added Mostovskoy.

"*Mais ce n'est pas votre métier,*" Gardi said reproachfully.

Ikonnikov-Morzh quickly retorted:

"That's just it, Mikhail Sidorovich; from your point of view, too, it's exactly the same, don't you see? But I don't want an absolution of sins. Don't tell me that the guilty ones [*vinovaty*] are those who are compelling you, and that you are not guilty [*vinoven*] because you are not free. I *am* free! I am building a Vernichtungslager. I am answerable to the people who will be choked by gas here. I can say 'no'! What power can stop me, if I find in myself the power to be fearless in the face of my own destruction? I will say 'no!' *Je dirai non, mio padre, je dirai non!*"

Gardi's hand touched the grey head of Ikonnikov.

"*Donnez-moi votre main,*" he said.

"All right, now here comes the admonishing by the shepherd of his wayward sheep's pride," said Chernetsov, and Mostovskoy, with a knee-jerk reaction of ideological sympathy, nodded in agreement.

But Gardi did not admonish Ikonnikov. He took Ikonnikov's dirty hand to his lips and kissed it.[27]

The priest Gardi tries to soothe Ikonnikov's conscience by telling him that many of the prisoners in the camp, including the priest himself, are working on this same project. We are all slaves to the current situation, Gardi insists. It can't be helped. God will pardon us, he tells Ikonnikov, who replies that he does not want to be absolved of this sin, as the priest Gardi offers to do for Ikonnikov on God's behalf. Ikonnikov insists that, even as a prisoner in a Nazi concentration camp, he is responsible for others and he is free. "I have to answer to the people who will be gassed here [as if I were facing them now],"[28] Ikonnikov tells the priest.

Ikonnikov insists that, even as a prisoner in a Nazi concentration camp, he is responsible (or "guilty"/ *vinovat, vinoven*) and that he is free.

He must answer to—respond to—the people who will be gassed in the chambers he will have consented to build. "The I who am building an extermination camp [and here Grossman writes the German word *Vernichtungslager* in Cyrillic letters as фернихтунслагерь] is the very same I who am now answering [*otvechaiu*] to those who will be gassed," Ikonnikov says. The Russian verb *otvechat'* is the precise equivalent to the French *répondre*, which means "to respond to," "to answer to," to be responsible for," and even "to answer for," the other. By suddenly writing the German word *Vernichtungslager* (extermination camp) in Cyrillic letters rather than in Roman, as he had just previously done, Grossman is emphasizing that the speaker of these words, whose native tongue is Russian, is now taking full responsibility for his actions, that he is owning them.

Ikonnikov realizes, as if this realization were a revelation from beyond, that he has the ability, the freedom, to say no. The priest Gardi has just told Ikonnikov that he, Ikonnikov, and the other prisoners are all slaves in the concentration camp and that God will therefore pardon them for their actions. Even the Communists, who scorn religion, Ikonnikov suggests, routinely expect forgiveness for their betrayal of individual, irreplaceable human lives—though the Communists expect this forgiveness from the abstract principle of the allegedly ineluctable and just march of history toward a classless society rather than from God. Ikonnikov begs to differ. Don't tell me, he says, that the only guilty or responsible ones (*vinovaty*) are those who are ordering us to act in a shameful manner, who are telling me that I am "a slave" and that I am "not guilty or responsible because" I am "not free." He declares that I, Ikonnikov, *am* free (*Ia svoboden*). As Levinas writes in *Totality and Infinity*, published at roughly the same moment (1961) Grossman completed *Life and Fate*, "To be free is to have time to forestall one's own abdication under the threat of violence" (*Être libre, c'est avoir du temps pour prévenir sa proper déchéance sous la menace de la violence*).[29] My oppressors do not have the power, Ikonnikov asserts, to force me to build an extermination camp and thus to betray my responsibility to the other so long as I am able to draw on my moral power to accept my own extermination at the hands of the Nazis and say no. Thus Ikonnikov concludes, in an impassioned mixture of Russian, French, and Italian: "*Ia skazhu 'net'! Je dirai non, mio padre, je dirai non!*" ("I will say 'no'! I will say no, my father, I will say no!").

Gardi places his hands on Ikonnikov's head. The priest is deeply moved, overcome by Ikonnikov's words. Gardi then asks Ikonnikov—with all the politesse of addressing the Other with the formal version of the second person in French—to give him his hand (*Donnez-moi votre main*), a command that contrasts with the more intimate *ty* of Ikonnikov's previous address, in Russian, to Gardi. Chernetsov caustically remarks that he fully expects that the shepherd—that is, the priest Gardi—will now admonish his charge, Ikonnikov, for the alleged pride this particular wayward sheep has just shown by refusing the priest's generous offering of God's forgiveness. Mostovskoy nods in supercilious agreement. But Gardi hardly admonishes Ikonnikov. The priest rather honors Ikonnikov's deep spiritual wisdom by kissing Ikonnikov's dirty hand, a hand that has been dirtied by digging—at first in ignorance—the foundations of a gas chamber. Petitioners sometimes kiss the hand of a Roman Catholic priest, especially immediately following the priest's inauguration. Here the tables are turned. The priest Gardi kisses the hands of the nonbeliever Ikonnikov who has now, in effect, just been inaugurated as a priest of the creed of senseless kindness, of responsibility for the Other, of answering for the Other, even at the risk of certain death and with no reward, such as gaining immortal life for one's own soul in a world to come. Ikonnikov here thinks God—a God in whom he does not "believe"—beginning with, or on the basis of, the ethical relation, and for this he receives the priest's wholehearted blessing.

The great novelist and nonbeliever Vasily Grossman is here thinking God in a manner that is precisely parallel to the reflections of Levinas, an observant Jew, in two of his Talmudic readings.

In the first Talmudic passage, Levinas speculates on the significance or meaning of God for the moral life. Levinas remarks that, according to the Talmud, God is perhaps my permanent refusal of a history that would put up with my private tears—that is, with however I might rationalize the harm I have done to the Other facing me, and which haunts me. The Jewish tradition gives its practitioners the opportunity, during the month of Elul and in the Days of Awe that include the high holidays of Rosh Hashannah and Yom Kippur, to ask forgiveness from those they may have harmed. In the tractate *Yoma* from the Talmud, the rabbis debate the issue of whether one must, in fact, ask forgiveness from the party one has offended.

Is it possible, the Talmud asks, for us to bypass this unpredictable and painful process of interpersonal relations by asking forgiveness, instead, directly from God? The Talmud consists of the Mishnah, or the Oral Law, compiled toward the end of the second century of the Common Era; and the Gemara, compiled some three centuries later. The passage from the Talmud to which I now wish to turn ponders the wisdom of the Mishnah (the Oral Law) that stipulates that, on Yom Kippur, God will not forgive transgressions committed against others if the transgressor has not first sought out the offended party and asked for forgiveness from him or her individually. In the Gemara, Rabbi Yossef bar Helbe, like the priest Gardi in *Life and Fate*, wishes to absolve the transgressor of the necessity of seeking forgiveness from the offended party. Rabbi Yossef argues that the transgressor may short-circuit this delicate and uncertain process by seeking forgiveness directly from God.

In his commentary on this Talmudic passage, Levinas notes that "the text of the Gemara rises [up] against this . . . overly virile proposition . . . which puts the universal order above the interpersonal order." Levinas continues:

> No, the offended individual must always be appeased, approached, and consoled individually. God's forgiveness—or the forgiveness of history—cannot be given if the individual has not been honored [*respecté*]. God is perhaps precisely this permanent refusal of a history that would put up with our private tears. [*Dieu n'est peut-être que ce refus permanent d'une histoire qui s'arrangerait de nos larmes privées.*][30]

For the Talmud, as Levinas understands it here, God is not equivalent to the ineluctable march of a providential or imagined grand narrative of human destiny that can dispense with my responsibility for the Other who is facing me. God is rather thought on the basis of ethics. God is the word that comes to mind when, as the priest Gardi recognizes at the end of our passage from Grossman's *Life and Fate*, I refuse to come to too easy a truce with the painful awareness of the harm I have done, or may be tempted to do, to a unique and irreplaceable other. God is the word that comes to mind when, before I dare to seek an all-encompassing forgiveness, I say *Je dirai non, mio padre, je dirai non!*

Ikonnikov's *Je dirai non, mio padre, je dirai non* is the precise equivalent, as well, of Levinas's understanding of a stunning remark made by one particular Talmudic commentator on the identity of the Messiah in a second passage from the Talmud we now wish to consider. The passage is from the treatise *Sanhedrin* (98b4). The commentator's name is Rav Nachman, a Talmudic scholar who died in the year 320 of the Common Era. Some of the rabbis cited in this section of *Sanhedrin* say that the name of the Messiah is Shiloh (meaning "a gift" [*shai*] "to him" [*l'o*]); some say his name is Chaninah (meaning "mercy"); still others say his name is Menachem the son of Chizkiah, for the name "Menachem" means "comforter." Rav Nachman offers a different interpretation. "If he [the Messiah] is of the living," Rav Nachman remarks, "then he might well be (like) Me" (*kegon 'ana'*; *c'est alors Moi*, in Levinas's translation of the Talmudic text). As Levinas remarks of this passage from the Talmud, Rav Nachman is saying "the Messiah is Myself [*Moi*]; to be Myself is to be the Messiah. . . . The fact of not evading the burden imposed by the suffering of others defines"[31] what it means to be a self, to be *Moi*. The Roman Catholic priest Gardi, who first offers, in the name of God, to absolve Ikonnikov of his responsibility for the Other through a perhaps premature and preemptive act of forgiveness, is taught this holy truth by the nonbeliever Ikonnikov in our passage from *Life and Fate* when Ikonnikov says "*Je dirai non, mio padre, je dirai non!*"

The protagonist of Grossman's novel is Viktor Shtrum, a nuclear scientist who is racing, on behalf of the Soviets, against the Nazis to be the first to split the atom and thus to determine the outcome of the war and of the postwar world. A nonbeliever who is oblivious to his own Jewishness at the beginning of the book, Shtrum establishes a rapport with Judaism in the course of the novel, and even with the word "God" and how that word might signify in a meaningful way for a modern, rational consciousness. There is much of Vasily Grossman in Viktor Shtrum. Primo Levi's great work of testimony, *Se questo è un uomo* (*If This Is a Man*, known in English as *Survival in Auschwitz*), is pure Levi, and Levi's text, like Grossman's, bears witness to its author's discovery of his relationship to Judaism—to the Jewish people, to Jewish texts, to Jewish experience, and to what we might call the Jewish capacity or tendency to think God, outside of the question of God's existence or nonexistence, through the ethical relation.

In February and March 1981, Radio France-Culture broadcast a series of interviews with Levinas conducted by Phillipe Nemo. The interviews, which form the basis of Levinas's book *Ethics and Infinity*, trace the thinker's development from his days as a student to his most recent work on the question and meaning of God. The last interview broaches the question of the relation of philosophy to religion. Nemo suggests to Levinas that one of the purposes of religion is to "give men consolations."[32] Levinas agrees that religion "is not identical to philosophy, which does not necessarily bring the consolations which religion is able to give." Religion may indeed offer consolations to the religiously observant, Levinas agrees, but the offering of consolations for the painful difficulties of life is not, for him, the essence of religion. Levinas goes so far as to say that such consolations are a secondary phenomenon and one that should not, moreover, be sought as an end in itself. Levinas goes on to assert boldly that "only a humanity that also can do without these consolations may perhaps be worthy of them [*n'est peut-être digne de ces consolations qu'une humanité qui peut aussi s'en passer*]."[33] The Bible, for Levinas, consists, first and foremost, of instances of ethical witness that only later become "religions" in which "men find consolations."[34]

The Roman Catholic priest Gardi, in the passage from *Life and Fate*, attempts to offer the consolations of religion to those who, under admittedly crushing circumstances, are tempted to betray their responsibility to others. We shall now, in concluding this section of this chapter, comment on a short passage from Primo Levi's *Se questo è un uomo* that clarifies what Levinas means when he says that "only a humanity that can do without the consolations of religion are perhaps worthy of them." For Levinas, there is an indissoluble link between the word "God" and ethical responsibility, a link that is completely severed by that creation of Ivan Karamazov, the Grand Inquisitor. The Grand Inquisitor, in stark contrast to Levinas, has no confidence in man's capacity to rise to the supreme dignity of his responsibility "without the reward of heaven and eternity. Though if there were anything in the other world," the Grand Inquisitor cynically continues, "it would certainly not be for such as they."[35]

In the thirteenth chapter ("October 1944") of *Se questo è un uomo*, we find Levi describing an action of a believer who, for Levi, is not worthy of the consolations of religion. Levi has just described the process, in Auschwitz, of the Nazis' selection of those who will go to the gas chamber and those who will have been spared this fate, at least for the moment. Depending on the particular card the prisoners are given, they go either to the left, "the bad side" (*die schlechte Seite*),[36] or to the right. Those selected for the bad side now know that, within two days, they will be gassed. An old man named Kuhn, having learned that he is one of those who will be spared, has just returned to his bunk. His young neighbor, Beppo the Greek, was not so lucky. Levi observes:

> I see and hear old Kuhn praying aloud, with his beret on his head, swaying backwards and forwards violently. Kuhn is thanking God because he has not been chosen [for selection to the gas chamber]. Kuhn is out of his senses. Does he not see Beppo the Greek in the bunk next to him, Beppo who is twenty years old and is going to the gas chamber the day after tomorrow and knows it and lies there looking fixedly at the light without saying anything and without even thinking any more? Can Kuhn fail to realize that next time it will be his turn? Does Kuhn not understand that what has happened today is an abomination, which no propitiatory prayer, no pardon, no expiation by the guilty, which nothing at all in the power of man can ever clean again? If I was God, I would spit at Kuhn's prayer.[37]

Grossman and Levi show how those who demonstrate their belief in God can, through their very display of belief, betray the responsibility to their neighbor that this same God, according to the biblical text, above all so rigorously and so relentlessly commands.

"He Didn't Believe in God, but Somehow It Was as if God Were Looking at Him"

The protagonist of Grossman's novel, as we have noted, is the Jewish nuclear physicist Viktor Shtrum. The novel, with its focus on Shtrum, tells the story of Shtrum's moral struggles. Shtrum is a thoroughly assimilated Jew, as was Grossman himself. In the course of the novel, as Shtrum embraces his identity as a Jew, he at the same time imagines himself not so much as believing in God but rather, through responding to the command of ethical responsibility, as bearing witness to God, to the word "God," in a manner that accords with a radical and deeply Jewish understanding of the word "God" as embraced by Levinas.

When the word "God" appears in *Life and Fate* it sometimes signifies (1) unquestioned authority, and in this sense—from a Jewish perspective— God would here mean its opposite, that is, idolatry. At other times (2) the word is associated with the Greek, and more specifically with the Platonic and Aristotelian, understanding of reason or *noesis* as a divine force in man, as the way in which mortals can participate in divine immortality. And then there is (3) the Hebraic understanding of God as a commanding ethical responsibility. All three meanings appear in the section of the novel in which Grossman portrays Shtrum's great moral struggle, but it is, in the end, the ethical understanding that predominates.

As the massive novel draws to its conclusion, Grossman focuses on Viktor's struggle. The momentum of the great Battle of Stalingrad, a battle that would decide the fate of the entire world, has now shifted decisively in favor of the Soviets. Fascism will be defeated. But now an even greater battle will be decided: the battle for men's souls in the totalitarian Soviet state. Viktor is the head of an institute dedicated to research on nuclear physics. The state is engaged in an antisemitic campaign. Viktor has been targeted, as have other Jews in his institute. The state is requiring that Viktor confess to a political crime that he has not committed. Viktor has expressed some criticisms of the state in private conversations, it is true, but he is hardly a traitor. Viktor's wife, from whom he has become increasingly estranged emotionally, urges him, for the family's sake, to capitulate. It is a moment of great moral crisis for Viktor. He has a life-changing decision to make. Just before he makes that decision, he goes to

visit his mentor, Dmitry Petrovich Chepyzhin, who has left the institute,
apparently, precisely because he did not want his scientific research to be
compromised by politics. Chepyzhin is a moral man, but in his conversation with Viktor, Grossman makes Chepyzhin the spokesman for what
I have called the Greek or Platonic-Aristotelian (i.e., the noetic), rather
than the Hebraic-ethical, notion of the divine.

The reader is struck by how, in an officially atheist Soviet society, two
nuclear physicists can make such easy reference to God. "One might
think that only God was able to limit Infinity," Chepyzhin tells Viktor.
Chepyzhin continues: "Beyond a cosmic boundary, we have to admit
the presence of a divine power. Right?" To which Viktor responds, "Of
course."[38] Viktor is completely preoccupied with the meeting, sched-
uled for the next day at the institute, at which he is expected to confess.
Chepyzhin, who has distanced himself from politics, wants to talk about
the joys of scientific discovery, of pure research, that will allow him not
only to participate in the divine, but even to surpass God!

Chepyzhin, sounding very much like Grossman himself, argues passionately for freedom as "the fundamental principle of life,"[39] as the
essence of the transformation of inanimate matter into living matter. In
a rapturous monologue, Chepyzhin imagines that "one day man will be
endowed with all the attributes of the deity—omnipresence, omnipotence
and omniscience. . . . Omnipresence—formerly an attribute of God, will
have become one more conquest of reason. But man won't just stop there.
After attaining equality with God, he will not stop. . . . The abyss of time
and space will be overcome. Man will finally be able to look down on
God."[40] Viktor does not doubt that science may well proceed with the
extraordinary triumphs, straining credibility, as envisioned by Chepyzhin.
But this brings Viktor "not joy, but utter despair."[41] "We think we're so
wise," Viktor says,

> yet on this very day the Germans are slaughtering Jewish children
> and old women as though they were mad dogs. And we ourselves
> have endured 1937 [Viktor is referring to one of Stalin's purges] and
> the horrors of collectivization—famine, cannibalism, and the depor-
> tation of millions of unfortunate peasants. . . . You say man will be
> able to look down on God—but what if he also becomes able to look
> down on the Devil? What if he eventually surpasses *him*? You say life
> is freedom. Is that what people in the camps think? . . . Do you think
> this man of the future will surpass Christ in his goodness? . . . What I
> want to know is—do you believe in the evolution of kindness, moral-
> ity, mercy? Is man capable of evolving in that way?[42]

Viktor concludes that today's science—he is no doubt thinking here particularly of nuclear science—must "be entrusted only to men of spiritual understanding, to prophets and saints." Instead it is being left to apparatchiks like Sokolov in Viktor's own laboratory, who is clever but very timid, "who prostrates himself before the State and believes there is no power except that of God," as docs Markov, also in Viktor's laboratory, who "hasn't the slightest inkling of questions of good and evil, of love and morality."[43] "God" here signifies an amoral force that commands our unquestioning obedience.

But is Viktor capable of bearing witness to God as a moral force? Viktor is very clear-sighted and honest, in this passage, about his own vanity and egoism. He observes that his colleague Savostyanov thinks of science "as another kind of sport," that "solving a particular problem is the same as setting a new athletic record. All he cares about is getting there first. And I'm no better."[44] Grossman named his protagonist "Viktor" for good reason! Viktor is obsessed with being victorious, with winning, with triumphalism. But Viktor is also self-aware. He wonders painfully if he can bear witness to God in the Jewish sense of the word. "Where can I find faith, strength, determination?" he asks Chepyzhin, now speaking "with a strong Jewish accent." "What can I say?" Viktor continues. "You know what's happened—and now I'm being persecuted just because. . . ."[45] Viktor jumps up without finishing his sentence, drops his teaspoon to the floor, begins to tremble all over, thanks Chepyzhin and leaves in tears, careful to avoid looking at Chepyzhin, his moral model, "in the face." Let us take the liberty of finishing Viktor's sentence. Viktor is being persecuted because . . . he is a Jew. As Viktor remarked earlier in this chapter, he has been accused of "dragging science into the swamp of Talmudic abstraction, cutting it off from reality."[46] Those who see the discussions in the Talmud as abstract exercises in splitting hairs, however, fail to take note of the kind of profound ethical engagement that we discovered in our earlier discussion of forgiveness in the Talmudic tractate *Yoma* and of the meaning of the Messiah in *Sanhedrin*. Will Viktor, at the meeting at the institute the following day, choose to assimilate, to capitulate, and thus to betray the very meaning of moral truth, truth that is persecuted precisely because it is true?

Viktor appears to be headed toward making a public confession of a political crime he never in fact committed. He then abruptly changes his mind and chooses not to repent. As soon as he arrives at this decision, Viktor says that he "felt calm and thoughtful. He didn't believe in God [*On ne veril v Boga*], but somehow it was as though God were looking at him. Never in his life had he felt such happiness, such humility. Nothing on earth could take away his sense of rightness now."[47] Grossman continues: "He thought of his mother. Perhaps she had been standing beside him when he had so unaccountably changed his mind. Only a minute before he had sincerely wanted to make a hysterical confession. Neither God nor his mother had been in his mind when he had to come to that last unshakeable decision. Nevertheless, they had been there beside him."[48]

By not confessing to crimes he never committed, Viktor stays true to his conscience. And for Viktor, as he remarks to his family after he makes his fateful decision not to engage in the charade of a pretended repentance in order to save his own skin, "socialism is, first of all, the right to a conscience [*sovest'*]."[49] There is, however, perhaps a touch too much of virility and of heroism, of triumphalism, in Viktor's victorious struggle to maintain his integrity in the passage from *Life and Fate* in which he makes his "last unshakeable decision" not to repent. Viktor himself "had been conscious of something wooden in his voice as he made his speech about conscience."[50] His decision hardly costs him, in the end, his career or his life, as becomes vividly clear when, remarkably, he later receives an admiring telephone call from Stalin himself. The virile Man of Steel, the very embodiment of the totalitarian state, wants to make sure that Viktor has all the means necessary to pursue his important scientific research, which Stalin no doubt hopes, but does not explicitly mention, will help secure the atomic bomb for the Soviet state before its rivals reach that same goal. In the wake of the approving phone call from Stalin, Viktor's anxiety about some of the less than positive things he had said in the past about the regime dramatically lessens and then all but disappears, but with that vanished anxiety Viktor also begins to lose his empathy for those who suffer at the hands of the all-powerful Soviet state. When he was a pariah awaiting state arrest, "his head had been full of thoughts about life, truth and freedom, thoughts about God [*o Boge*]."[51] Now, after being officially embraced by Stalin and thus morally compromised, Viktor's head is no longer "full of thoughts . . . about God."

Not long after his triumph, Viktor is pressured to sign a public letter denouncing two innocent men, two doctors—one of whom was certainly Jewish—absurdly accused of assassinating a famous Russian author. At first he responds with moral horror at the prospect that he could possibly sign such a letter, and in urging his colleagues to back off from pressuring him to sign, Viktor evokes God, whom he clearly associates with conscience, with ethics: "Oh my God [*Nu Bozhe moi*]!" Viktor exclaims. "Please understand that I have a conscience. . . . I'm under no obligation. . . . You must allow me the right to a clear conscience."[52] Viktor is convinced of the doctors' innocence, but his overweening desire to be regarded as a true "patriot," a real "Russian," and "a true Soviet citizen"[53]—not as a Jewish misfit, that is—is part of what persuades him to sign the letter. He signs the letter and is then immediately consumed with an overwhelming sense of remorse.

When Viktor made up his mind not to repent for his alleged and non-existent crime(s), he had felt indescribably happy and imagined that God, along with his mother, was by his side. He now feels that he has committed a "terrible sin."[54] He has utterly lost his moral authority. Just after signing the document, one of his laboratory assistants, Anna Stepanovna Loshakova, a Jew whom Viktor had defended when the state dismissed her because she was Jewish, tells Viktor that she wants him to know "how much you have done for me and for others [*drugikh*]"[55] and that his manifest responsibility for others "is more important than any great discovery." Those with no power or prestige in the Soviet hierarchy— "mechanics, cleaners and caretakers"—to a person all say, she remarks, that Viktor is "a righteous person [*pravil'nyi chelovek*],"[56] the equivalent, in the Hebrew tradition, of a *tzadik*, a "righteous one." And righteous ones, in this tradition, are those who are especially favored by God.

At the conclusion of the chapter in which he shamefully signs the letter, Viktor receives a telephone call from Chepyzhin, who tells Viktor that he, Chepyzhin, had been quarreling with some prominent officials over the letter which he, Chepyzhin, clearly refuses to sign. "Have you heard about this letter?" he asks Viktor. Viktor manages to respond to Chepyzhin with a tepid half-truth. Grossman then vividly imagines Viktor's sense of shame at his betrayal of responsibility, as Viktor comments: "God, God [*Bozhe, Bozhe*], what had he done?"[57] Here the word "God," stated twice, bears powerful witness to Viktor's commanding sense of responsibility to others that he has just shamefully betrayed.

Turned Inside Out: God, Transcendence, Hope

The word "God" appears for the final two times in a brief chapter (58 in the Russian text)[58] toward the end of *Life and Fate*. This chapter is preceded by a slightly longer chapter in which the word "God" also appears, but with different associations. The juxtaposition is suggestive. In modernist fashion, Grossman often juxtaposes chapters of varying lengths with little or no explicit commentary explaining the artistic reasons for the juxtapositions. I mentioned earlier that Grossman is struggling with at least three associations that come to mind when we say the word "God": (1) God understood as a principle to which believers owe total obedience;

(2) God as reason (*noesis*); and (3) God as the word par excellence that
bears witness to my inescapable and untransferable responsibility for
a unique and irreplaceable Other. The juxtaposed endings of these two
chapters guide the reader toward embracing as authoritative the third of
these associations that come to mind when Vasily Grossman writes the
word "God" in *Life and Fate*.

These two chapters are set in a hut near the Lubyanka, the notorious
prison in Moscow that held many political prisoners in the Stalin era.
Chapter 57 ends with a passage that contains a chilling Soviet version of
Dostoevsky's famous chapter, in *The Brothers Karamazov*, on the Grand
Inquisitor. Both chapters 57 and 58 take place in the environs of the
Lubyanka, and both feature Nikolay Grigorevitch Krymov, the dedicated,
even fanatical, Bolshevik who is the husband of Zhenya, Viktor's sister-in-
law. Zhenya is a lively and free-spirited artist who early in the novel had
left Krymov for the dashing and imposing tank commander, Novikov.
Krymov is devastated by Zhenya's leaving him, especially now that Krymov, a true-believing and rigid Communist, has himself been arrested and
imprisoned for no apparent reason. Krymov has now become a victim of
the very regime to which he is so devoted. He refuses to confess, despite
repeated beatings and torture. And he continues to believe in the justice
of the Communist Party's cause. He trusts that, in the end, justice and
equality—and even freedom—will ultimately prevail.

One of the major subplots of the novel is the love triangle between
Zhenya, Novikov, and Krymov. Zhenya believes in the autonomy of the
self, of the modern woman's right and ability to make her own choices,
including the choice to leave her husband for another man. But a gnaw-
ing sense of obligation draws her to return to Krymov, especially after
his arrest, despite her belief in her own autonomy. "I don't like saints,"
she remarks at one point in the novel. "There's usually some kind of hys-
teria underneath. . . . I'd rather have an outright bitch. . . . It's of her
own free will that a woman. . . . goes to bed with a man, lives with him,
or decides to leave him."[59] Despite her belief in the complete autonomy
of the self, Zhenya somehow feels compelled to leave Novikov and to
return to Krymov. Zhenya's returning to Krymov bears witness to the
very sanctity that Zhenya derides, but which *Life and Fate* continually
extols. The novel tells of a number of remarkable examples of random,
apparently senseless acts of human kindness in the midst of unfathomable
human destruction. "Human history," for Grossman, "is not the battle
of good struggling to overcome evil. It is a battle fought by a great evil
struggling to overcome a kernel of human kindness. But if what is human
in human beings has not been destroyed even now, then evil will never

conquer."[60] So Levinas, in the penultimate paragraph of *Otherwise Than Being*, speaks of the great hope that is inspired by even "the little humanity that adorns the earth" (*le peu d'humanité qui orne la terre*).[61]

Let us return to the conclusion of part 3, chapter 57 of *Life and Fate* (chapter 56 in the Chandler translation). Krymov is speaking to Katsenelenbogen, a fellow prisoner in the Lubyanka. The two are discussing another prisoner named Dreling. Katsenelenbogen is a dedicated Communist who was a Chekist, a member of the first Soviet security organization set up by Lenin that later became the infamous KGB. Dreling is a Menshevik who refuses to bow to authority. Krymov, like Katsenelenbogen, is a devoted Communist, but he—in contrast to Katsenelenbogen—looks forward to the day when social equality will be achieved and the repressive measures of the Soviet state will no longer be necessary. Katsenelenbogen refers to "personal freedom"—the very freedom that permitted Ikonnikov to rise to his full humanity and to say "no" to building a gas chamber—as a "cave-man principle."[62] Krymov accuses Katsenelenbogen of ascribing "to the security organs all the attributes of the deity."[63] Katsenelenbogen agrees. "Yes, I believe in God," the avowed atheist paradoxically confesses to Krymov. He continues: "I'm an ignorant, credulous old man. Every age creates the deity in its own image. The security organs are wise and powerful; they are what holds sway over twentieth-century man. Once this power was held by earthquakes, forest-fires, thunder and lightning—and they too were worshipped."[64]

Krymov mentions the rebellious Dreling to Katsenelenbogen, who remarks, "that vile old man disturbs my faith."[65] For Katsenelenbogen, God means an amoral power that commands my absolute obedience. This is a god, moreover—to recall Levinas's wording in *Otherwise Than Being*—that is "un certain dieu," "a certain god" in the sense of a god in whom one can and must believe with certainty. Dreling's rebellious witness, for Katsenelenbogen, threateningly calls the existence of this god into question.

Grossman juxtaposes Katsenelenbogen's understanding of god with that which is signified by the last reference to God in the novel. This final reference to God appears at the conclusion of chapter 58 of the Russian text. Krymov's interrogators continue to insist that he sign the trumped-up confession they have prepared. Krymov refuses. Then another, very different kind of document, it turns out, requires his signature. Krymov is asked to sign for a parcel of food items that was left for him by his estranged wife Zhenya. Krymov is stunned. "'Oh God, oh God [*Bozhe, Bozhe*].' He began to cry."[66] The word "God," uttered here twice by the atheist Krymov, bears witness to Zhenya's totally unexpected gift, to the responsibility she has miraculously assumed for the Other, with no expectation of a reward, for her estranged and suffering husband Nikolay Grigorevich Krymov.

A totally unexpected gift, an act of kindness and of sacrifice given with no expectation of a reward, to which Krymov responds with the words "Oh God, oh God!" This, for both Levinas and Grossman, is how God appears after his death announced by Nietzsche, after the death of a certain god inhabiting the world behind the scenes, after the Shoah, after the Gulag.

I would like to bear witness, in concluding this chapter, to the context which inspired many of the insights I have developed here. In the spring quarters of 2010 and 2012, I taught a class on "Literature and Ethics: Levinas and Vasily Grossman's *Life and Fate*" at the Oregon State Penitentiary (2010) and the Oregon State Correctional Institution (2012). This context is relevant to the theme of this chapter on loss and hope. The physical setting in which I taught these classes was grim, but hope sprang out of this grimness.

My classes, as I have mentioned, are part of the national Inside-Out Prison Exchange program. In these classes, the students enact the ethical encounter in which the ego (the *Moi*) empties itself of its being, turns itself inside out (*à l'envers*).[67] In precisely this sense, Ikonnikov was turned inside out by his untransferable responsibility for each of the unique human beings who would perish in the gas chambers he was being ordered to build by his Nazi captors. Zhenya, similarly, was turned inside out by her sense of obligation to Krymov, despite her belief in the autonomy of a self that has a right to act in accordance with maximizing its own self-interest.

What does the prison context have to do with the relation between loss and hope, which is the subject of this chapter? I will end with the testimony of two of my Inside-Out students, whom I will identify by their first names only (students, as mentioned earlier, are known only by their first names in Inside-Out classes).

An inside student named Sam is here reflecting on how, during the class meetings of our Inside-Out class in spring 2012 on Grossman and Levinas, he miraculously felt he was no longer in prison:

> I can without a doubt say that this class has changed me forever. . . .
> A huge reason why this class had such a powerful effect on me was the atmosphere in every class meeting. I came from a world full of stereotypes, prejudice, and "violence against the other." And walked into a sanctuary. I wasn't judged for my circumstances or my past. I

was welcomed into a community where we respected, even admired, each other's differences. We encouraged participation and respected the right to just listen. After crossing the threshold into class, I felt free in every sense of the word. [68]

An inside student named Cannon describes the sense of hope he experienced in that same Inside-Out class in spring 2012 on Grossman and Levinas:

This class has been a wonderful and profoundly inspiring experience. See, over time I had begun to have fear and uncertainties about the capabilities between in here and out there. Time and experience had brought dread of the public stereotypically viewing us as Frankenstein-like abhorrences. To be viewed with fear and disdain, as those lost to humanity. I had even begun to fear the same for myself, that I might be losing the capability to reasonably and effectively interact with the "real people" of society. This class changed that. The way the professor and all the students treated us has reintroduced a long-lost sense of optimism. [69]

EPILOGUE

I have sought in this book "to find the traces of the coming of [the word] God to mind"[1] in the experience of being turned inside out, especially in the prison setting, by my untransferable responsibility to the Other in front of me. I tried to show how Dostoevsky and Vasily Grossman think God on the basis of ethics in their novels, and I commented on passages from the Bible and the Talmud that, I argued, could be understood as examples of thinking God, outside of ontology, on the basis of ethics. In my discussion of Dostoevsky's novel *The Idiot* in chapter 3, I showed how the God of the Bible is represented as the God both of ethics and of justice, and that justice demands that I take responsibility not only for the other in front of me, but for the third person who comes along, and then for all the other others. I related the tension between ethics and justice to my understanding of the significance of Jacob's limping after his wrestling match with the divine stranger in Genesis 32:32, and to the tragic ending of Dostoevsky's novel *The Idiot*. There Prince Myshkin, in the wake of his emotive responsiveness to the morally commanding and emotionally destitute face of Nastasya Fillipovna—despite his previous pledge to marry Aglaya Epanchina—finds himself fatally crazed and cradling the head of Nastasya's murderer, Rogozhin, in his arms.

I would like to conclude by sharing with you an incident that occurred during the closing ceremony of an Inside-Out class I taught in spring 2012 that bears witness to what Levinas means by the third party. In this class, we read Grossman's novel *Life and Fate* alongside the series of interviews with Levinas collected in the book *Is It Righteous to Be?* This was, once again, an extraordinary group of students who entered very deeply into the texts we read. The inside and outside students seemed, very early on in the class, to be comfortable with each other, so comfortable that I felt it was necessary to call a few of the outside students into my office on campus to remind them that it was important to remember, when we are inside, of precisely where we are: a prison. That it was important to be mindful of boundaries, to tighten things up. The students said they understood and were grateful for the reminder.

The final closing circle in an Inside-Out class is always a difficult rite of passage. The Inside-Out program has a no-contact rule following each class. That is, no contact is permitted between inside and outside students once the class is over. This rule is designed to protect both inside and outside students. Without this rule, inside students might be tempted to contact their fellow students from the outside to enlist their support in their legal battles. As a result, the purity of the inside-out classroom experience might be compromised. Inside students might come to class with an agenda. Outside students might be tempted to become involved in the private lives of the inside students in ways that would alarm the prison authorities, thus threatening the existence of a program that has, so far, been a very positive and often transformative experience for the inside students as well as for their classmates on the outside. Repercussions for inside students who break the no-contact rule are, moreover, far more severe for inside students than for outside students. So the closing circle is truly the end of something. This is a time when I've come to share with the students my own reflections on something positive we can find in those painful, fleeting closing moments. There is a way in which each of us in our Inside-Out classes is so fully present for the three hours a week that we come together, present in ways that we aren't always so present in our day-to-day lives. I tell the students that this is the result, in part, of our awareness, from the very first moment of the class, of how limited, how finite is our time together especially in the wake of the no-contact rule. If we brought this kind of awareness to our lives beyond the Inside-Out classroom, imagine how much more present we could be, how much more available to those around us!

I asked the students to share something that they will take away from the class and that will have a lasting impact on their lives. Sam, an inside student, shared the moving remarks I just cited near the end of chapter 5 about how grateful he was that in our classroom he consistently felt unjudged and welcomed by his classmates. It was then time for an outside student to say a few words. Bianca spoke of her high regard for all of the inside students, and said that she couldn't understand why they were being "punished" by serving a prison term or what good that punishment could possibly accomplish.

I, too, had a very high regard for the inside students in the class, but Bianca's comments made me uncomfortable, especially because a prison administrator was there with us at this charged moment and I was concerned about how this administrator would take Bianca's comment. Inside-Out classes would hardly be welcomed by prison officials if these officials thought that the explicit point of these classes was to dismantle the prison system or excuse criminal behavior. I decided that we should discuss Bianca's comments during our debriefing session the following evening when I met with the outside students separately. I drew the students' attention to the subject of our class: literature and ethics. Why, I asked the students, might someone feel uncomfortable with Bianca's saying that she couldn't understand why our classmates on the inside were being "punished"? No response from my students.

Was this non-response, I wondered, the effect of my outside students having been so completely turned inside out by the faces of their classmates on the inside, so hollowed out by the face of the Other, so transformed, that they had somehow become oblivious of the other others, of the victims of the crimes perpetrated by their classmates? We discourage our outside students from asking their classmates on the inside about their crimes, though sometimes inside students do voluntarily reveal this information to their classmates from the outside, especially in the context of how it relates to our discussions about responsibility for the Other. This struck me as an appropriate moment to remind the outside students about what Levinas means by "other others," which came up a number of times during our class discussions.

In our readings from *Is It Righteous to Be?* we confronted, on a number of occasions, what Levinas calls "the third party [*le tiers*]." Let us recall the passage from *Is It Righteous to Be?* that we cited earlier. When I encounter the Other, for Levinas, I am responsible for him or her—infinitely responsible, in fact. We are not just a pair, however. I and the Other in front of me are not "alone in the world." We are

> at least three. Two plus a third. If I heed the second person to the end, if I accede absolutely to his request, I risk, by this very fact, doing a disservice to the third one, who is also my other. But if I listen to the third, I run the risk of wronging the second one. This is where the State steps in. The State begins as soon as three are present. It is inevitable. Because no one should be neglected, yet it is impossible to establish with the multiplicity of humanity a relation of unique to unique, of face to face. One steps out of the register of charity between individuals to enter the political. Charity pursues its fulfillment in a demand for justice. It takes a referee, laws, institutions, an authority: hence the State, with its tyrannical authority.[2]

In the face-to-face relation, I am obligated to be charitable toward the Other, to respond to him or her: to exercise my respons-ability (the word "responsibility" is spelled, in French, "respons*a*bilité"), to exercise my *ability* to respond to, even to answer for, the Other. But I am also responsible to the third who comes along, and to all the other others. The Other, in the face-to-face relation, is infinite, cannot be limited, reduced, categorized. But now, with the appearance of the other others, I must compare incomparables. Here is where "justice" enters, and the state. My students and I clearly observed how, in Vasily Grossman's novel *Life and Fate*, set during the Battle of Stalingrad in Stalinist Russia, the original justice sought by Marxism devolved into totalitarianism, into cruelty and the murder of innocents in the name of pursuing the justice required by the state. Levinas even goes so far as to say that "justice constantly has a bad conscience" because "the demand of charity which precedes it remains and beckons it."[3] Justice can always be better. Our charity for the other, the bad conscience that accompanies judgment, demands that we work for more and more perfect justice in the world.

In *Life and Fate* Vasily Grossman describes how, even in the most horrendous and oppressive of situations—in a concentration camp, in a gas chamber, in a gulag, in the midst of bloody military conflicts—individual human beings perform extraordinary, unexpected, seemingly random acts of kindness. In their anthology, my students selected the following passage from *Life and Fate* as one of their favorites in the novel. We cited this passage earlier. It is spoken by Ikonnikov, Grossman's preacher of the creed of senseless kindness:

> Human history is not the battle of good struggling to overcome evil. It is a battle fought by a great evil struggling to overcome a small kernel of human kindness. But if what is human in human beings has not been destroyed even now, then evil will never conquer.[4]

Bianca, in her affection for her classmates from the inside, whom she was now seeing for the last time, had clearly tapped into the remarkable energy of irrepressible kindness generated by, and borne witness to in, Grossman's text. She had perhaps forgotten, for the moment, about the other others who had been harmed by her classmates from the inside.

Sister Helen Prejean, the author of the book *Dead Man Walking*, has said that one of her greatest regrets in her fight against the death penalty was that she did not at first reach out sufficiently to the families of the murder victims while she was spiritual adviser to the convicted killers Patrick Sonnier and Robert Willie. Sister Helen was turned inside out by her responsibility for Sonnier and Willie, whose faces she saw before and during their execution for their crimes. Just before Sonnier's execution, Sister Helen tells him, "I can't bear the thought that you would die without seeing one loving face. I will be the face of Christ for you. Just look at me."[5] Levinas remarks that "what I say about the face of the neighbor, the Christian probably says about the face of Christ."[6] This moment becomes the climax of the extraordinarily moving opera version of *Dead Man Walking*. While Sister Helen was turned inside out by the face of Patrick Sonnier, she soon came to regret that she had failed to pay sufficient attention to the other others, that is, to the victims and their families. Sister Helen had the courage to acknowledge her error, and she went on to found Survive, an organization that supports families of murder victims, of the other others.

In our debriefing session, I felt obliged to remind my outside students about these other others. My strong feeling was that Bianca's classmates on the inside hardly needed this same reminder. Surely Terry and Nat, judging from their commentary on a passage from *The Brothers Karamazov* I discussed in the "Prologue" to this book, did not need to be reminded. Perhaps it was sufficient, I felt, to have debriefed only with the outside students about Bianca's remarks. The Inside-Out teaching manual suggests that instructors, after we meet with our inside and outside students together for the last time, hold separate debriefing sessions with our inside and our outside students. The rationale for these separate final meetings is that, for all that the inside and outside students discover they have in common over the course of a class, it is also true that the very different environments they inhabit powerfully shape their individual responses to the class. There are things that students in each group may need to say that they might not feel comfortable expressing in the presence of the other group.

I later held a debriefing with the inside students. I hadn't intended to discuss Bianca's remarks, but Shawn, one of the inside students, wanted very much to know what the outside students had discussed during their debriefing session with me, especially in the wake of the prison administrator's unusual presence in the room during the final closing circle. One inside student applauded Bianca for saying what she believed. Two others, however, had misgivings. Sam remarked that at first he was glad to hear what Bianca had said, but he then came to feel almost embarrassed by Bianca's attempt to exonerate him. "It's not as if I'm not in prison for a reason," Sam concluded, almost surprised by his refusal to accept a free pass for failing to live up to his responsibility for the Other.

Sam, as did Terry and Nat in our class on *The Brothers Karamazov*, was here affirming Dostoevsky's insight—first articulated by Father Zosima's brother Markel and then adopted by Father Zosima himself—about the nature of the "I," about true subjectivity: "Each of us is responsible for everyone and everything, and I more than all the others."

Is it likely that Bianca would have made the same concluding remark that she did if she had taken an Inside-Out class that was focused exclusively on the criminal justice system or on *The Brothers Karamazov* rather than on *Life and Fate*, a novel that celebrates the eruption of spontaneous acts of charity in the context of totalitarian political oppression? When Inside-Out classes are offered in the field of criminal justice, students have the opportunity to learn just how complex a phenomenon crime is. Criminal acts are committed within a broad cultural context rife with injustice at every level. This, I take it, is the force of Father Zosima's insistence that "if I had been [more] righteous myself, perhaps there would have been no criminal standing before me."

If I were more righteous, perhaps there would be no prisons at all. But since there are prisons, it is my responsibility to do what I can to offer my students, inside and outside alike, the opportunity to be turned inside out by the other, to transcend labels and prejudices, and to help transform the prison environment into a more compassionate and just one. Each of us who has been turned inside out can then do everything in our power to create an increasingly just society for the benefit of each other, and for all the other others, inside and outside the prison walls until, one day, there are no prison walls and no prisons at all.

Epigraphs

The eleven epigraphs at the beginning of the book are from:

Gareth Reeves, *Nuncle Music* (Manchester, Eng.: Carcanet, 2010), 73.

Václav Havel, *Letters to Olga*, trans. Paul Wilson (New York: Knopf, 1988), 312.

Emmanuel Levinas, "God and Philosophy," in *Of God Who Comes to Mind*, trans. Bettina Bergo (Stanford, Calif.: Stanford University Press, 1998), 74.

Emmanuel Levinas, *Autrement qu'être ou au-delà de l'essence* (Dordrecht, Netherlands: Nijhoff, 1974); the French is cited from the Livre de Poche edition (Paris, 2001), 185. The English translation of this work is cited from *Otherwise Than Being, or, Beyond Essence*, trans. Alphonso Lingis (Pittsburgh: Duquesne University Press, 1981), 117.

Dostoevsky's letter to Maikov, March 25, 1870. Cited from Dostoevsky, *Complete Letters*, vol. 3 (1868–1871), ed. and trans. David A. Lowe (Ann Arbor, Mich.: Ardis, 1990), 248. I have modified Lowe's translation. The Russian text is cited from Dostoevsky, *Pis'ma*, vol. 2 (1867–1871), ed. A. S. Dolinina (Moscow: State Publishing House, 1930), 263.

Fyodor Dostoevsky, *The Brothers Karamazov*, trans. Constance Garnett, rev. Matlaw and Oddo (New York: W. W. Norton, 2011), second Norton Critical Edition, 202. This translation will be cited hereafter as the second Norton Critical Edition. I am aware that the phrase "turned inside out" is, in this passage, not a literal rendering of the Russian words *s drugogo kontsa* ("from the other end"), but I have chosen to cite the classic Garnett translation here both for its poetic resonance and for its obvious relation to the subject—and indeed to the title—of this book. The Russian is cited from Fyodor Dostoevsky, *Brat'ia Karamazovy* (Moscow: Eksmo, 2003), 241.

Emmanuel Levinas, *Carnets de captivité et autres inédits*, ed. Rodolphe Calin and Catherine Chalier, in *Oeuvres 1* (Paris: Bernard Grasset/IMEC, 2009), 196.

Levinas, *Carnets de captivité et autres inédits*, 240.

Emmanuel Levinas, "The Paradox of Morality: An Interview with Emmanuel Levinas," in *The Provocation of Levinas: Rethinking the Other,* ed. Robert Bernasconi and David Wood (London: Routledge, 1988), 177.

Turned Inside-Out: Literature, Art, and Testimony from the Inside-Out Prison Exchange Program, ed. Madeline, James, and Katie, vol. 2, summer 2010 (Eugene, Ore.: University of Oregon Publications, 2010), 50.

Havel, *Letters to Olga*, 145.

Prologue

1. Emmanuel Levinas, *Ethics and Infinity: Conversations with Philippe Nemo*, trans. Richard A. Cohen (Pittsburgh: Duquesne University Press, 1985), 85–86. Throughout this book, I will follow the convention of Alphonso Lingis, the translator of Levinas's two major philosophical works (*Totality and Infinity* and

Otherwise Than Being), by capitalizing the first letter of the word "Other" when referring to the person whom "I," as a subject, am facing.

2. Dostoevsky, *The Brothers Karamazov*, second Norton Critical Edition, 276–77.

3. *Dostoevsky and Levinas Face to Face* (Eugene, Oregon, 2011), ed. Aisha, Jordan, Eryn, Carmela, Kevin G., Nick, and Jeffrey (students in my spring 2011 Inside-Out class, "Ethics and Literature: Levinas and *The Brothers Karamazov*," taught at the Oregon State Correctional Institution), 44.

4. One of the inside students in the class, Kevin G., writes to me that "Terry's comment and Danny's response also triggered further reflections and conversations. I talked with several people afterwards, both students from the class and people not in it—friends, family, volunteers, etc.—about the pain and blame that follow in the wake of our crimes. Our friends and especially our families tend to blame themselves for our actions, thinking that if they had only done something different the crime wouldn't have occurred. We, in response, point out that they are not responsible for our actions."

5. My own translation. The Russian is cited from Dostoevsky, *Brat'ia Karamazovy*, 297. The English translation of this particular sentence is based on the version by Richard Pevear and Larissa Volokhonsky (New York: Farrar, Straus and Giroux, 2002). I have made alterations in their translation. The Pevear-Volokhonsky translation of *The Brothers Karamazov* is usefully literal. This accomplished team takes the equivalent approach, in the translation of Dostoevsky, to that of Richmond Lattimore in his Homeric translations. The Constance Garnett translation is more in line with the approach of Robert Fitzgerald in the field of Homeric translation: Garnett does not translate word for word, but she rather creates a kind of parallel and totally convincing work of verbal art. Where possible, I will cite the Garnett translation, as revised first by Robert Matlaw and then by Susan McReynolds Oddo in the most recent Norton Critical Edition (2011).

6. Emmanuel Levinas, *Is It Righteous to Be? Interviews with Emmanuel Levinas*, ed. Jill Robbins (Stanford, Calif.: Stanford University Press, 2001), 133.

Given the emphasis in this book on the impact of Dostoevsky's incarceration on his fiction, it is worth noting that the sentence just quoted from *The Brothers Karamazov* on my responsibility for the other—which was to become the mantra of Levinas—perhaps finds one of its sources in the convict Bulkin's insistence, when accompanying his fellow convict Varlamov on a series of visits to other inmates one Christmas night, that what Varlamov was telling the inmates, to their great delight, was in fact nothing but lies. "It was as if," our narrator remarks, "he [Bulkin] made himself responsible to answer for [*obiazannost' otvechat' za*] Varmalov's actions, as if all of Varmalov's faults lay on his [Bulkin's] conscience" (Fyodor Dostoevsky, *Notes from the House of the Dead*, trans. Boris Jakim [Grand Rapids, Mich.: Erdmans, 2013], 175; translation modified). The Russian is cited from Fyodor Dostoevsky, *Zapiski iz mertvogo doma* (Moscow: Eksmo, 2005), 175.

7. Fyodor Dostoevsky, *The House of the Dead*, trans. Constance Garnett in *The House of the Dead* and *Poor Folk*, trans. Garnett (New York: Barnes and Noble, 2004), 99; Dostoevsky, *Zapiski iz mertvogo doma*, 302. Unless otherwise noted, translations into English of *The House of the Dead* will be cited from the Garnett translation.

8. Dostoevsky, *The Brothers Karamazov*, second Norton Critical Edition, 202.

9. Levinas, *Ethics and Infinity*, 22; Emmanuel Levinas, *Éthique et infini* (Paris: Fayard et Radio-France, 1982; rpt. Le Livre de Poche, 2012), 12. Levinas's phrase "the meaning of life" can be found in the concluding sentence of *Anna Karenina*, uttered by Tolstoy's character Levin, whose thought so clearly reflects Tolstoy's own: "My life, my whole life [*vsia moia zhizn'*], regardless of all that may happen to me, is not only not meaningless [*ne bessmyslenna*], as it was before, but it possesses the unquestionable meaning [*smysl*] of the goodness [*dobra*] with which I have the power to invest it" (Tolstoy, *Anna Karenina* [Moscow: Eksmo, 2011], 797). Levin is not sure whether he would call his epiphany an epiphany of faith in God or not. "Whether this is faith or not faith, I don't know" (*A vera—ne vera—ia ne znaiu*), Levin remarks. Levin is here, in anticipation of Levinas, thinking God on the basis of ethics.

10. See Seán Hand, "Salvation through Literature: Levinas's *Carnets de captivité*," *Levinas Studies* 8, ed. Jeffrey Bloechl (Pittsburgh, Pa.: Duquesne University Press, 2013), 45–65.

11. Levinas, *Carnets de captivité et autres inédits*, ed. Calin and Chalier, in *Oeuvres 1*.

12. Levinas, *Otherwise Than Being*, 185.

13. Emmanuel Levinas, *Dieu, la mort, et le temps* (Paris: Grasset, 1993), 155; Levinas, *God, Death, and Time*, trans. Bettina Bergo, ed. and anno. Jacques Rolland (Stanford, Calif.: Stanford University Press, 2000), 137.

14. This is a strikingly contemporary aspect of Levinas's thought that allies him with influential religious thinkers like the Dalai Lama. Buddhism's current appeal is attributable, in large part, to the fact that Buddhism—I am thinking particularly of Mahayana Buddhism—is, like the thought of Levinas, deeply ethical, spiritually alive, and at the same time skeptical about "theism" in the strictly ontological sense of the word. For Levinas and Buddhism, see Steven Shankman, *Other Others: Levinas, Literature, Transcultural Studies* (Albany: State University of New York Press, 2010), 18, 19, 48, 49, 168 n. 46, and 187 n. 44. See also Steven Shankman, "(m)Other Power: Shin Buddhism, Levinas, *King Lear*," in *From Ritual to Romance and Beyond: Comparative Literature and Comparative Religious Studies*, ed. Manfred Schmeling and Hans-Joachim Backe (Würzburg, Germany: Königshausen & Neumann, 2011), 231–39.

15. See http://vimeo.com/5193052 for an award-winning documentary video that was made about my spring 2009 class on "Literature and Ethics" that I taught at the Oregon State Penitentiary.

16. Levinas, *Autrement qu'être*, 185; *Otherwise Than Being*, 117.

17. Levinas, *Otherwise Than Being*, 185.

18. Peter Atterton, "Art, Religion, and Ethics Post Mortem Dei: Levinas and Dostoevsky," *Levinas Studies: An Annual Review*, vol. 2 (2007), 105–32. Atterton sees Ivan in *The Brothers Karamazov* as exemplifying Levinas's view of ethical asymmetry, and of God without theodicy. For me, however, as I discuss in chapter 3 (the fifth section, titled "'Come, take me instead of him': Responsibility as Transcendence in *The Brothers Karamazov*"), what is notable about Ivan is the fact that he does not take personal responsibility for his father's murder until the trial scene when—having become a kind of holy fool, with "brain fever"—he says of his falsely accused brother Dmitry, "Take me instead of him!"

19. Jacques Rolland, *Dostoïevski: La question de l'autre* (Paris: Verdier, 1983); Val Vinokur, *The Trace of Judaism: Dostoevsky, Babel, Mandelstam, Levinas* (Evanston, Ill.: Northwestern University Press, 2008); and Susan McReynolds, *Redemption and the Merchant God: Dostoevsky's Economy of Salvation and Antisemitism* (Evanston, Ill.: Northwestern University Press, 2008).

20. Joseph Frank, *Dostoevsky: The Years of Ordeal, 1850–1859* (Princeton, N.J.: Princeton University Press, 1983; rpt. 1990), 69–162.

21. Paul I. Contino, "Dostoevsky and the Prisoner," in *Literature and the Public Sphere*, ed. Susan Van Zanten Gallagher and M. D. Walhout (New York: St. Martin's, 2000), 32–52.

22. Havel, *Letters to Olga*, 312.

Chapter 1

1. On the subject of Levinas's writings during his captivity, see Howard Caygill, "On Levinas's Prison Notebooks," *Radical Philosophy* 160 (March–April 2010), 27–35; and Hand, "Salvation through Literature: Levinas's *Carnets de captivité*."

2. Levinas, *Ethics and Infinity*, 48. The French is cited from *Éthique et infini*, 38.

3. Levinas, *Ethics and Infinity*, 50.

4. Emmanuel Levinas, *Existence and Existents*, trans. Alphonso Lingis (Pittsburgh, Pa.: Duquesne University Press, 1978; rpt. 2003), 56. The French is cited from *De l'existence à l'existant* (Paris: Vrin, 1963; rpt. Édition de Poche, 1990), 100.

5. Levinas, *Existence and Existents*, xxvii.

6. Levinas, *Carnets de captivité et autres inédits*, 202. Fyodor Dostoevsky, *Crime and Punishment*, trans. Richard Pevear and Larissa Volokhonsky (New York: Vintage Books, 1992), 459; Fyodor Dostoevsky, *Prestuplenie i nakazanie* (Moscow: Russian Language, 1984), 343.

7. Levinas, *Carnets de captivité et autres inédits*, 202.

8. Dostoevsky, *The House of the Dead*, trans. Garnett, 99; Dostoevsky, *Zapiski iz mertvogo doma*, 118. Kevin G. writes to me: "There have been many debates and discussions—and even rather vehement arguments—amongst inmates, even recently, about the use of the word 'home' while in prison. Some people refer to their cell as a home, as do officers when they say things like, 'Go home!' For many of us, accepting prison as our 'home' is an acknowledgement of giving up. It becomes the final piece of institutionalization. Even for those of us who have no release date and have already spent multiple decades 'locked up,' calling prison 'home' is something we bristle at. There's that other saying that 'Home is where the heart is' and our hearts are not here in prison. Although we have dear friends here, our hearts are truly with those whom we call family on the outside, particularly our sons and daughters, nieces and nephews."

9. Levinas, *Carnets de captivité et autres inédits*, 202.

10. Dostoevsky, *Crime and Punishment*, trans. Pevear and Volokhonsky, 459; Dostoevsky, *Prestuplenie i nakazanie*, 343.

11. Joseph Frank, *Dostoevsky: The Years of Ordeal*, 93. This is Frank's translation of a letter Dostoevsky wrote from Omsk dated February 22, 1854.

12. Dostoevsky, *House of the Dead*, part 2, chapter 3. Frank is translating the Russian text corresponding to *Zapiski iz mertvogo doma*, 253. The italics (*morally* unbearable) are mine. In the letter just mentioned to his brother of February

22, 1854, Dostoevsky says, "Often I lay sick in the hospital" (*Selected Letters of Fyodor Dostoevsky*, ed. Joseph Frank and David I. Goldstein, trans. Andrew R MacAndrew [New Brunswick, N.J.: Rutgers University Press, 1987], 60).

13. The translation is indebted both to *House of the Dead*, trans. Garnett, 301 and *Notes from the House of the Dead*, trans. Jakim, 306. Gorianchikov's self-absorption, no doubt based on Dostoevsky's own experience in the prison camp in Omsk, is reflected in that of Raskolnikov in *Crime and Punishment* at the very beginning of the novel as well as in the novel's epilogue. In the novel's third paragraph, Dostoevsky, in introducing the reader to the novel's protagonist, says that Raskolnikov was isolated and absorbed or immersed (*uglubit'sia*) in himself (*Prestuplenie i nakazanie*, 16). Note the repetition of the verb *uglubit'sia*, meaning "to become absorbed in," in the passage from *Crime and Punishment*. In the epilogue, in a letter to Raskolnikov's sister and her husband, Sonya says that, in her recent meeting with Raskolnikov in prison in Siberia, Raskolnikov seemed "immersed in himself" (*ugblublen v samogo sebia* [*Prestuplenie i nakazanie*, 402]).

14. "Getting Out of Being by a New Path" is the title of Jacques Rolland's introduction to Levinas's *On Escape*, trans. Bettina Bergo (Stanford, Calif.: Stanford University Press, 2003).

15. Levinas, *Ethics and Infinity*, 52; Levinas, *Éthique et infini*, 50.

16. Ibid.

17. *Ethics and Infinity*, 98.

18. Ibid.

19. Emmanuel Levinas, "The Name of a Dog, or Natural Rights," in *Difficult Freedom: Essays on Judaism*, trans. Seán Hand (Baltimore: Johns Hopkins University Press, 1990), 152–53; Levinas, *Difficile liberté* (Paris: Albin Michel, 1976), 234. This essay first appeared in 1975.

20. Levinas, *Carnets de captivité*, 202.

21. Dostoevsky, *Selected Letters of Fyodor Dostoevsky*, 58.

22. Dostoevsky, *House of the Dead*, 11, translation modified; Dostoevsky, *Zapiski iz mertvogo doma*, 12.

23. Dostoevsky, *House of the Dead*, 25.

24. Ibid., 30.

25. Dostoevsky, *House of the Dead*, 40; Dostoevsky, *Zapiski iz mertvogo doma*, 47.

26. Dostoevsky, *House of the Dead*, 67–68.

27. Ibid., 72.

28. Ibid., 81.

29. Ibid., 73.

30. Ibid., 77–78.

31. Fyodor Dostoevsky, *Winter Notes on Summer Impressions*, trans. David Patterson (Evanston, Ill.: Northwestern University Press, 1988), 48–49.

32. Emmanuel Levinas, "The Rights of the Other Man," in *Alterity and Transcendence*, trans. Michael B. Smith (New York: Columbia University Press, 1999), 149.

33. Genesis 4:9.

34. Dostoevsky, *House of the Dead*, 85; Dostoevsky, *Zapiski iz mertvogo doma*, 102.

35. Dostoevsky, *House of the Dead*, 86; Dostoevsky, *Zapiski iz mertvogo doma*, 103.

36. Dostoevsky, *House of the Dead*, 86.

37. Dostoevsky, *Winter Notes on Summer Impressions*, 40. The Russian is cited from the fifth volume of the collected works of Dostoevsky (Leningrad: Nauka, 1973), 72.

38. Levinas, *Ethics and Infinity*, 86.

39. Dostoevsky, *Winter Notes on Summer Impressions*, 40. In the suppressed chapter "At Tikhon's" from Dostevsky's penultimate great novel *Demons*, responsibility to the Other is commanded, as in this passage from *Winter Notes on Summer Impressions*, by the face of a violated young girl (named Matryosha in *Demons*). Totsky's violation of the adolescent beauty Nastasya Fillipovna Barashkova lies at the core of the action of *The Idiot*, the major novel that preceded the publication of *Demons*.

40. Dostoevsky, *Winter Notes on Summer Impressions*, 426. Dostoevsky attributes this expression to a Pole he calls "M." in *House of the Dead*, 282.

41. Dostoevsky, *A Writer's Diary*, ed. and intro. Gary Saul Morson, trans. and anno. Kenneth Lantz (Evanson, Ill.: Northwestern University Press, 1994), 132.

42. Ibid., 135 (*A Writer's Diary*, February 1876, chapter 1.3). The Russian is cited from Dostoevsky's *Polnoe sobranie sochinenii v tridtsati tomakh* [*Complete Collected Works in Thirty Volumes*] (Leningrad: Nauka, 1981), 22:49.

43. For Levinas on the face, see particularly the whole of chapter 7 of *Ethics and Infinity* and, for a fuller and more philosophically rigorous articulation, see section 3 ("Exteriority and the Face") of Levinas's first magnum opus, *Totality and Infinity: An Essay on Exteriority*, trans. Alphonso Lingis (Pittsburgh: Duquesne University Press, 1969), 187–247.

44. Levinas, *Ethics and Infinity*, 78.

45. Ibid.

46. On Levinas and Dostoevsky, see Val Vinokur, *The Trace of Judaism*; Atterton, "Art, Religion, and Ethics Post Mortem Dei: Levinas and Dostoyevsky"; Alain Toumayan, "I More Than the Others," *Yale French Studies*, no. 104, "Encounters with Levinas" (2004): 55–66; Jill Robbins, *Altered Reading: Levinas and Literature* (Chicago: University of Chicago Press, 1999); and Rolland, *Dostoïevski et la question de l'autre*.

47. Dostoevsky, *Selected Letters*, 63.

48. Dostoevsky, *House of the Dead*, 95.

49. Ibid., 40.

50. Ibid., 134. I have slightly modified the Constance Garnett translation, changing Garnett's now dated verb "jarred on" to "disrupted" as a translation of the Russian verb *narushal* (Dostoevsky, *Zapiski iz mertvogo doma*, 160).

51. Dostoevsky, *Crime and Punishment*, 546.

52. Ibid. The word "godless [one]," that is, "atheist" (*bezbozhnik*), will reappear in Dostoevsky's *Writer's Diary* (March 1877) to describe what the Jewish people, according to Dostoevsky, most decidedly are *not*.

53. Dostoevsky, *Prestupleniye i nakazanie*, 405.

54. Dostoevsky, *Zapiski iz mertvogo doma*, 63.

55. Dostoevsky, *House of the Dead*, 53.

56. What is meant by the phrase "God saved them"? Was this a matter of luck, or of providence working independently of men's actions, or was "the news of the theft of the vodka . . . invented on the spur of the moment to save" Gorianchikov

and the other gentlemen inmates? Were Gorianchikov and the other gentlemen convicts saved by an inmate who answered the call of responsibility for his neighbor? There is a suggestion, then, in the text of *House of the Dead*, that one of the convicts may have prevented Gazin from murdering Gorianchikov and his fellow gentlemen inmates. Dostoevsky is perhaps here thinking the word "God" on the basis of ethics, as he does in the novels of his maturity that we discuss in chapter 3.

57. Dostoevsky, *Complete Letters*, 3:248; the Russian text is cited from Dostoevsky's *Pis'ma*, vol. 2, 263.

58. Dostoevsky, *Selected Letters*, 68; the Russian text is cited from Dostoevsky's *Pis'ma*, vol. 1 (1832–1867), ed. A. S. Dolinina (Moscow: State Publishing House, 1928), 142.

59. Levinas, "The Name of a Dog, or Natural Rights," in *Difficult Freedom*, 153.

60. Dostoevsky, *House of the Dead*, 92.

61. Levinas, *Carnets de captivité*, 207. My own translation, as will be all translations from the *Carnets de captivité et autres inédits*.

62. In the first version of these reflections, as the editors of the *Carnets de captivité* inform us (213, note a), Levinas had originally written "Jesus," which he changed to "Jonah" in the revised version.

63. See Levinas, *Carnets de captivité et autres inédits*, 148, for Levinas's description of what he calls the specifically "Judeo-Christian"—as opposed to "pagan"—"category" of "the just who suffer." See also *Carnets de captivité*, 179: "In persecution, I find the original meaning of Judaism, its initial emotion."

64. A minimum of ten adults (a minyan) are necessary for a complete Jewish religious service.

65. In the first version of this text, as mentioned in note 62, above, Levinas had written "Jesus," which he revised with a typewriter in order to substitute the name "Jonah." Perhaps because the typewritten name was barely legible, he then crossed it out and rewrote it again, by hand, and underlined it.

66. Levinas, *Carnets de captivité*, 211–13.

67. In an entry in *A Writer's Diary* published in 1877, Dostoevsky comments that there "were several Jews" in the prison camp at Omsk (in *House of the Dead* there is just one), and that "no one excluded them or persecuted them. . . . And yet these same Jews," Dostoevsky continues, "shunned the Russians in many respects: they did not want to eat with them; they regarded them almost haughtily (and this, of all places, in prison!); and, in general, they showed loathing and aversion toward the Russians" (*A Writer's Diary*, trans. Lantz, 356–57).

Chapter 2

1. Dostoevsky, *The Brothers Karamazov*, second Norton Critical Edition, 202.

2. Levinas, *God, Death, and Time*, 137.

3. Emmanuel Levinas, *Of God Who Comes to Mind*, trans. Bettina Bergo (Stanford, Calif.: Stanford University Press, 1998), xi; Levinas, *De Dieu qui vient à l'idée* (Paris: Vrin, 1982; rpt. 2004), 7.

4. Levinas, *Of God Who Comes to Mind*, ix; Levinas, *De Dieu qui vient à l'idée*, 5–6.

5. Emmanuel Levinas, "To Think God on the Basis of Ethics," in *God, Death, and Time*, 136.

6. Ibid., 137.

7. Ibid., 138, translation modified.

8. Ibid.,139; *Dieu, la mort et le temps*, 158.

9. Ibid.

10. Emmanuel Levinas, "Witnessing and Ethics," in *God, Death, and Time*, 199; Levinas, *Dieu, la mort et le temps*, 228.

11. *Tanach: The Torah, Prophets, Writings*, ed. Rabbi Nosson Scherman, ArtScroll Series/Stone Edition (Brooklyn, N.Y.: Mesorah Publications, 1996; rpt. 2003), 1121.

12. Cited from Levinas, *God, Death, and Time*, 199. The English translation, based on *The New Oxford Annotated Bible with the Apocrypha*, revised standard version, ed. Herbert G. May and Bruce Metzger (New York: Oxford University Press, 1977), is revised for consistency with the French, which cites the *Bible de Jérusalem* (Paris: Éditions de Cerf, 1986); see Levinas, *God, Death, and Time*, 285, footnote 7.

13. *Turned Inside-Out: Literature, Art, and Testimony from the Inside-Out Prison Exchange Program*, 50.

14. Emmanuel Levinas, "God and Philosophy," *Of God Who Comes to Mind*, 56; "Dieu et la philosophie," *De Dieu qui vient à l'idée*, 95.

15. *Oxford Latin Dictionary*, 604.

16. Ibid., 633.

17. Delhomme is the author of *La Pensée et le reel: Critique de l'ontologie* (Paris: Presses Universitaires de France, 1967) and *L'impossible interrogation* (Paris: Desclée, 1971). Cited in Levinas, *Of God Who Comes to Mind*, 197 (n. 1).

18. Etienne Gilson, *Reason and Revelation in the Middle Ages* (New York: Scribner's, 1938). This brief survey of Gilson's book and his distinction between reason and faith is drawn from my article "Reason and Revelation in the Pre-Enlightenment: Eric Voegelin's Analysis and the Case of Swift," *Religion and Literature* 16, no. 2 (Summer 1984): 1–24.

19. Saint Augustine, *On the Gospel of St. John* 29.6.

20. Levinas, "God and Philosophy," 57.

21. See book 6 of the *Republic* and my commentary in *Other Others*, 76–77 and "Ghosts and Responsibility: The Hebrew Bible, Confucius, Plato," in *Rethinking Ghosts in World Religions*, ed. Mu-chou Poo (Brill, 2009), esp. 77.

22. Levinas, "God and Philosophy," 57; Levinas, "Dieu et la philosophie," 96.

23. Levinas, "God and Philosophy," 57.

24. Levinas, "God and Philosophy," 57; Levinas, "Dieu et la philosophie," 96.

25. Ibid.

26. Levinas, "God and Philosophy," 55.

27. Levinas, "God and Philosophy," 57; Levinas, "Dieu et la philosophie," 96.

28. Levinas, "God and Philosophy," 58; Levinas, "Dieu et la philosophie," 97.

29. Ibid.

30. Levinas, "God and Philosophy," 59; Levinas, "Dieu et la philosophie," 98–99. In his *Prison Notebooks*, Levinas appears to characterize as "sleepers" those around him who are content to continue to live their lives oblivious to the true horror of their situation and of the plight of the world. Levinas remarks: "To sleep. One hears the sounds of people who continue to live. It is an agitation that underlines the sensible behavior [*la sagesse*] of the sleeper. Like the sound of the sea" (*Carnets de captivités*, 79).

31. Levinas, "God and Philosophy," 59; Levinas, "Dieu et la philosophie," 99.

32. *Tanach*, 1549.

33. Levinas, "Dieu et la philosophie," 102.

34. Levinas, "God and Philosophy," 62; Levinas, "Dieu et la philosophie," 104.

35. Levinas, "God and Philosophy," 63; Levinas, "Dieu et la philosophie," 105.

36. Ibid.

37. Levinas, "God and Philosophy," 63; Levinas, "Dieu et la philosophie," 107. Translation altered for accuracy.

38. Earlier in this paragraph Levinas makes an allusion to Plato's theory of reminiscence, which is articulated by Socrates: that knowledge is *anamnesis*, recollection. Levinas asks if an idea can be placed in thought and yet "renounce its literary heritage of Socratic nobility." Can there be a thought that is not a remembered thought, a thought that does not already have its origin in consciousness? As Levinas well knew, and consistently acknowledged, it was this same Plato and this same Socrates who answered a perhaps surprising "yes" to this question. We are referring here to what Socrates says in the sixth book of the *Republic* just before he sets out to describe the so-called divided line of knowledge—divided, that is, between the realms of the visible and the invisible. True knowledge is knowledge of that which is beyond sense, of the ideas themselves. But above all these ideas is the idea of the good itself, which, Socrates insists, isn't truly an idea that is like knowledge and truth. The very existence and essence of objects of knowledge are dependent upon the good, Socrates asserts, although "the good itself is not essence but is still *beyond being or essence* [*epeikeina tês ousias*], exceeding it in dignity or age [*presbeia*] and in power" (509c). The good, for Plato, is more venerable than—that is, comes before—ontology, the science of being. "Beyond being": a demonically hyperbolic expression (*daimonias hyperbolês*), Glaucon remarks. The very impetus for Platonic philosophizing in the *Republic* begins with the philosopher's attempt to analyze, and to offer an antidote to, the corruptions of Athenian society that led to the Peloponnesian War and its devastating impact on Athens. Philosophy, in the Platonic sense, begins with a concern for others, with an attempt to better human society by imagining a world of ideas—such as justice—against which contemporary existence can be measured and found wanting. The *Republic* begins with Socrates generously accepting an invitation, issued by the young Glaucon and Polemarchus, to join these young people in a discussion about the nature of justice. Living in a time of corruption, they wonder if justice even exists. Platonic philosophizing thus begins with Socrates's answering the call to responsibility for the other.

39. Levinas, "God and Philosophy," 65; Levinas, "Dieu et la philosophie," 108.

40. Ibid.

41. Ibid.

42. Levinas, "God and Philosophy," 66; Levinas, "Dieu et la philosophie," 109.

43. Levinas, "God and Philosophy," 69.

44. Michael Morgan, *Discovering Levinas* (Cambridge: Cambridge University Press, 2007), 197.

45. Emmanuel Levinas, "Meaning and Sense," in *Emmanuel Levinas: Basic Philosophical Writings*, ed. Adrian T. Peperzak, Simon Critchley, and Robert Bernasconi (Bloomington: Indiana University Press, 1996), 64. Originally translated into English by Alphonso Lingis in *Collected Philosophical Papers* (The Hague:

Martinus Nijhoff, 1987), the translation was revised by Bernasconi and Critch-ley for inclusion in *Basic Philosophical Writings*. This same essay appeared in Levinas, *Humanisme de l'autre home* (1972) and was translated, with the title "Signification and Sense," by Nidra Poller in *Humanism of the Other* (Urbana: University of Illinois Press, 2003), 9–44.

46. Levinas, *Ethics and Infinity*, 106.

47. Gate Two, chapter 3, "The Formula of the *Berachot*," trans. Rabbi Avraham Yaakov Finkel (Brooklyn: Judaica, 2009), 80–81. In conversation with me, Georges Hansel, an inspiring commentator on the Talmud and also the son-in-law of Levinas, mentioned the prayer I discuss in the text as an example of what Levinas is describing in the passage from *Ethics and Infinity*. See also Levinas, "The Name of God according to a Few Talmudic Texts," chapter 8 of *Beyond the Verse: Talmudic Readings and Lectures*, trans. Gary Mole (Bloomington and Indianapolis: Indiana University Press, 1994), especially p. 122, where Levinas reflects, in commenting on the Talmudic tractate Berakhot 12a, on how "[t]he Thou becomes He in the Name, as if the Name belonged simultaneously to the correctness of being addressed as Thou and to the absolute of holiness. And it is without doubt this essential ambiguity—or enigma—of transcendence that is preserved in the standard expression in the Talmud for designating God: 'The Holy One, blessed be He.' " This chapter was first published, in French, in 1982.

48. See Longinus, *On the Sublime*, sections 26 and 27. In section 27, Longinus comments on the power of a writer's switching from indirect to direct speech, which he refers to as *apostrophe*. Levinas, in contrast, is commenting on the opposite, that is, on the startling transformation of "thou" into "he." It is perhaps not by chance that, startlingly for an ancient Greek rhetorical theorist, Longinus (*On the Sublime*, chapter 9) finds the epitome of what he means by the sublime not in any work of Greek literature but rather in the biblical utterance "let there be light, and there was light" (Genesis 1:3).

49. Levinas, "God and Philosophy," 69.

50. Levinas, "God and Philosophy," 69; Levinas, "Dieu et la philosophie," 115.

51. Levinas, "God and Philosophy," 72.

52. Levinas, "Dieu et la philosophie," 119.

53. Gen. 23–25, trans. Alter.

54. Gen. 18:27; Levinas, "God and Philosophy," 72.

55. Levinas, "God and Philosophy," 72; Levinas, "Dieu et la philosophie," 119.

56. *The Torah: With Rashi's Commentary Translated, Annotated, and Eluci-dated*, Vol. II, Shemot/Exodus, ed. Rabbi Yisrael Isser Zvi Herczeg et al., The Sapirstein Edition, the ArtScroll Series (Brooklyn, New York: Mesorah Publica-tions, 1995; rpt. 1999), 187.

57. Levinas, "God and Philosophy," 72–73; Levinas, "Dieu et la philosophie," 119–20.

58. Levinas, "God and Philosophy," 74; Levinas, "Dieu et la philosophie," 121.

59. Levinas, "God and Philosophy," 75; Levinas, "Dieu et la philosophie," 123.

60. Levinas, *Of God Who Comes to Mind*, 201, n. 34.

61. Levinas, "God and Philosophy," 76; Levinas, "Dieu et la philosophie," 124.

62. Ibid.

63. Levinas, "God and Philosophy," 77.

64. Ibid.

65. Ibid.

66. Ibid.

67. Levinas, "God and Philosophy," 78; Levinas, "Dieu et la philosophie," 127.

68. Ibid.

69. Ibid.

Chapter 3

1. Upon his release from the prison camp in Omsk, Dostoevsky wrote a letter (February 22, 1854) to his brother Mikhail urging him to send him "Hegel without fail, especially Hegel's *History of Philosophy*. My whole future is linked with it!" (*Selected Letters of Fyodor Dostoevsky*, ed. Frank and Goldstein, 63). Steven Cassedy wonders if Dostoevsky's knowledge of Hegel ever went beyond "a popularized notion of certain Hegelian phrases and concepts" (*Dostoevsky's Religion* [Stanford, Calif.: Stanford University Press, 2005], 27).

2. Dostoevsky, *Crime and Punishment*, 261; Dostoevsky, *Prestuplenie i nakazanie*, 201.

3. Dostoevsky, *Crime and Punishment*, 261; Dostoevsky, *Prestuplenie i nakazanie*, 202.

4. Dostoevsky, *Crime and Punishment*, 261.

5. Dostoevsky, *Crime and Punishment*, 261; Dostoevsky, *Prestuplenie i nakazanie*, 202.

6. Ibid.

7. Ibid.

8. Ibid.

9. Levinas, *God, Death, and Time*, 293, n. 34.

10. Dostoevsky, *Crime and Punishment*, 517.

11. Dostoevsky, *Crime and Punishment*, 517; Dostoevsky, *Prestuplenie i nakazanie*, 386.

12. Ibid.

13. Ibid.

14. Ibid.

15. Dostoevsky, *Crime and Punishment*, 549; Dostoevsky, *Prestuplenie i nakazanie*, 408.

16. Ibid.

17. Ibid.

18. Ibid.

19. Dostoevsky, *Crime and Punishment*, 549.

20. Fyodor Dostoevsky, *Demons*, trans. Richard Pevear and Larissa Volokhonsky (New York: Alfred A. Knopf, 1994), 501.

21. Dostoevsky, *The Idiot*, trans. Richard Pevear and Larissa Volokhonsky (New York: Vintage Books, 2001), 218. Later in the novel (part 3, chapter 6), Ippolit Terentyev comments on how corrosive to religious belief is the subject of this Holbein painting. If "all those believers [*verovavshie*]" in Jesus "and those who worshiped him had seen a corpse like this," Terentyev comments, "how could they believe [*poverit'*], looking at such a corpse, that this sufferer would resurrect?" Terentyev even wonders if Jesus himself had been able, on the eve of his execution, to see this image of him painted by Holbein, whether "he would have gone to the cross and died as he did" (*The Idiot*, trans. Richard Pevear

and Larissa Volokhonsky, 408–9 [translation modified]; the Russian is cited from Fyodor Dostoevsky, *Idiot* [San Bernadino, Calif.: Planet Books, 2013], 293).

22. Dostoevsky, *The Idiot*, 220.

23. Ibid.

24. Ibid. *The Idiot*, 220–21.

25. Ibid., 221.

26. Dostoevsky, *Demons*, 253; Fyodor Dostoevsky, *Besy* (St. Petersburg: Azbuka, 2011), 252.

27. Homer, *Iliad* 6, ll. 232–36. In a letter dated January 1, 1840, Dostoevsky tells his brother Mikhail, "Homer (a legendary man, he was perhaps like Christ, an incarnation of God sent to us) can be compared only to Christ and not to Goethe. Try to understand him, brother, try to grasp the meaning of the *Iliad* (admit it—you haven't really read it, have you?). Don't you realize that in the *Iliad* Homer gave to the whole ancient world a scheme for spiritual and earthly life with the same force as Christ gave it to the modern world? Now, as a lyricist with a purely angelic nature and with a Christian and childlike poetic spirit, Victor Hugo stands alone, and there is no one who can be compared to him in this, neither Schiller (Christian poet though he be) nor Shakespeare as a lyric poet . . . nor Byron, nor Pushkin. Only Homer, who has the same unshakable belief in his vocation, with his childlike belief in the god of poetry whom he serves, draws his poetry from a source similar to Victor Hugo's" (Dostoevsky, *Selected Letters*, 19).

28. Dostoevsky, *The Idiot*, 223.

29. Vinokur, *The Trace of Judaism*, 20.

30. Dostoevsky, *The Idiot*, 611.

31. Emmanuel Levinas, *Is It Righteous to Be?* 193–94. This chapter is entitled "In the Name of the Other." The original interview was conducted by Luc Ferry, Raphaël Hadas-Lebel, and Sylvaine Pasquier and was published in French in *L'Express* (July 9, 1990). The translator is Maureen V. Gedney.

32. *The Torah: With Rashi's Commentary Translated, Annotated, and Elucidated*, Vol. I, Bereshit/Genesis, The Saperstein Edition, ArtScroll Series (Brooklyn, N.Y.: Mesorah Publications, 1995), ed. Rabbi Yisrael Isser Zvi Herczeg et al., 371.

33. Deut. 16.20.

34. Levinas, *Otherwise Than Being*, 157 (V.3 ["From the Saying to the Said, or the Wisdom of Desire"]); the French reads, "Paix, paix au prochain et au lointain" (Levinas, *Autrement qu'être*, 245).

35. Levinas, *Otherwise Than Being*, 158.

36. Ibid.

37. Dostoevsky, *Complete Letters*, 3:248; the Russian text is cited from Dostoevsky's *Pis'ma*, 2:248.

38. Dostoevsky, *Demons*, 116; Dostoevsky, *Besy*, 125.

39. Dostoevsky, *Demons*, 619; Dostoevsky, *Besy*, 592.

40. Kirillov's belief in unbelief is anticipated by Prince Myshkin in Dostoevsky's earlier novel, *The Idiot*. The Russian people, according to Myshkin (part 4, chapter 7), "don't simply become atheists, but they absolutely *believe* [*uveruiut*] in atheism, as in a new faith" (the Russian is cited fom *Idiot*, 389; my own translation).

41. Dostoevsky, *Demons*, 559 (translation modified); Dostoevsky, *Besy*, 584.

42. Kirillov's determination to kill himself as an act of sheer will and pure human agency is anticipated by Ippolit Terentyev in *The Idiot*, particularly in part 3, chapter 5.

43. Dostoevsky, *Demons*, 231; Dostoevsky, *Besy*, 232.

44. Dostoevsky, *Demons*, 232.

45. Dostoevsky, *Demons*, 235; Dostoevsky, *Besy*, 236.

46. Dostoevsky, *Demons*, 236; Dostoevsky, *Besy*, 237. Dostoevsky associated such ecstatic moments with the sensations he experienced just before the painful, even unbearable onslaught of an epileptic fit. See Myshkin's reflections on his epilepsy (part 2, chapter 5), where the Prince recalls his sensing, in such ecstatic moments, a glimpse of the/a "supreme being" (*vysshego bytiia* [162]).

47. Dostoevsky, *Demons*, 239; Dostoevsky, *Besy*, 239.

48. Robert Heilman recalls Voegelin making this comment to him in conversation during the final years of Voegelin's life when he lived, in retirement, in Palo Alto, California. See Robert Heilman, *The Professor and the Profession* (Columbia: University of Missouri Press, 1999), 102.

49. See Eric Voegelin, "Reason: The Classic Experience," in *Anamnesis* (Notre Dame, Ind.: University of Notre Dame Press, 1978), especially 91–97 on "The Tension of Existence."

50. Dostoevsky, *Demons*, 619.

51. Dostoevsky, *Brat'ia Karamazovy*, 297.

52. Levinas, *Otherwise Than Being*, 149.

53. Levinas, *Autrement qu'être*, 230.

54. Levinas, "God and Philosophy," in *Of God Who Comes to Mind*, 69.

55. Levinas, *Otherwise Than Being*, 147; translation slightly modified.

56. For a fine presentation and analysis of the many Kantian "antinomies" of belief in Dostoevsky's thought and fiction, see Cassedy, *Dostoevsky's Religion*, especially chapter 4 ("Belief Is Expressed in Antinomies").

57. Dostoevsky, *Brat'ia Karamazovy*, 251.

58. Dostoevsky, *The Brothers Karamazov*, second Norton Critical Edition, 200.

59. Dostoevsky, *The Brothers Karamazov*, trans. Pevear and Volokhonsky, 264; Dostoevsky, *Brat'ia Karamazovy*, 272.

60. Dostoevsky, *The Brothers Karamazov*, second Norton Critical Edition, 226.

61. Dostoevsky, *Winter Notes on Summer Impressions*, trans. Patterson, 49. The italics are mine.

62. Dostoevsky, *The Brothers Karamazov*, second Norton Critical Edition, 655–56.

63. Dostoevsky, *The Brothers Karamazov*, trans. Pevear and Volokhonsky, 264; Dostoevsky, *Brat'ia Karamazovy*, 273.

64. Dostoevsky, *The Brothers Karamazov*, second Norton Critical Edition, 254. On Saint Alexis, see Victor Terras, *A Karamazov Companion* (Madison: University of Wisconsin Press, 1981; rpt. 2002), 22, n. 51.

65. Trans. John Dryden, *Plutarch's Lives* (Edinburgh: C. Elliot, 1795), 6 vols., 4:211. See also l. 117 of Alexander Pope's *Epistle to Dr. Arbuthnot*, where the poet compares his own distorted physique to that of Alexander the Great: "*Ammon's great Son* [i.e., Alexander the Great] one shoulder had too high" (Pope, *Imitations of Horace, with An Epistle to Dr. Arbuthnot and The Epilogue to the*

Satires, ed. John Butt [London: Yale University Press, 1939; rpt. 1969], 104. There are other classical allusions in this chapter that ally Ivan with the classical pagan world. The Grand Inquisitor claims that he has taken up "the sword of Caesar" (*The Brothers Karamazov,* second Norton Critical Edition, 228) rather than the love, gentleness, and righteousness of Christ. The wizened, ninety-year-old Grand Inquisitor banishes Jesus, who has suddenly and miraculously come back to earth, and orders him never to come back again. Jesus responds to his banishment neither with words nor with anger, but rather by kissing the Grand Inquisitor. "The kiss," Ivan tells Alyosha, "glows [or burns] in his heart [i.e., in the heart of the Grand Inquisitor], but the old man adheres to his idea [that Christ must be banished]." "'And you with him, you too [*i ty*]?' cried Alyosha, mournfully" (ibid.). Alyosha's mournful "you too/*i ty*" recalls the Latin words *et tu* ("even you," "you, too") of the bleeding Caesar's famous (and famously disputed) last words (*et tu, Brute*) that he utters to his erstwhile friend and supporter Brutus, who joined in the violent and bloody republican rebellion against the now fatally wounded emperor Caesar on the Ides of March. The Latin phrase appears in Shakespeare's play *Julius Caesar,* III.1.87. Dostoevsky, an avid Shakespearean, could well have come across the Latin phrase in Shakespeare's play.

66. Levinas, *Otherwise Than Being,* 117; Levinas, *Autrement qu'être,* 185.

67. Dostoevsky, *Brat'ia Karamazovy,* 702.

68. Dostoevsky, *The Brothers Karamazov,* second Norton Critical Edition, 576.

69. Ibid.

70. Ibid., 524.

71. Ibid., 577; Dostoevsky, *Brat'ia Karamazovy,* 704.

72. See my article "From Solitude to Maternity: Levinas and Shakespeare," *Levinas Studies: An Annual Review,* vol. 8 (2013), 67–79.

73. Levinas, *Of God Who Comes to Mind,* 69; Levinas, *De Dieu qui vient à l'idée,* 2nd ed., 113–14. Then comes a sentence that, in 1975 (Levinas did not mention Grossman in print until 1984), anticipates Levinas's later preoccupation with Vasily Grossman's novel *Life and Fate,* which I discuss in chapter 5 of this book. By means of this "turning around," Levinas says, "the Desirable escapes Desire." Or, as Levinas often states this phenomenon (and in fact does so in this very passage): ethics—the call to responsibility for the Other—is the non-erotic par excellence. Levinas continues, "The goodness of the Good—of the Good that neither sleeps nor slumbers [the language here, as discussed earlier, is reminiscent of the description of God's unsleeping moral vigilance in Psalm 121]—*inclines the movement it calls forth to turn it away from the Good and orient it toward the other, and only thus toward the Good*" (italics are mine). Here Levinas articulates the chief moral insight of Grossman's great novel, which prefers concrete and senseless acts of human kindness to an adherence to abstract notions of the Good that, for Grossman, have historically resulted in murder and cruelty committed in the name of the perpetrator's idea of the "Good." See Ikonnikov's scribblings, part 2, chapter 15 of Vasily Grossman, *Life and Fate,* trans. Robert Chandler (New York: New York Review of Books, 1985; rpt. 2006) (chapter 16 in the Russian text). In the same section of his essay "God and Philosophy," Levinas goes on to discuss the relation between goodness and *il*-leity. "Intangible, the Desirable separates itself from the relationship with Desire that it calls forth

and, by this separation or holiness, remains a third person: He [*Il*] at the root of the You [*Tu*]. He [*Il*] is Good in this very precise, eminent sense: He [*Il*] . . . compels me to goodness [*m'astreint à la bonté*]" (Levinas, *Of God Who Comes to Mind*, 69; Levinas, *De Dieu qui vient à l'idée*, 114). Levinas is here describing the transcendence of illeity. I am attempting, in this book, to show how Dostoevsky and Vasily Grossman, in their novels, are charting this same itinerary of an illeity conceived outside of ontology, outside of the question of God's existence.

74. See Levinas, "God and Philosophy," in *Of God Who Comes to Mind*, 68–69. Like Levinas's awakened I, Ivan's is here being "faithful to an engagement that it never made." Ivan's I is being "sobered up from the ecstasy of intentionality."

75. Levinas, "God and Philosophy," 68.

76. Ibid., 71.

77. Ibid.

78. Levinas, "God and Philosophy," 71; Levinas, "Dieu et la philosophie," 117.

79. Levinas, "God and Philosophy," 72; I have substantially altered the translation.

80. Dostoevsky, *The Brothers Karamazov*, second Norton Critical Edition, 579.

81. Levinas, *Autrement qu'être*, 234

82. Dostoevsky, *The Brothers Karamazov*, second Norton Critical Edition, 581; Dostoevsky, *Brat'ia Karamazovy*, 708.

83. Dostoevsky, *The Brothers Karamazov*, second Norton Critical Edition, 630 (translation slightly modified); Dostoevsky, *Brat'ia Karamazovy*, 774.

84. Levinas, *Otherwise Than Being*, 147.

85. Dostoevsky, *Brat'ia Karamazovy*, 773.

86. Ralph E. Matlaw, "On Translating *The Brothers Karamazov*," in *The Brothers Karamazov*, second Norton Critical Edition, 672.

87. Ibid.

88. As Joseph Frank remarks, "An obvious 'miscarriage of justice' (the title of the entire Book 12) has occurred on the legal level, though Dimitry has inwardly accepted the justice of suffering for his parricidal impulses" (Frank, *Dostoevsky: The Mantle of the Prophet, 1871–1881* [Princeton, N.J.: Princeton University Press, 2002], 698).

89. Levinas, *Otherwise Than Being*, 150; *Autrement qu'être*, 234.

90. Ibid.

91. *Oxford Latin Dictionary*, ed. P. G. W. Glare (Oxford: Clarendon, 1996), 827.

92. See Morgan, *Discovering Levinas*, 189. Morgan refers the reader to Levinas's essay "Meaning and Sense" included in *Basic Philosophical Writings*, ed. Peperzak, Critchley, and Bernasconi, 61 and 64.

93. Levinas, *Otherwise Than Being*, 150.

94. Ibid., 151.

95. Dostoevsky, *The Brothers Karamazov*, second Norton Critical Edition, 242; Dostoevsky, *Brat'ia Karamazovy*, 289.

96. Levinas, *Otherwise Than Being*, 150.

97. Dostoevsky, *The Brothers Karamazov*, second Norton Critical Edition, 524.

98. Dostoevsky employs this same patronymic, with the same intent, in the scene in which Fyodor bids Ivan farewell, for the last time, as Ivan leaves

Fyodor's house for his journey to Moscow. The old man accompanies his son onto the steps of his house, where Ivan had been staying and is about to kiss Ivan good-bye when "Ivan Fyodorovich made haste to hold out his hand, obviously avoiding the kiss" (Dostoevsky, *The Brothers Karamazov*, second Norton Critical Edition, 241). Dostoevsky uses the same patronymic, to the same effect, three more times before Ivan sets off in his carriage.

99. Dostoevsky, *The Idiot*, trans. Pevear and Volokhonsky, 583; Dostoevsky, *Idiot* (Russian text), 415.

100. Levinas, *Ethics and Infinity*, 48.

101. Levinas, *Éthique et infini*, 38.

102. Levinas, *Of God Who Comes to Mind*, ix.

103. Ibid., 198, n. 11. The English translation of Descartes's *Third Meditation* is from the English translation of J. Cottingham, R. Stroothoff, and D. Murdoch in *Descartes: Selected Philosophical Writings* (Cambridge: Cambridge University Press, 1988), 97, as cited in *Of God Who Comes to Mind*, 198, n. 11.

104. See the "Foreword" to the Pevear-Volokhonsky translation of *The Idiot*, xii: "'*Stavrogin is everything*,' Dostoevsky wrote in a note to himself dated August 16, 1870."

105. Dostoevsky, *Demons*, 420.

106. Ibid., 601.

107. Ibid., 600.

108. Ibid.

109. Dostoevsky, *Demons*, 604; Dostoevsky, *Besy*, 578.

110. Ibid.

111. David I. Goldstein comments as follows on the reader's response to Lyamshin's scream: "There is, to be sure, nothing heroic in Lyamshin's act. Nor is it an act of civic courage or contrition. It is neither noble nor virtuous, but it is, nonetheless, a profoundly human act, arising out of an organic, human revulsion to an act of cold-blooded murder" (Goldstein, *Dostoevsky and the Jews* [Austin, Tex.: University of Texas Press, 1981], 84).

112. Dostoevsky, *Demons*, 670.

113. Goldstein, *Dostoevsky and the Jews*, 84–85.

114. Trans. Goldstein, *Dostoevsky and the Jews*, 52. Svidrigailov says that he wishes to shoot himself "in front of an official witness" (*pri ofitsial'nom' svidetele* [Dostoevsky, *Crime and Punishment*, 510; Dostoevsky, *Prestuplenie i nakazanie*, 381]). The Jewish fireman does not wish to be such a witness.

115. Havel, *Letters to Olga*, 145.

116. Dostoevsky, *Demons*, 419; Dostoevsky, *Besy*, 406.

117. *The Dalai Lama: A Policy of Kindness*, ed. Sidney Piburn (Ithaca, N.Y.: Snow Lion Publications, 1990), 18. The episode with the Dalai Lama had an overwhelmingly positive effect on our class. Jeff was not offended by the Dalai Lama's response to his question. He was, rather, very grateful for the emotional support he received from his classmates, inside and out. Elizabeth established a special connection with the class as a result of her having been singled out as the questioner, and for having endured what many perceived as a dismissive response from His Holiness. As an inside student named Michael remarked in our class anthology (22), "special thanks to Elizabeth for taking one for the team!"

Chapter 4

1. See Joseph Frank, "Dostoevsky and Anti-Semitism," in *Between Religion and Rationality* (Princeton, N.J.: Princeton University Press, 2010), 159–72.

2. Ibid., 160.

3. Ibid.

4. Ibid., 161.

5. Dostoevsky, *The Brothers Karamazov*, trans. Pevear and Volokhonsky, book 11, chapter 3, p. 583. The Russian is cited from Dostoevsky, *Brat'ia Karamazovy*, 596.

6. Ibid.

7. Frank, "Dostoevsky and Anti-Semitism," 171.

8. Ibid., 167.

9. Ibid., 169.

10. Dostoevsky, *Polnoe sobranie sochinenii*, 26:147. Frank (172) is here citing the translation of Kenneth Lanz, Dostoevsky, *A Writer's Diary* (August 1880), 504.

11. Frank, "Dostoevsky and Anti-Semitism," 172.

12. See McReynolds, *Redemption and the Merchant God*, 219, n. 19. "The real life prototype, Isai Bumstehl," McReynolds writes, "was a jeweler imprisoned for murder, whipped and branded. The records say that he was a convert to Greek Orthodoxy." If Bumstehl was a convert to Greek Orthodoxy, then Dostoevsky's unsympathetic representation of Isai Fomich's praying on the eve of the Sabbath must have been drawn from elsewhere. David I. Goldstein believes that Bumstehl was in fact a Jew and that the inaccuracies in Dostoevsky's description of Isai Fomich Bumshtein's Friday evening Sabbath observances were composed "at the expense of factual truth, to heighten the comic effect to the plane of the grotesque" (Goldstein, *Dostoevsky and the Jews*), 25. James P. Scanlan, in the introduction to Boris Jakim's recent English translation of *House of the Dead*, appears to endorse Goldstein's belief that the real-life prototype for Bumshtein was in fact a practicing Jew and not a convert. See Dostoevsky, *Notes from the House of the Dead*, trans. Jakim, xiv–xv.

13. Dostoevsky, *House of the Dead*, 69; Dostoevsky, *Zapiski iz mertvogo doma*, 84.

14. Dostoevsky, *House of the Dead*, 70; Dostoevsky, *Zapiski iz mertvogo doma*, 84.

15. Dostoevsky, *House of the Dead*, 139–40.

16. Ibid., 120.

17. Dostoevsky, *House of the Dead*, 120; Dostoevsky, *Zapiski iz mertvogo doma*, 144–45.

18. Dostoevsky, *House of the Dead*, 120; Dostoevsky, *Zapiski iz mertvogo doma*, 144.

19. Ibid.

20. Dostoevsky, *House of the Dead*, 120.

21. Ibid., 68.

22. David I. Goldstein reports on the inaccuracies in Dostoevsky's representation of Isai Fomich Bumshtein's observance of the Jewish Sabbath in his masterful *Dostoevsky and the Jews*, 24–30.

23. Levinas, "God and Philosophy," 71; Levinas, "Dieu et philosophie," 115.

24. Leonid Tsypkin, *Summer in Baden-Baden*, trans. Roger and Angela Keys (London: Hamish Hamilton/Penguin, 2005), 115–16.

25. Dostoevsky, *The Brothers Karamazov*, trans. Pevear and Volokhonsky, 584; translation modified.

26. Tsypkin, *Summer in Baden-Baden*, 115.

27. Frank, "Dostoevsky and Anti-Semitism," 160. Cited by Frank, ibid.

28. Dostoevsky, *A Writer's Diary*, 361.

29. Frank, "Dostoevsky and Anti-Semitism, 161.

30. The Russian is cited from Leonid Tsypkin, *Leto v Badene* (Moscow: Novoe Literaturnoe Obozrenie, 2013), 153.

31. Tsypkin, *Summer in Baden-Baden*, 115; translation modified.

32. Dostoevsky, *Polnoe sobranie sochinenii*, 25:75, 82, trans. Lantz; Dostoevsky, *A Writer's Diary* (March 1877), 349. Dostoevsky's claim that every Jew, without exception, is close to God, is refuted by his correspondent Avraam-Uriya (assimilated to Arkady Grigorevich) Kovner, a secular Jew whose critical response to Dostoevsky's antisemitic attitudes elicited the articles Dostoevsky wrote on "The Jewish Question" in the March 1877 issue of *A Writer's Diary*. Would you advise today's many young secular Jews who claim to be nonbelievers, Kovner asks Dostoevsky, "to convert to Christianity, when they are unable to believe in any organized religion?" (cited by Goldstein, *Dostoevsky and the Jews*, 133).

33. Dostoevsky, *A Writer's Diary*, trans. Lantz, 365.

34. Ibid., 349.

35. Ibid., 366.

36. Dostoevsky, *Selected Letters of Fyodor Dostoevsky*, trans. MacAndrew, 439.

37. Ibid., 438.

38. Ibid.

39. Levinas, *Autrement qu'être*, 233.

40. Dostoevsky, *Polnoe sobranie sochinenii*, 30.1:17, trans. MacAndrew; Dostoevsky, *Selected Letters*, 450; translation slightly modified.

41. Dostoevsky, *Brothers Karamazov*, second Norton Critical Edition, 646; Dostoevsky, *Brat'ia Karamazovy*, 795.

42. Ibid.

43. Tolstoy, *The Gospel in Brief: The Life of Jesus*, trans. Dustin Condren (New York: Harper Perennial, 2011), viii.

44. Franz Rosenzweig, *The Star of Redemption*, trans. William W. Hallo (Notre Dame, Ind.: University of Notre Dame Press, 1970; rpt. 1985), 341.

45. Ibid., 341–42.

46. Rosenzweig, *Star of Redemption*, 342; Franz Rosenzweig, *Der Stern der Erlösung* (Frankfurt: Suhrkamp, 1988), 380.

47. In contrast to Christianity, there is no *credo* (meaning "I believe") in the Jewish liturgy. The closest approximation in the Jewish liturgy to the Christian *credo* is the *Shema Israel* ("Listen, O Israel, HASHEM is our God, HASHEM is [or will be] [the only] one"). Even here, however, immediately following the recitation of the *Shema*, the worshipper is commanded not necessarily to believe in God, but rather to *love* him: ("You shall love [*ve'ahavtah*] HASHEM your God with all your heart, with all your soul, and with all your resources/strength"). This part of the liturgy is drawn from Deuteronomy 6:4–5.

48. Dostoevsky, *Polnoe sobranie sochinenii*, 25:82. Dostoevsky, *A Writer's Diary*, trans. Lenz, 359; translation slightly altered.

49. Emmanuel Levinas, *In the Time of the Nations*, trans. Michael B. Smith (Bloomington: Indiana University Press, 1994), 164.

50. Trans. Ralph E. Matlaw, Dostoevsky, *The Brothers Karamazov*, second Norton Critical Edition, 667.

51. Dostoevsky, *Crime and Punishment*, 321; Dostoevsky, *Prestuplenie i nakazanie*, 245.

52. Dostoevsky, *Crime and Punishment*, 325; Dostoevsky, *Prestuplenie i nakazanie*, 248.

53. Dostoevsky, *Crime and Punishment*, 327; Dostoevsky, *Prestuplenie i nakazanie*, 249.

54. Dostoevsky, *Demons*, 253.

55. Dostoevsky, *Demons*, 251; Dostoevsky, *Besy*, 252.

56. See the chapter "Textes messianiques" in Levinas, *Difficile liberté*, 137.

57. Ibid. Stavrogin is an avowed atheist who, at the same time, according to his one-time disciple Shatov, had insisted, in words Dostoevsky lifts from one of his own letters, that "if someone proved" to him "mathematically that the truth is outside Christ," he, Stavrogin, would rather "agree to stay with Christ than with the truth" (*Demons*, 249, with reference to Dostoevky's letter to N. D. Fonvizin [1854]). See Dostoevsky, *Selected Letters*, 68.

58. Dostoevsky, *Selected Letters*, p. 354; translation modified. The Russian is cited from Dostoevsky, *Pis'ma*, vol. 2 (Leningrad: State Publishing House, 1930), 348.

59. Dostoevsky, *The Brothers Karamazov*, second Norton Critical Edition, 666.

60. Ibid.

Chapter 5

1. The epigraph is from Vasily Grossman, *Life and Fate*, trans. Chandler, 833. Vladimir Korolenko (1853–1921) was a Ukrainian-Russian writer of short stories.

2. Mystical Christianity is another matter. The distinction between mystical and dogmatic theology—that is, between *theologia mystica* and *theologia dogmatica*—goes as far back as the church fathers. See Eric Voegelin's comments on this distinction as recorded in *Eric Voegelin's Thought: A Critical Appraisal* (Durham, N.C.: Duke University Press, 1982), 190. See also the Thomistic distinction between *fides informis* and *fides caritate formata*, *Summa* 2–2, q. 4, a. 3–6, q. 6, q. 23, a. 6, a. 8.

3. This is how Levinas understands the famous phrase *ve'ahavta lere'akha kamokha* from Leviticus 19:18, usually translated as "you shall love your neighbor as yourself." Levinas suggests another way to translate this phrase. See *Of God Who Comes to Mind*, 90 (translation modified in what follows); *De Dieu qui vient à l'dée*, 144: "What does 'as yourself' [*kamokha*] signify? Buber and Rosenzweig were here very uneasy about the translation. They said to each other, does not 'as yourself' mean that one loves oneself most? . . . They translated it, 'love your neighbor, he is like you.' But if one first agrees to separate the last word of the Hebrew verse, *kamokha*, from the beginning of the verse, one can

read the whole thing still otherwise. 'Love you neighbor; this work is like your-self'; 'love your neighbor; this is yourself'; 'it is this love of the neighbor which is yourself.'"

4. Emmanuel Levinas, *Is It Righteous to Be?*, 133.

5. Vasily Grossman, *Dobro vam* [*Good to You*], in *Povest', Rasskazy, Ocherki* (Moscow: Vagrius-Agfar, 1998), 199.

6. See Morgan, *Discovering Levinas*, 1–13.

7. Levinas, *Otherwise Than Being*, v.

8. Ibid., 185.

9. Ibid., 150.

10. Ibid., 151.

11. Ibid.

12. Levinas made a number of inspiring comments on Grossman's novel that are scattered throughout the interviews collected in *Is It Righteous to Be?* On Grossman's life and work, see Frank Ellis, *Vasily Grossman: The Genesis and Evolution of a Russian Heretic* (Oxford: Berg, 1994); and John Garrard and Carol Garrard, *The Bones of Berdichev: The Life and Fate of Vasily Grossman* (New York: Free, 1996).

13. Grossman, *Life and Fate*, trans. Chandler, 531.

14. Levinas, *Is It Righteous to Be?*, 89.

15. Grossman, *Life and Fate*, 29.

16. Ibid.

17. Ibid.

18. See Father Patrick Desbois, *The Holocaust by Bullets: A Priest's Journey to Uncover the Truth behind the Murder of 1.5 Million Jews* (New York: Palgrave Macmillan, 2008).

19. Grossman, *Life and Fate*, 27–28.

20. Levinas, *Is It Righteous to Be?* 89. The French reads: "Il n'y a pas de Dieu, il n'y a pas de bien, il y a la bonté" (*Les Nouveaux Cahiers* 82 [1985]: 33).

21. Levinas, *Autrement qu'être*, 233.

22. Grossman similarly believes that Raphael's inspiring *Sistine Madonna* "is a purely atheistic expression of life and humanity, without divine participa-tion" (Grossman, "The Sistine Madonna," in *The Road: Stories, Journalism, and Essays*, trans. Robert and Elizabeth Chandler, with Olga Mukovnikova [New York: New York Review Books, 2010], 166). In Levinas's terms, God is not pres-ent, does not appear, does not participate in Being, but the Madonna's maternal devotion may be said to *bear witness to God* in the sense that, when Viktor refuses to repent to the Stalinist authorities for a crime he did not commit, he imagines that God—along with his mother—was standing beside him. Dosto-evsky shared Grossman's admiration for Raphael's *Sistine Madonna*. As Robin Feuer Miller informs us, Dostoevsky's "favorite painter was Raphael, his favorite painting the *Sistine Madonna*. Dostoevsky's second wife, Anna Grigor'evna Dos-toevskaia, has written about her first visit with Dostoevsky to the Royal Picture Gallery in Dresden. 'My husband went past all the rooms and took me straight to the *Sistine Madonna*—the painting he considered the finest manifestation of human genius. . . . Fyodor Mikhailovich prized the works of Raphael more than anything else in painting and considered the *Sistine Madonna* his greatest work'" (*Dostoevsky's Unfinished Journey* [New Haven, Conn.: Yale University

Press, 2007], 9; Miller is here citing a passage from Anna Grigor'evna Dostoevs-kaia, *Dostoevsky: Reminiscences*, trans. Beatrice Stillman [New York: Liveright, 1975], 117–19).

23. Grossman, *Life and Fate*, 29.

24. Ibid.

25. Ibid. See Grossman, *Life and Fate*, 404–11, for the remarkable text of Ikon-nikov's "scribblings" on the evils paradoxically committed throughout human history by those devoted to abstract notions of the Good. These would be a series of betrayals, for Levinas, of a God thought on the basis of ethics, outside of ontology.

26. Levinas, *Of God Who Comes to Mind*, 69.

27. My own translation of the Russian text cited from Vasily Grossman, *Zhizn' i sud'ba* (Moscow: Eksmo, 2011), 310–11, with some words drawn from the Chandler translation, 304–5.

28. In the phrase *pred liud'mi* (literally, "before the people"), the force of the preposition *pred*, meaning "before" or "in front of," is "in front of others," that is, "before people's *faces*."

29. Levinas, *Totality and Infinity*, trans. Lingis, 237; Emmanuel Levinas, *Totalité et infini: Essai sur l'extériorité* (The Hague: Martinus Nijhoff, 1971; rpt. Paris: Livre de Poche), 265.

30. Emmanuel Levinas, *Nine Talmudic Readings*, trans. with intro. Annette Aronowicz (Bloomington: Indiana University Press, 1994), 20. I have slightly altered this translation. The French is cited from Emmanuel Levinas, *Quatre lectures talmudiques* (Paris: Les Éditions de Minuit, 1968), 44. The Talmudic passage on which Levinas comments is from the Tractate *Yoma*, 85a–85b.

31. Levinas, *Difficult Freedom*, 89; *Difficile liberté*, 137. The Hebrew/Aramaic of the Gemara is cited from the Schottenstein edition of *Talmud Bavli*, vol. 49, *Tractate Sanhedrin*, vol. 3 (Brooklyn, N.Y.: Mesorah Publications, 3rd edition, 2008).

32. Levinas, *Ethics and Infinity*, 118.

33. Levinas, *Éthique et infini* (Paris: Fayard, 1982), 127, my own translation.

34. Levinas, *Ethics and Infinity*, 118.

35. Dostoevsky, *The Brothers Karamazov*, second Norton Critical Edition, 226.

36. Primo Levi, *Survival in Auschwitz: The Nazi Assault on Humanity*, trans. Stuart Woolf (New York: Touchstone, 1996), 128.

37. Levi, *Survival in Auschwitz*, 129–30.

38. Grossman, *Life and Fate*, 690.

39. Ibid.

40. Ibid., 691.

41. Ibid., 692.

42. Ibid.

43. Ibid., 693.

44. Ibid.

45. Ibid.

46. Ibid., 687.

47. So, too, does Pierre, the protagonist and spiritual seeker of Tolstoy's *War and Peace*, the novel upon which *Life and Fate* is modeled, tell the Mason who

wishes to induct him into the order of the Masons, that he, Pierre, is a nonbeliever. "I do not believe . . . do not believe in God" (*Ia ne veriu, ne veriu v Boga*), Pierre nervously confesses to the Mason (Tolstoy, *War and Peace,* vol. 1 [Moscow: Astrel, 2010], 427 [vol. 2, part 2, chapter 2]). Though Pierre is a nonbeliever, he strives for moral goodness, as does Tolstoy's Levin, and as does Grossman's Viktor. Through the character of Pierre, Tolstoy—as does Grossman through Viktor—"thinks God" on the basis of ethics, as Tolstoy does also through his character Nekhlyudov in his last novel, *Resurrection.*

48. Grossman, *Life and Fate,* 697–98.

49. Grossman, *Zhizn' i sud'ba,* 655; Grossman, *Life and Fate,* 699.

50. Grossman, *Life and Fate,* 701.

51. Grossman, *Zhizn' i sud'ba,* 821; Grossman, *Life and Fate,* 828.

52. Grossman, *Zhizn' i sud'ba,* 830; Grossman, *Life and Fate,* 837 (translation altered). While the phrase "O Bozhe" can mean simply "Oh my gosh," an expression of surprise uttered with no explicit reference to God, the word "Bozhe" nonetheless is literally an address to God, just as in English the person who exclaims, in stunned surprise and perhaps even in horror, "Oh my God," isn't necessarily a believer.

53. Grossman, *Life and Fate,* 834.

54. Ibid., 841.

55. The word for "the Other," in Levinas's sense, in Russian would be *drugoi.* Grossman, *Zhizn' i sud'ba,* 831; Grossman, *Life and Fate,* 838.

56. Ibid.

57. Grossman, *Zhizn' i sud'ba,* 832; Grossman, *Life and Fate,* 839 (translation modified). Chandler's translation ("Heavens, what had he done?") omits, or only indirectly alludes to, Grossman's and Viktor's direct and repeated reference to the word "God" (*Bozhe*).

58. Chapter 57 in the Chandler translation of *Life and Fate.*

59. Grossman, *Life and Fate,* 705.

60. Ibid., 410.

61. Levinas, *Autrement qu'être,* 283; Levinas, *Otherwise Than Being,* 185.

62. Grossman, *Life and Fate,* 846.

63. Ibid.

64. Ibid.

65. Ibid.

66. Grossman, *Zhizn' i sud'ba,* 840; Grossman, *Life and Fate,* 847.

67. Levinas, *Autrement qu'être,* 185; Levinas, *Otherwise Than Being,* 117.

68. *Zhizn' i sud'ba* [*Life and Fate*], an anthology of student writings from my spring 2012 Inside-Out class on "Literature and Ethics: Levinas and Vasily Grossman's *Life and Fate,*" ed. Pepe, Abs, Seth, Talon, Steve, Carolina, Robyn, and Anna, published by Oregon Corrections Enterprises, Oregon State Correctional Institution, Salem, Oregon (2012), 7.

69. Ibid.

Epilogue

1. Levinas, *Of God Who Comes to Mind,* preface to the second edition, ix.

2. Levinas, *Is It Righteous to Be?* 193–94.

3. Ibid., 194.

4. Grossman, *Life and Fate*, 410.

5. Helen Prejean, *Dead Man Walking: An Eyewitness Account of the Death Penalty in the United States* (New York: Vintage Books, 1994), 37.

6. Levinas, *Is It Righteous to Be?* 280. For a Levinasian reading of *Dead Man Walking*, see Patricia Molloy, "Face to Face with the Dead Man: Ethical Responsibility, State-Sanctioned Killing, and Empathetic Impossibility," *Alternatives: Global, Local, Political* 22, no. 4 (October–December 1997): 467–92.

BIBLIOGRAPHY

Aisha, Jordan, Eryn, Carmela, Kevin G., Nick, eds. *Dostoevsky and Levinas Face to Face*. Eugene, Ore.: University of Oregon Publications. 2011. Anthology of student writings compiled for "Ethics and Literature: Levinas and *The Brothers Karamazov*," Inside-Out class taught at the Oregon State Correctional Institution, 2011.

Atterton, Peter. "Art, Religion, and Ethics Post Mortem Dei: Levinas and Dostoevsky." *Levinas Studies: An Annual Review*, vol. 2 (2007): 105–32.

Bernasconi, Robert, and David Wood. "The Paradox of Morality: An Interview with Emmanuel Levinas." In *The Provocation of Levinas: Rethinking the Other*. London: Routledge, 1988.

Butt, John, ed. *Imitations of Horace, with An Epistle to Dr. Arbuthnot and The Epilogue to the Satires*. 1939. London: Yale University Press, 1969.

Calin, Rodolphe, and Catherine Chalier, eds. *Carnets de captivité et autres inédits*, *Oeuvres 1*. Paris: Bernard Grasset/IMEC, 2009.

Cassedy, Steven. *Dostoevsky's Religion*. Stanford, Calif.: Stanford University Press. 2005.

Caygill, Howard. "On Levinas's Prison Notebooks." *Radical Philosophy* 160 (March–April, 2010): 27–35.

Contino, Paul I. "Dostoevsky and the Prisoner." In *Literature and the Public Sphere*, edited by Gallagher and Walhout. New York: St. Martin's, 2000.

Delhomme, Jeanne. *La Pensée et le reel: Critique de l'ontologie*. Paris: Presses Universitaires de France, 1967.

———. *L'impossible interrogation*. Paris: Desclée, 1971.

Desbois, Father Patrick. *The Holocaust by Bullets: A Priest's Journey to Uncover the Truth behind the Murder of 1.5 Million Jews*. New York: Palgrave Macmillan, 2008.

Descartes, René. *Descartes: Selected Philosophical Writings*. Translated by J. Cottingham, R. Stroothoff, and D. Murdoch. Cambridge: Cambridge University Press, 1988.

Dostoevskaia, Anna Grigor'evna. *Dostoevsky: Reminiscences*. Translated by Beatrice Stillman. New York: Liveright, 1975.

Dostoevsky, Fyodor. *Besy*. St. Petersburg: Azbuka, 2011.

———. *Brat'ia Karamazovy*. Moscow: Eksmo, 2003.

———. *The Brothers Karamazov: A Revised Translation; Contexts; Criticism*. 2nd edition. Edited with a revised translation by Susan McReynolds Oddo. New York: W. W. Norton, 2011.

———. *The Brothers Karamazov*. Translated by Richard Pevear and Larissa Volokhonsky. New York: Farrar, Straus and Giroux, 2002.

———. *Crime and Punishment*. Translated by Richard Pevear and Larissa Volokhonsky. New York: Vintage Books, 1993.

———. *Demons*. Translated by Richard Pevear and Larissa Volokhonsky. New York: Alfred A. Knopf, 1994.

———. *Fyodor Dostoevsky, Complete Letters, III: 1868–1871*. Edited and translated by David A. Lowe. Ann Arbor, Mich.: Ardis, 1990.

———. *The House of the Dead* and *Poor Folk*. Translated by Constance Garnett. With an introduction by Joseph Frank. Notes by Elena Yuffa. New York: Barnes and Noble, 2004.

———. *The Idiot*. Translated by Richard Pevear and Larissa Volokhonsky. New York: Vintage Books, 2003.

———. *Idiot*. Russian text. San Bernadino, Calif.: Planet Books, 2013.

———. *Notes from the House of the Dead*. Translated by Boris Jakim. Grand Rapids, Mich.: Erdmans, 2013.

———. *Pis'ma*, vol. 2 (1867–1871). Edited by A. S. Dolinina. Moscow: State Publishing House, 1930.

———. *Polnoe sobranie sochinenii v tridtsati tomakh*. Leningrad: Nauka, 1972–90.

———. *Prestuplenie i nakazanie*. Moscow: Russian Language, 1984.

———. *Winter Notes on Summer Impressions*. Translated by David Patterson. Evanston, Ill.: Northwestern University Press, 1988.

———. *A Writer's Diary*. Edited by Gary Saul Morson. Translated by Kenneth Lantz. Evanston, Ill.: Northwestern University Press, 2009.

———. *Zapiski iz mertvogo doma*. Moscow: Eksmo, 2005.

Ellis, Frank. *Vasily Grossman: The Genesis and Evolution of a Russian Heretic*. Oxford: Berg, 1994.

Frank, Joseph. *Between Religion and Rationality*. Princeton, N.J.: Princeton University Press, 2010.

———. *Dostoevsky: The Mantle of the Prophet, 1871–1881*. Princeton, N.J.: Princeton University Press, 2002.

———. *Dostoevsky: The Years of Ordeal, 1850–1859*. Princeton, N.J.: Princeton University Press, 1990.

Frank, Joseph, and David I. Goldstein, eds. *Selected Letters of Fyodor Dostoevsky*. Translated by Andrew R. MacAndrew. New Brunswick, N.J.: Rutgers University Press, 1987.

Garrard, John, and Carol Garrard. *The Bones of Berdichev: The Life and Fate of Vasily Grossman*. New York: Free, 1996.

Gilson, Etienne. *Reason and Revelation in the Middle Ages*. New York: Scribner's, 1938.

Glare, P. G. W. *Oxford Latin Dictionary*. Oxford: Clarendon, 1996.

Gobineau, Arthur. *The Inequality of the Human Races*. New York: H. Fertig, 1999.

Goldstein, David I. *Dostoevsky and the Jews*. Austin: University of Texas Press, 1981.

Grossman, Vasily. *An Armenian Sketchbook*. Translated by Robert Chandler and Elizabeth Chandler. New York: New York Review of Books, 2013.

———. *Life and Fate*. Translated by Robert Chandler. 1985. New York: New York Review of Books, 2006.

———. *Povest', Rasskazy, Ocherki*. Moscow: Vagrius-Agfar, 1998.

———. *The Road: Stories, Journalism, and Essays*. Translated by Robert Chandler and Elizabeth Chandler with Olga Mukovnikova. New York: New York Review of Books, 2010.

———. *Zhizn' i sud'ba*. Moscow: Eksmo, 2011.

Hand, Seán. "Salvation through Literature: Levinas's *Carnets de captivité*." In *Levinas Studies* 8, edited by Jeffrey Bloechl. Pittsburgh, Pa.: Duquesne University Press, 2013.

Havel, Václav. *Letters to Olga*. Translated by Paul Wilson. New York: Knopf, 1988.

Heilman, Robert. *The Professor and the Profession*. Columbia: University of Missouri Press, 1999.

La Bible de Jérusalem. Paris: Éditions de Cerf, 1986.

Levi, Primo. *Se questo è un uomo*. Turin: Einaudi, 1989.

———. *Survival in Auschwitz: The Nazi Assault on Humanity*. Translated by Stuart Woolf. New York: Touchstone, 1996.

Levinas, Emmanuel. *Autrement qu'être ou au-delà de l'essence*. Dordrecht, Netherlands: Nijhoff, 1974.

———. *Basic Philosophical Writings*. Edited by Adrian T. Peperzak, Simon Critchley, and Robert Bernasconi. Bloomington: Indiana University Press, 1996.

———. *Beyond the Verse: Talmudic Readings and Lectures*. Translated by Gary Mole. Bloomington and Indianapolis: Indiana University Press, 1994.

———. "Cinq ans derrière les barbelés." In *Le Magazine de France*. Paris: Programmes de France, 1945.

———. *Collected Philosophical Papers*. Translated by Alphonso Lingis. The Hague: Martinus Nijhoff, 1987.

———. *De Dieu qui vient à l'idée*. 1982. Paris: Vrin, 2004.

———. *De l'existence à l'existant*. 1963. Paris: Vrin, 1990.

———. *Dieu, la mort, et le temps*. Paris: Grasset, 1993.

———. *Difficile liberté*. Paris: Albin Michel, 1976.

———. *Difficult Freedom: Essays on Judaism*. Translated by Seán Hand. Baltimore: Johns Hopkins University Press, 1990.

———. *Ethics and Infinity: Conversations with Philippe Nemo*. Translated by Richard A. Cohen. Pittsburgh: Duquesne University Press, 1985.

———. *Éthique et infini*. 1982. Paris: Fayard et Radio-France, 2012.

———. *Existence and Existents*. Translated by Alphonso Lingis, 1978. Pittsburgh, Pa.: Duquesne University Press, 2003.

———. *God, Death, and Time*. Translated by Bettina Bergo. Stanford, Calif.: Stanford University Press, 2000.

———. *Humanisme de l'autre homme*. Montpellier, France: Fata Morgana, 1972

———. *Humanism of the Other*. Translated by Nidra Poller. Urbana: University of Illinois Press, 2003.

———. *In the Time of the Nations*. Translated by Michael B. Smith. Bloomington: Indiana University Press, 1994.

———. "Meaning and Sense." In *Emmanuel Levinas: Basic Philosophical Writings*, edited by Adrian T. Peperzak, Simon Critchley, and Robert Bernasconi. Bloomington: Indiana University Press, 1996.

———. "The Name of God according to a Few Talmudic Texts." In *Beyond the Verse: Talmudic Readings and Lectures*. Translated by Gary Mole. Bloomington and Indianapolis: Indiana University Press, 1994.

———. *Nine Talmudic Readings*. Translated by Annette Aronowicz. Bloomington: Indiana University Press, 1994.

————. *Oeuvres 1: Carnets de captivités et autres inédits.* Edited by Rodolphe Calin and Catherine Chalier. Paris: Bernard Grasset/IMEC, 2009.

————. *Of God Who Comes to Mind.* Translated by Bettina Bergo. Stanford, Calif.: Stanford University Press, 1998.

————. *Otherwise Than Being, or, Beyond Essence.* Translated by Alphonso Lingis. Pittsburgh, Pa.: Duquesne University Press, 1981.

————. *Quatre lectures talmudiques.* Paris: Les Éditions de Minuit, 1968.

————. "The Rights of the Other Man." In *Alterity and Transcendence,* translated by Michael B. Smith. New York: Columbia University Press, 1999.

————. "Signification and Sense." In *Humanism of the Other,* translated by Nidra Poller. Urbana: University of Illinois Press, 2003.

————. *Totalité et infini: Essai sur l'extériorité.* The Hague: Martinus Nijhoff, 1971.

————. *Totality and Infinity: An Essay on Exteriority.* Translated by Alphonso Lingis. Pittsburgh, Pa.: Duquesne University Press, 1969.

Madeline, James, and Katie, eds. *Turned Inside-Out: Literature, Art, and Testimony from the Inside-Out Prison Exchange Program,* vol. 2. Eugene, Ore.: University of Oregon Publications, 2010.

McReynolds, Susan. *Redemption and the Merchant God: Dostoevsky's Economy of Salvation and Antisemitism.* Evanston, Ill.: Northwestern University Press, 2008.

Miller, Robin Feuer. *Dostoevsky's Unfinished Journey.* New Haven, Conn.: Yale University Press, 2007.

Molloy, Patricia. "Face to Face with the Dead Man: Ethical Responsibility, State-Sanctioned Killing, and Empathetic Impossibility." *Alternatives: Global, Local, Political* 22, no. 4 (October–December 1997): 467–92.

Morgan, Michael L. *Discovering Levinas.* Cambridge: Cambridge University Press, 2007.

The New Oxford Annotated Bible with the Apocrypha, revised standard version. Edited by Herbert G. May and Bruce Metzger. New York: Oxford University Press, 1977.

Pepe, Abs, Seth, Talon, Steve, Carolina, Robyn, and Anna, eds. *Zhizn' i sud'ba* [*Life and Fate*]. Salem, Ore.: Oregon Corrections Enterprises, Oregon State Correctional Institution, 2012. An anthology of student writings from spring 2012 Inside-Out class on "Literature and Ethics: Levinas and Vasily Grossman's *Life and Fate.*"

Plutarch. *Plutarch's Lives.* Translated from the original Greek. Wth notes critical and historical; and a life of Plutarch. 6 volumes. Edinburgh: C. Elliot, 1795.

Prejean, Sister Helen. *Dead Man Walking: An Eyewitness Account of the Death Penalty in the United States.* New York: Vintage Books, 1994.

Rashi. *The Torah: With Rashi's Commentary Translated, Annotated, and Elucidated.* Volume I, Bereshit/Genesis. Edited by Rabbi Yisrael Isser Zvi Herczeg et al. The Saperstein Edition. ArtScroll Series. Brooklyn, N.Y.: Mesorah Publications, 1995.

————. *The Torah: With Rashi's Commentary Translated, Annotated, and Elucidated.* Volume II, Shemot/Exodus. Edited by Rabbi Yisrael Isser Zvi Herczeg et al. The Saperstein Edition. ArtScroll Series. Brooklyn, N.Y.: Mesorah Publications, 1995. Reprint, 1999.

Reeves, Gareth. *Nuncle Music.* Manchester, Eng.: Carcanet, 2013.

Robbins, Jill. *Altered Reading: Levinas and Literature.* Chicago: University of Chicago Press, 1999.

———. ed. *Is It Righteous to Be? Interviews with Emmanuel Levinas.* Stanford, Calif.: Stanford University Press, 2001.

Rolland, Jacques. *Dostoïevski: La question de l'autre.* Paris: Verdier, 1983.

———. "Introduction." In *On Escape,* by Emmanuel Levinas. Translated by Bettina Bergo. Stanford, Calif.: Stanford University Press, 2003.

Rosenzweig, Franz. *Der Stern der Erlösung.* Frankfurt: Suhrkamp, 1988.

———. *The Star of Redemption.* 1970. Translated by William W. Hallo. Notre Dame, Ind.: University of Notre Dame Press, 1985.

Sandoz, Ellis. *Eric Voegelin's Thought: A Critical Appraisal.* Durham, N.C.: Duke University Press, 1982.

Scherman, Rabbi Nosson, ed. *Tanach: The Torah, Prophets, Writings,* 1996. Brooklyn, N.Y.: Mesorah Publications, 2003.

Shankman, Steven. "From Solitude to Maternity: Levinas and Shakespeare." *Levinas Studies: An Annual Review,* vol. 8 (2013): 67–79.

———. "Ghosts and Responsibility: The Hebrew Bible, Confucius, Plato." In *Rethinking Ghosts in World Religions,* edited by Mu-chou Poo. Leiden: Brill, 2009.

———. *Other Others: Levinas, Literature, Transcultural Studies.* Albany, N.Y.: State University of New York Press, 2010.

———. "(m)Other Power: Shin Buddhism, Levinas, *King Lear.*" In *From Ritual to Romance and Beyond: Comparative Literature and Comparative Religious Studies,* edited by Manfred Schmeling and Hans-Joachim Backe. Würzburg, Germany: Königshausen & Neumann, 2011.

———. "Reason and Revelation in the Pre-Enlightenment: Eric Voegelin's Analysis and the Case of Swift." *Religion and Literature* 16, no. 2 (Summer 1984): 1–24.

Stubbert, Tiffany. "Inside Looking Out." Online video. Vimeo, 2009. Web. http://vimeo.com/5193052.

Talmud Bavli. Vol. 49: *Tractate Sanhedrin,* Volume 3. Brooklyn, N.Y.: Mesorah Publications. 3rd edition, 2008.

Terras, Victor. *A Karamazov Companion.* 1981. Madison: University of Wisconsin Press, 2002.

Tolstoy, Leo. *Anna Karenina.* Moscow: Eksmo, 2011.

———. *The Gospel in Brief: The Life of Jesus.* Translated by Dustin Condren. New York: Harper Perennial, 2011.

———. *Voina i Mir* [*War and Peace*]. 2 volumes. Moscow: Astrel, 2010.

Toumayan, Alain. "I More Than the Others." *Yale French Studies,* no. 104 (2004): 55–66.

Tsypkin, Leonid. *Leto v Badene.* Moscow: Novoe Literaturnoe Obozrenie, 2013.

———. *Summer in Baden-Baden.* Translated by Roger and Angela Keys. London: Hamish Hamilton/Penguin, 2005.

Vinokur, Val. *The Trace of Judaism: Dostoevsky, Babel, Mandelstam, Levinas.* Evanston, Ill.: Northwestern University Press, 2008.

Voegelin, Eric. *Anamnesis.* Notre Dame, Ind.: University of Notre Dame Press, 1978.

Volozhiner, Rabbi Chaim. *Nefesh Hachaim.* Translated by Rabbi Avraham Yaakov Finkel. Brooklyn, N.Y.: Judaica, 2009.